DATE DUE

MAY 3 1993			

THE CHINESE ARMY AFTER MAO

THE CHINESE ARMY AFTER MAO

ELLIS JOFFE

HARVARD UNIVERSITY PRESS
CAMBRIDGE, MASSACHUSETTS
1987

Library of Congress Cataloging-in-Publication Data

Joffe, E. G. H. (Ellis G. H.)
    The Chinese Army after Mao.
    Includes index.
    1. China. Chung-kuo jen min chieh fang chün—
History. I. Title.
UA837.J64 1987   355′.00951   87–131
ISBN 0–674–54849–3

Contents

Contents

Preface

Since the end of the Maoist period, and especially since Deng Xiaoping consolidated his position as China's paramount power-holder in the late 1970s, China has been swept by breathtaking changes which Deng has aptly termed 'a second revolution'. Distinguished by a dramatic drive to modernization, this 'revolution' has jettisoned long-cherished Maoist principles and has reshaped all sectors of Chinese society in new ways. Not all the sectors, however, have received equal attention in accounts by outside observers. In most accounts, the spotlight has been turned primarily on economic and social developments; military modernization has figured much less prominently.

The reasons for this are not hard to see. For one thing, modernization of the armed forces concerns a relatively narrow sector of society and is less sensational than developments in other sectors. For another, changes in the armed forces are much less visible to visitors and information about them is harder to come by. Above all, China's future appears to depend first and foremost on economic progress, which tends to overshadow changes in other sectors.

But these changes have been significant. In the military sector, fundamental and far-reaching reforms have been carried out in the post-Mao period. When the new leadership took over, the People's Liberation Army (PLA) was in a state of stagnation. Dominated for almost two decades by an outdated doctrine and deeply involved in political activities, the PLA had lost its capacity to fight and function as a modern military force. Conventional weapons and equipment had become obsolete and professional standards had declined drastically. To overcome these defects, the Deng leadership launched a series of reforms designed to modernize the Chinese armed forces and to make them capable of defending China effectively against a modern army.

These reforms have been determined by China's economic capabilities and the leadership's threat perceptions. Convinced that China is not confronted with a direct military danger, the leadership has strictly limited defence spending and has refrained from acquiring costly weapons. However, slow technological progress has been abundantly compensated for by sweeping changes in areas that require few resources but enhance the army's ability to wage war. Many of these changes are in initial stages, and the PLA still faces a long march to modernization. Nevertheless, by the mid-1980s it has already undergone a major transformation and, in comparison with the army of Maoist days, has acquired an entirely new look.

The transformation of the PLA in the post-Mao period is the subject of this book. Chapter 1 surveys the development of the PLA during the Maoist era and highlights the reasons for its decline as a professional force. Chapter 2 analyses the basic outlook – internal and external – of the new leadership as the basis for understanding its policy of military modernization. How this policy was formulated and what it means for the military establishment is the subject of Chapter 3. The next three chapters look at the vast changes that have taken place in the PLA since the end of the 1970s. Chapter 4 examines the revision of Maoist military doctrine in line with the requirements of modern warfare. Chapter 5 focuses on the modernization of weapons and equipment. Chapter 6 surveys the whole range of reforms that have been introduced to raise the professional quality of the armed forces. Chapter 7 traces the withdrawal of the PLA from politics and describes the state of civil–military relations in the post-Mao period.

Acknowledgements

It is my pleasure and obligation to acknowledge the help I received in preparing this book. I am most grateful to the Harry S. Truman Research Institute of the Hebrew University, and particularly to its Director, Professor Harold Z. Schiffrin, for giving me support and excellent working conditions for many years. To the Warden and Fellows of St Antony's College, Oxford, I am very grateful for electing me as a senior associate member during the academic year 1984/5 and providing me with an ideal environment for writing the first draft. To Gerald Segal I am indebted for his comments on the manuscript and for countless hours of discussion. I would like to thank Cecile Panzer, Director of the superb Truman Library, and Riccardo Schwed, of the China section, for responding without fail to my many requests. Janette Lasken and Rachel Blumenfeld helped in collating materials. Sarah Lemann did a splendid job in typing the manuscript. Above all, I am grateful to Pamela Lubell – a scrupulous, resourceful and knowledgeable researcher – for research assistance and editorial advice. The responsibility for the contents is, needless to say, solely mine.

1

The Maoist Legacy

The modernization of the Chinese armed forces, given China's limited resources and vast defence needs, is an awesome undertaking under the most favourable circumstances. However, the circumstances faced by the post-Mao leadership were anything but favourable. During the Maoist period the PLA had fallen far behind advanced armies in the acquisition of conventional weapons and its overall professional competence had declined sharply. The modernization efforts of the new leaders were thus beset from the outset by problems caused by the PLA's deterioration during the preceding years. An assessment of their efforts, therefore, has to begin at the base line set by these problems.

On the face of it, the decline of the PLA's military capabilities under the Maoist leadership seems incongruous and puzzling. For this was a leadership which attached supreme importance to military force and which took as an article of faith Mao's dictum that 'political power grows out of the barrel of the gun'. It was a leadership which fervently aspired to enhancing China's prestige and influence in the international arena, where military power is a prime indicator of a nation's standing. It was a leadership which throughout its history operated under perceived threats to China's security, first from the United States and later from the Soviet Union.[1] And it was a leadership which was ready to resort to the calculated use of force when it decided that this was necessary to protect or advance China's national interests.

How then did it come about that a leadership which was highly sensitive to the value of its armed forces was responsible for their decline? The conventional answer is that China's military backwardness is a function of its economic poverty and technological inadequacies. This is, of course, true – but only up to a point. The constraints imposed by China's level of development on all sectors of society are well known and their significance need not be elaborated.[2] On closer examination, however, these constraints fall short of providing more than a limited explanation for the state of the PLA during the Maoist period, for two main reasons.

First, the same constraints have been present throughout the history of the People's Republic, but they did not prevent important advances during two notable periods. One was in the early and mid-1950s, when the PLA was converted from a guerrilla army with antiquated equipment and outdated tactics into a fairly modern and professional army. The second period began when the Chinese embarked on their post-Mao programme of military modernization in which a central component has been the improvement of the PLA's weapons and equipment.

The second reason is that the deterioration of the PLA extended to areas – such as doctrine, leadership, organization and training – the improvement of which, unlike hardware, is not a drain on resources but which are no less crucial to the army's capabilities. In all these areas, professional criteria were disregarded for long stretches during the Maoist period and quality was severely damaged. This disregard was not dictated by economic considerations.

In short, China's level of development sets clear limits to the modernization of its armed forces but does not determine their performance within these limits. How the military actually performs depends decisively on the policies of the leadership and their implications. Therefore, the main explanation for the condition of the armed forces during the Maoist period has to be sought not in objective circumstances, but in the policies of the Maoist leadership and their consequences.

The policies which turned out to be inimical to the modernization of the PLA were not, of course, formulated with this purpose in mind. Mao's credentials as an advocate of a strong army were never in doubt, nor was his commitment to its modernization, a goal which he believed would be best achieved by his policies. However, from the late 1950s, Maoist policies had exactly the opposite effect on the PLA. Not only did they prove fundamentally incompatible with the requirements of modernization but, worse still, they lent themselves to extreme interpretations and abuses by radical leaders, who subverted the programmes of the professional military for ideological and political reasons.

Thus, regardless of their original intent, Maoist policies impeded the progress of the PLA for almost twenty years. Although these years also witnessed spectacular achievements in nuclear technology and some advances in select sectors of the conventional forces, modernization as a sustained and single-minded policy for the military could not be resumed until after Mao's death and the downfall of his radical supporters. In the interim, surging advances in military technology and techniques bypassed the PLA, leaving a legacy of backwardness. And it is with this legacy that his successors have had to grapple in their efforts to modernize the PLA.

Military Modernization in the 1950s: A Brief Beginning

The immediate origins of Maoist military policies lie in the interaction between developments in the armed forces and the dramatic changes which swept over the Chinese scene in the second half of the 1950s. These changes, which culminated in the abandonment of the Soviet model of national development and the launching of the Great Leap Forward, had profound implications for the military. These implications can be best appreciated when viewed against the process of military modernization which the new policies disrupted.[3]

When the Chinese Communists came to power in 1949, one of their most urgent tasks was to convert their victorious but primitive army into an armed force capable of defending China from external enemies. This was a monumental and multi-faceted task. Although a superb guerrilla force, as a national defence army the PLA was a military anachronism. Its equipment was heterogeneous and obsolete. It lacked naval or air arms. Its command structure was decentralised and rudimentary. Its communications and logistics systems were simplistic. Its soldiers were irregulars and its commanders lacked the skills and attitudes necessary in a modern army.

The leadership was united in its awareness of the need to overcome these deficiencies without delay. In his inaugural address upon the establishment of the new regime, Mao himself stressed that China required a 'completely modernized armed force', and this objective was incorporated into China's provisional constitution. Similar statements were made by other top leaders.[4] This consensus proved critical to the success of military modernization in the early years because it provided the impetus essential for a concerted campaign. Leadership consensus, however, was not enough. It had to be supplemented by capital and technological knowhow, and these were sorely lacking. China had just emerged from more than three decades of civil strife and foreign invasion which had ravaged the country, and the tasks of rehabilitation had first claim on resources. In addition, China's military leadership, while highly proficient in commanding unconventional forces, possessed neither the knowledge nor the skills vital to transforming them into a conventional army.

These difficulties became quickly apparent. Although China's leaders continued to talk about the need for military modernization, there was a gap between declaration and action. Some steps – such as massive demobilization and the establishment of military academies – were taken but these did not add up to a full-scale drive. Such a drive could not get under way without extensive aid.

For this the Chinese turned to the Soviet Union. However, Soviet military aid was not immediately forthcoming. Although the Sino-Soviet Treaty of

1950 presumably contained secret provisions for Soviet military assistance to China,[5] Stalin was clearly in no hurry to provide it to the Chinese in substanti al quantities until compelled to do so by circumstances.

The circumstances stemmed from China's intervention in the Korean War – in the initiation of which the Chinese took no part, and in the waging of which they originally had no intention of participating. However, the turn of events on the battlefield thwarted China's original intentions. The unexpected commitment of UN troops to the conflict reversed the initial victories of the North Koreans and pushed their crumbling armies back across the 38th Parallel. As UN troops moved into North Korea, the Chinese issued repeated warnings that they would not remain idle if the advance continued. These warnings went unheeded. Perceiving a threat to their national security, the Chinese intervened massively.[6]

The long-term impact of this intervention on the Chinese military can hardly be overestimated. Although reluctant to acknowledge it publicly during the Maoist period, the Chinese themselves have done so in recent years: 'The war of resisting US agression and aiding Korea enables us to realize more clearly from our personal experience that it is impossible to win a modern war without meeting the requirements of modern warfare and without strengthening modernization in various respects.'[7]

Their 'personal experience' was highly traumatic. The Chinese armies that crossed the Yalu in late October 1950 still consisted of the same tough but poorly equipped infantrymen who had fought in the civil war. They were still equipped with outdated small arms and had no armour or air support. Their logistics system was inadequate and was further hampered by the absence of standardization. They had no modern communications.

Although reluctant to intervene and aware of their technological inferiority, the Chinese did not embark on a suicidal mission. They were confident that their superiority in numbers and non-material qualities – morale and motivation, as well as tested doctrine and tactics – would be an effective counterpoise to their weaknesses. In short, the Chinese were prepared to enter the Korean War because they still put primary reliance on the 'human element'.

This reliance was the source of the 'human wave' attacks which the Chinese used to overrun key enemy tactical positions by sheer force of numbers and human tenacity. Initially they were able to rout the UN forces, but their success was short-lived. They could not sustain their offensives because their primitive logistics system and UN air interdiction forced them to regroup and resupply after an attack. And they were hampered by inadequate mobility, which resulted from their total lack of air support, unfamiliarity with terrain and poor communications. For their part, UN forces quickly learned to absorb the Chinese thrusts and then to counter-attack along a firm battleline which deprived the Chinese of the ability to manoeuvre on the enemy's flanks, which was crucial to their tactics. These counter-attacks, moreover, were supported by murderous firepower which incessantly pounded the Chinese troops.

By the summer of 1951 the Chinese had suffered enormous losses, and their hardships were aggravated by inadequate supplies and equipment. The effect on morale was devastating, and since high morale was crucial to reliance on the 'human element', its erosion led to increasing disintegration of frontline units.

To stem this trend, the Soviets began to send large quantities of military equipment to the Chinese. This enabled the Chinese high command to start reorganizing and re-equipping its forces. New units were established consisting of artillery and heavy weapons, tanks, armoured cars, trucks, and anti-aircraft guns. An air force, non-existent when the Korean War broke out, came into being and by the end of 1951 was able to challenge UN air superiority. The flow of Soviet arms and equipment enabled the Chinese to maintain a stalemate on the battlefield until a truce was reached.[8] At the same time, it laid the basis for the future modernization of the PLA.

The lessons learned by the Chinese military leaders on the Korean battlefield were crucial for this modernization. They learned that their rich storehouse of combat experience provided no solutions to the manifold problems of modern warfare. They learned that their hitherto successful strategy and tactics, based on the superiority of the 'human element', had severe limitations and liabilities. And they learned, above all, that their army would have to undergo a total transformation before it could again confront a modern military force. This transformation dominated the development of the PLA until the late 1950s.

Developments in two interrelated arenas outside the military establishment – Sino-Soviet relations and Chinese national development policies – were instrumental in facilitating the transformation. Until the late 1950s these developments created the conditions essential to the modernization of the PLA, highlighting the integral connection between military policies and China's international posture and national politics. It was when changes occurred in these two arenas that the modernization of the PLA was disrupted.

Sino-Soviet relations in the mid-1950s have been rightly labelled the 'honeymoon' period in their history. The death of Stalin, who had harboured deep suspicion of Mao, and the jockeying for power among his successors, who needed Chinese support, made the new Soviet leaders much more sensitive to China's status and receptive to its requirements than Stalin had ever been. The Chinese, for their part, intent on rebuilding the country quickly and content with their international position after the Korean War, were prepared to accept Soviet leadership in foreign affairs. This temporarily defused the most potentially divisive issue in Sino-Soviet relations – the question of authority in the Communist bloc. As a result, the two countries co-operated closely for several years.

One result of this co-operation was the wholehearted adoption by the Chinese of the Soviet model of national development, which stressed centralization, specialization and professionalism. Although the Chinese would soon discard this model because, in addition to other reasons, it proved to be incompatible with Maoist revolutionary values, in the early 1950s they were not yet aware of the full extent of this incompatibility. Another result was the extension of Soviet credits to China, primarily for the purchase of complete plants. A third was the large-scale transfer of Soviet technology to China, primarily through the dispatch of Soviet experts to advise the Chinese.

Without this co-operation military modernization could not have been carried out. Leadership consensus on the suitability of the Soviet model to China was vital to the reorganization of the PLA along professional lines which departed from Maoist revolutionary principles. The readiness of China's leaders, including Mao, to sanction this departure was especially important in the military sector, where technical and organizational complexities threw its divergence from Maoist principles into particularly sharp relief.

Second, Soviet military equipment was indispensable to the PLA's modernization. The supply begun during the Korean War was accelerated and expanded after the ceasefire, reaching an estimated cost of US$2 billion by 1957. Although most of this cost was in credits rather than grants, the burden it put on the Chinese was more than offset by the fact that they were able to arm the PLA with fairly modern weapons which they could not have acquired in any other way.

Equally indispensable was Soviet expertise, which the Chinese needed to operate their new weapons and to revamp the PLA's organization and concepts. Shortly after the signing of the 1950 Treaty a Soviet military mission was set up in Peking and until the end of the decade several thousand Soviet advisers were sent to China – estimates range from three to six thousand. Many Chinese officers went to the Soviet Union to study. Soviet manuals were translated into Chinese and incorporated into the modernization programmes of the PLA. Although the Chinese later realized that the Soviet 'advanced experience' which they were assimilating so assiduously in the mid-1950s was completely out of step with their own revolutionary traditions, 'learn from the Soviet army' was the standard operational slogan during the heyday of military modernization.

Heading the modernization programme was the updating of weapons. Within the limits imposed by what was available from the Soviets, the Chinese high command proceeded to weld its light infantry divisions into a much more complex and better-equipped army, possessing basic service and support arms. The most striking advance was in the air force, which by the mid-1950s contained some 4,000 combat aircraft. The Soviets, to be sure, did not give the Chinese their latest weapons, and the quantities were far from enough to mechanize all the ground forces of the PLA. Nonetheless, the gap between Chinese weapons in the mid-1950s and the state of the art was not nearly as glaring as it was to become in later years. Although still outdated by US and Soviet standards, the PLA's prospects for further progress were highly favourable.

These prospects were also based on the advances made by the Chinese in areas other than hardware, for the Chinese leaders understood from the outset that military modernization not only entailed the acquisition of new weapons, but also necessitated far-reaching changes in leadership, training, education and organization. These changes altered the traditional revolutionary character of the PLA and laid the essential foundation for the development of a modern army.

The first change was in the make-up of the leadership. The Chinese high command was well aware of the urgent need to replace the Red Army commanders, who had risen from the ranks and whose formal training was haphazard, with a corps of officers skilled in modern military specialities and prepared to make military life their vocation. Such an officer corps was vital to the success of military modernization and the leaders made a concerted effort to meet this need. They established military academies for the training of new officers, who had to fulfil educational rquirements before being accepted, and advanced academies for veterans. They promulgated 'Regulations on the Service of Officers', which for the first time in the history of the Red Army instituted a system of ranks, regular channels of entry into the officer corps, and professional criteria for advancement, as well as insignia. They conferred military titles and honours on army leaders and introduced a differentiated pay scale. They took measures to provide for the continuous military education of officers. The Chinese, in short, created a professional officer corps. [9]

The institutionalization of a professional officer corps was followed by the introduction of conscription, which replaced the traditional practice of recruiting 'volunteers' to the Red Army for indefinite periods through appeals to patriotism and self-interest or through social pressures. Taken together, these measures underlined the distinction between the continuous flow of recruits, who enlisted for fixed periods and then returned to civilian life, and the permanent nucleus of professional officers, who were responsible for training the enlisted men and advancing the military profession. The PLA was thus put on a regular footing.

The modernization of equipment and the rationalization of recruitment were complemented by the reorganization of the command structure. For more than three years after the establishment of the regime vast power remained in the hands of generals who controlled the great regions into which the country had initially been divided. In 1952 the Peking leadership initiated a far-reaching process of centralization, which lasted two years and in the course of which senior military officials were transferred from the field armies to the capital, and a host of new organs were established to manage the military establishment. At the same time, the country was divided into military regions and districts. The new structure – especially the General Staff with its functional departments and their specialized subdepartments, as well as the headquarters of the various arms and sevices – was not only integral to the modernization of the PLA, but also indicated how complex and diverse the PLA had become in the space of a few short years.

In addition to modernizing the PLA over the short haul, the Chinese were also eager to develop their capacity to continue this process on their own in the long run. To this end, they made an effort to build a defence industry and to create a research and development capacity – an effort which, in view of China's later isolation, proved to be of critical importance. Although Stalin had been reluctant to help the Chinese build an independent capability to produce arms, his successors laid the foundation for China's defence industries, which in the mid-1950s began to manufacture Soviet-designed weapons systems. By the end of the decade Chinese production of Soviet weapons ran the full gamut from small arms to tanks, submarines and aircraft.

The achievements of military modernization in the 1950s were wide-ranging. Looking at it from a post-Mao perspective, the PLA's Chief of Staff, Yang Dezhi, affirmed:

> the contributions made by the Central Military Commission under Peng Dehuai in the early 1950s in regularizing the army in accordance with the instructions of the Central Committee Chairman Mao Zedong. The major measures taken at that time were: many regulations were laid down for routine service, formations, discipline and combat; important systems were set up for military service, cadre salaries, military ranks and so on; the establishment of the whole army was unified; large numbers of military, political, logistics, and technical schools were set up; and regular training was launched.

These measures, Yang pointed out, 'unified the army by regular forms within the short space of a few years, changed the original situation in which each base had its own methods, and changed the guerrilla war habits, with the result that the building of the army forged ahead in big strides and started to embark on the road to modernization and regulation'. [10]

What the chief of staff did not point out was that the 'big strides' taken by the PLA towards modernization were inevitably accompanied by a wholesale departure from Maoist military principles and practices. Forged in the fires of revolutionary warfare, the Maoist military model was the wellspring of the Red Army's inner strength. Based on the superiority of the 'human element', it had enabled the Chinese Communists to confront enemies possessing immeasurably greater material resources.

The Maoist model had several unique features designed to cultivate the 'human element'. It emphasised voluntaristic motivation and conscious discipline. It encouraged comradely relations, informality and egalitarianism between the ranks, based on long years of close and intimate association. It minimized distinctions between commanders and ordinary soldiers and drew soldiers into group decision-making in the administration of daily life, and even in the planning of military operations. It attached supreme significance to close co-operation with the civilian population. It accorded paramount importance to political work in the army and gave a pivotal role to a complex political apparatus, led by political commissars, to conduct it.

The Maoist military model was a singular product of the revolutionary struggle from which it emerged and was supremely suited to that milieu. It was, however, largely unsuited to the post-revolutionary milieu of a modernizing army. As a result, fundamental features of the model were rapidly discarded, either deliberately or by default, as the PLA rationalized its organization and procedures.

Thus, the many-faceted military 'democracy' of revolutionary days was replaced by relations between the ranks based on elaborate hierachy, rigid discipline and status consciousness. This led to estrangement between officers and rank and file which, in the view of the leadership, dangerously undermined the traditional internal unity of the army. Garrison life also insulated the army from the civilian population.

Most serious from the vantage point of the leadership was the erosion of the political control apparatus in the armed forces, which was supposed to be based on the joint leadership of units by military commanders and political commissars under the overall direction and supervision of Party committees at every level of the military hierachy down to the company. This apparatus, however, fell into disarray because professional officers opposed it on the grounds that a dual system of command, while applicable to revolutionary warfare, was incompatible with the requirements of a modern army. For this reason they ignored the Party committees and shunted the political commissars aside, introducing instead the 'single commander' system, in which the military commander had ultimate authority in his unit.

The seriousness of this erosion was underlined by the fact that it could not have occurred without at least the tacit support of the PLA's high command. And such support was given by top commanders to their subordinates because these commanders, led by Marshal Peng Dehuai, who became minister of defence after commanding Chinese forces in Korea, became converted to a professional military viewpoint in the course of the Korean War and of overseeing the modernization of the PLA. Consequently, they continued to pay lip-service to the political control system but failed to ensure its actual operation because, like professional officers throughout the armed forces, they concluded that this system was inimical to the combat efficiency of the army, which now became their primary concern.

Underlying the resistance of professional officers to Maoist military practices was their view that the Maoist doctrine of 'people's war', with its belief in the superiority of the 'human element' as a counterweight to technological inferiority, had outlived its usefulness. In contrast to Party leaders, who gave precedence to political and ideological factors on which the superiority of the 'human element' depends, the professional military argued that the success of an army in a modern war depends first and foremost on its material resources and professional competence. In short, while the Party leaders wanted to build a modern army around an unchanging core of revolutionary rules, the officers rejected these rules because they interfered with the needs of a modern army.

The challenge posed by the professional military to the Party's sacrosanct principles of army-building provoked a forceful reaction from Party leaders designed to stem the trend towards professionalism in the armed forces. However, this reaction to internal developments in the PLA was greatly intensified and magnified by changes that occurred in the two areas outside the army that had been critical to the modernization of the PLA: Sino-Soviet relations and China's national development policy. As these changes merged into a tidal wave of anti-professionalism, they brought to a halt the military modernization of the 1950s.

The Soviet Connection and the Chinese Army

The deterioration of Sino-Soviet relations in the second half of the 1950s had a profoundly adverse effect on the modernization of the PLA, because its progress was predicated on the expectation that the Chinese would continue to receive Soviet military equipment and to absorb Soviet methods of operation. However, the Soviet military connection was increasingly jeopardized, and finally severed, by the more and more critical attitude of the Chinese leadership towards the Soviet Union. This attitude had two main sources.

One was the disenchantment of the Chinese leadership with the Soviet model of development. Having pinned high hopes on Stalinist methods of industrialization as the way to building up national power in China in a short time, the Chinese had become disappointed by the gap which had developed between industrial and agricultural production, and by the inability of the agricultural sector to provide the surplus required by their ambitious industrial goals. More important for the military was the growing concern of many leaders, most notably Mao, over the socio-political consequences of importing Soviet methods of operation. These consequences were sharply at variance with the revolutionary experience and post-revolutionary expectations of the Chinese leaders, for under Soviet influence the Chinese revolution was becoming routinized and China's revolutionaries were becoming bureaucratized. As a foremost recipient of Soviet influence, the military establishment became a prime target for the Party leadership's attempts to stem the drift away from revolutionary values. By the end of the decade these attempts were reinforced by other factors and developed in a full-scale negation of military professionalism which, while varying in intensity, remained a major obstacle to military modernization throughout the remainder of the Maoist period.

Reinforcing the disenchantment of the Chinese leadership with the internal effects of the Soviet connection was its growing dissatisfaction with the international strategy laid down by the Kremlin for the Communist bloc. During the period of amicable relations between China and the Soviet Union, the Chinese accepted the Soviet line in global politics, which was based on the assumption that the strategic superiority of the United States and the destructiveness of nuclear weapons compelled the Communist bloc to pursue a policy of coexistence rather than confrontation with the West. Dependent on the Soviet nuclear shield and wary of America's designs, as reflected in its active anti-China policy after Korea, the Chinese could hardly do otherwise, even though their basic global and regional aims – the attainment of great-power status and the absorption of Taiwan – remained unfulfilled. In the mid 1950s the Chinese tried to achieve these aims by a flexible and friendly policy, typified by the 'five principles of coexistence' and the 'spirit of Bandung'. But while this policy greatly improved China's image, it hardly brought the Chinese closer to realizing their ambitions. From their vantage point, a new course of action was in order when conditions became appropriate.

Conditions became appropriate, in the estimate of Peking, in the autumn of 1957 due to Soviet achievements in military technology, as illustrated by the Russian launching of an ICBM and the orbiting of earth satellites.[11] This development had a galvanizing effect on the Chinese and opened new vistas for them. They now believed that the strategic balance of power in the international arena had shifted decisively in favour of the bloc, a belief expressed in Mao's famous meteorological metaphor, 'the East wind prevails over the West wind'. They thought that the bloc should exploit this new-found superiority to launch a frontal assault on the bastions of 'imperialism' through active support of 'national liberation' wars. And they were prepared to accept the risk of local wars in the conviction that, because of its inferior position, the West would not dare to escalate them into a general war.

This was a risk the Russians were not prepared to take. They did not share Peking's evaluation of the new military balance, and they did not draw the same conclusions with respect to the possibilities for action. The Russians did not claim in 1957, as the Chinese did, that the strategic balance had shifted in favour of the bloc, and they were reluctant to foment local conflicts for fear that these might escalate into a nuclear confrontation with the more powerful United States over issues peripheral to Russia's vital interests. What the Russians wanted was to use their achievements in weapons technology not to launch an offensive against the United States, but to reach an accommodation with it. This course was unacceptable to the Chinese for it meant that the two superpowers, having satisfied their basic global interests, would freeze the status quo – leaving the Chinese outside with their fundamental ambitions unfulfilled.

In the ensuing months and years these deeply divergent assessments of the global power balance were to become the prime factor fuelling the Sino-Soviet conflict. However, in 1957, when these differences were just emerging, a new and momentous issue was injected into the Sino-Soviet relationship, which was to have an enormous impact not only on the evolution of this relationship, but also, and more specifically, on the Sino-Soviet military connection and on the internal development of the PLA. This was the issue of Soviet nuclear aid to China.

This issue did not surface as a divisive force in the alliance until 1958. Although the Soviets began to assist China in a non-military nuclear programme in 1955, the Chinese did not attempt to develop a nuclear military capability, but relied on their treaty with the Soviet Union to deter a nuclear attack by the United States on China. In 1956, however, their sights were already set on such a capability, as indicated by Mao's statement that 'in the not-too-distant future' China would possess its 'own atomic bombs'.[12] However, Mao also warned the military that they would have to reduce the military budget in order to provide funds for the industrial underpinning of a nuclear programme, implying that this was to be a long-term indigenous effort. But impatience apparently overcame other considerations so that a year or so later the Chinese were evidently putting pressure on the Soviets to supply them with concrete aid for the development of military nuclear technology. The result was one of the strangest and most significant events in the history of Sino-Soviet relations: a secret agreement 'on new technology for national defence' signed on 15 October, 1957 and according to which the Soviet Union was to provide China with 'a sample of an atomic bomb and technical data concerning its manufacture'.[13]

In retrospect, it seems that this agreement was inevitably doomed to failure. China's heightened desire for an early independent nuclear capability derived from its dissatisfation with the posture and policies of the Soviet leadership, to which it was now turning for aid that was intended to support policies that were strongly disapproved of by this very leadership. The Soviets, for their part, were put in an impossible dilemma. On the one hand, they wanted to placate the Chinese and to retain their support for Soviet leadership of the bloc, which they could not do by blatantly refusing to help the Chinese. This was apparently the main reason for their signing the agreement. On the other hand, however, they had no intention of helping the increasingly dissident and even, in the Soviet view, reckless Chinese acquire a capability that would enable them to pursue an independent course that undermined and endangered basic Soviet policies.

These difficulties became apparent in the aftermath of the agreement. Presumably phrased in general terms, the agreement left the details to be subsequently worked out, and when the time came for concrete steps, the Soviets held back. They probably tried to fend off Chinese pressure by proposing to deploy nuclear weapons in China on the condition that the Soviets retained full control over them, a proposal that was rejected out of hand by the Chinese.[14] By early 1958, Chinese statements reflected pessimism about the prospect for receiving outside aid for their nuclear programme, and in mid-year they reached a fateful decision: China would proceed with the long-term development of its own nuclear capability on the basis of self-reliance.[15]

Freed from a central reason for following the Soviet line, the Chinese stepped up their attacks on Soviet policies, and also involved the Soviets against their will in the Taiwan Straits crisis of 1958.[16] By mid-1959 the Soviets obviously were fed up: on 20 June, the Chinese later claimed, they 'unilaterally tore up' the defence agreement, as one sanction against China's rising defiance. In 1960 the Soviets abruptly cut off all aid to China. The Sino-Soviet conflict was moving inexorably toward a climax.

The Great Leap Forward and the Return to 'People's War'

The adoption of a strategy based on the premises that China could acquire nuclear weapons only over the long haul by its own efforts, and that the Soviet Union was an unreliable military ally, had major implications for the armed forces. The starting point was that, given China's limited resources, concentration on an indigenous nuclear programme meant that it would inevitably have to be carried out at the expense of further large-scale development of the conventional forces. Though a far-reaching decision, it was never publicly specified during the Maoist period. However, in 1983, the Minister of Defence Zhang Aiping mentioned it explicitly:

> In the 1950s when our country was under blockade, encirclement and imperialist threat, the state emphasized the modernization of our national defence and allocated a larger amount of funds to it.
>
> Nevertheless the funds were still limited and fell far short of demands posed by various aspects of our national defence modernization. If we had used those funds equally in all areas and tried to develop everything, we would have achieved nothing or would have succeeded in minor projects and failed in major projects. Therefore, we had to concentrate the limited amounts of funds on projects that were most important, most urgently needed and could have an impact on the whole situation .... In 1956 the CPC Central Committee decided that developing guided missiles and atomic energy were the two key projects in our national defence modernization .... Our work in developing guided missiles and atomic bombs started relatively late but the speed of development was relatively quick. One important reason for this was that we ... gave priority to key tasks and concentrated our resources of labour, materials and funds.[17]

This decision disrupted the all-round modernization of China's conventional forces just when they were beginning to catch up with other modern armies, and was one of the main reasons for the gap that developed between them and these armies in the following years.

The freezing of further large-scale progress of the conventional forces was feasible in the view of the Maoist leadership because these forces had reached a level that was adequate to the defence of China. This belief was based on the publicly articulated assumption of the Chinese leaders that even if they could not deter a nuclear strike, such a strike would have to be followed by a ground invasion, because this was the only way to subjugate China. And against a ground invasion the Chinese could mount a superior defence despite their technological inferiority.

Such a defence, however, could not be based on a conventional strategy of positional warfare employed by a regular army with sophisticated weapons, but had to fall back upon Mao's doctrine of 'people's war', which relied on the superiority of the 'human element' and a mobile strategy of defence-in-depth to overcome technological inadequacies. Consequently, Mao's doctrine of 'people's war', which had been shelved as an operational concept during the period of modernization, was vigorously revived and became the source of guidelines for all the activities of the PLA.

The revival applied not only to the strategy and tactics of a 'people's war' but also to preparing the armed forces for this kind of war. These two aspects of the doctrine were inseparable. If waging the war dictated primary reliance on the superiority of the 'human element', then all practices in the armed forces had to be directed towards ensuring the high personal quality of the troops and their close co-operation with the civilian population. Thus, improvement of morale and close-combat skills became the primary concern of the leadership. Political work was strengthened and political control over the armed forces reasserted. Soviet-influenced attitudes were denounced and professionalism was denigrated.

The leadership's distrust of the professional army was also manifested in the reactivation of the militia on an unprecedented scale. Dating back to the early days of the Red Army, the militia had always functioned in response to limited needs and had been relatively small. After the introduction of conscription, it had fallen into a state of oblivion. With the return to 'people's war', a frenetic campaign under the slogan 'everyone a soldier' swept the nation, and the vastly expanded militia was portrayed as having the same importance to China's defence as the PLA.

The revival of the 'people's war' doctrine and its associated practices was inseparable from the far-reaching changes that took place on the national scene towards the end of the decade. Cut adrift from the Soviet model by their dissatisfaction with its effects and by the lessening prospect of substantial Soviet aid, Chinese leaders needed an alternative strategy that would enable them to continue the momentum of development by their own efforts. After almost two years of policy debates and oscillations, they converged behind Mao and his bold new approach to China's development problems – the Great Leap Forward.

Rooted in their own revolutionary experience, the Great Leap was inspired by Mao's revolutionary ideology, which had been submerged during the heyday of Soviet influence , but which now surfaced with fresh force and new dimensions. Looking at their current problems through the prism of their past experience, the Chinese leaders came to the conclusion that the methods which had brought them success in the revolutionary struggle could also be applied to the present. These methods sprang from Mao's basic belief that properly organized and motivated masses could move mountains through sheer human will power.

The Great Leap was conceived by Mao not only as a strategy of development, but also as a strategy that would preserve China's revolutionary character in the midst of modernization. In effect, this became the primary objective. By highlighting such elements as mass participation, egalitarianism, the supremacy of 'reds' over 'experts', and the dominance of the Party, the Chinese sought to create an environment in which economic development could proceed without the country succumbing to the materialistic pressures that characterize post-revolutionary societies. The result was a highly charged evangelical atmosphere, in which revolutionary principles reigned supreme and bureaucratic methods of operation were derided.

The consequences of these changes for the PLA and its future evolution were calamitous. First, they shattered leadership consensus on the urgent need for military modernization not only because of pragmatic considerations of resource allocation, but also for ideological reasons. This was because a PLA that operated according to professional maxims was now viewed as riven with unacceptable attitudes. Furthermore, as the foremost bastion of professionalism, the PLA was subjected to severe attacks by Maoist ideologues, which created a politically charged atmosphere that cowed officers and undermined military competence. Even after the Great Leap collapsed, the attitudes towards military modernization and, in particular, military professionalism, which were spawned by radical Maoist ideology endured in one form or another until the end of the Maoist period. Under these circumstances, the continuation of all-round military modernization was a mission impossible.

The policies of the Great Leap aroused growing dissent among military leaders, headed by Defence Minister Marshal Peng Dehuai, and led to the most serious leadership struggle since the establishment of the Communist regime. The arena for this struggle was the Lushan Conference of the Central Committee, held in July–August 1959, and the immediate spark that ignited it was Peng's bitter indictment of the Great Leap and its economic consequences.[18] But the background to Peng's challenge was provided by his disapproval of the foreign and military policies pursued by Mao and his colleagues.[19] Peng favoured continued reliance on Soviet aid for the development of China's nuclear programme, and reliance on the Soviet nuclear shield while this development was in progress. In the conventional field, Peng and his colleagues advocated the continued development of the PLA along the Soviet model and with Soviet aid in the direction of a modernized and mechanized army.

However, in the months preceding the Lushan Conference it had become increasingly clear to the Chinese that the price which the Soviets put on such aid was China's acceptance of the Soviet line in international affairs, and to some extent in internal affairs as well. This was a price that Peng was prepared to pay, or at least negotiate, for what he considered the overriding interest of national security. What Peng was not prepared to do was to tolerate the damage done to the armed forces by the introduction of the full panoply of Maoist policies and practices.

Peng's attempt to bring about a policy change was defeated by Mao, and he was dismissed and severely criticized. Peng's dismissal was the final signal that the PLA had entered a new period in which his brand of military professionalism had no place. In the post-Mao period, Peng was posthumously rehabilitated and praised,[20] and again it was a signal that the PLA had entered a new period – but this time military professionalism had been given pride of place.

The Leadership of Lin Biao: A Precarious Balancing Act

Peng's replacement as defence minister was Marshal Lin Biao, who a dozen years later was to play the central part in the most bizarre and sensational episode in the history of Chinese Communism: the alleged plot to assassinate Mao. But until he fell out with the Chairman, Lin was a faithful curator of the revolutionary values of which Mao was the creator. A firm believer in Maoist military principles, as well as a brilliant and experienced battlefield commander, Lin did not hold an active post during the period of modernization because, among other reasons, he presumably was dissatisfied with the direction which the Soviet-influenced PLA was taking. Upon assuming command of the PLA, Lin was entrusted with implementing the two-pronged policy of nuclear development and 'people's war'.[21]

Lin's immediate task was to set the military house in order and to soothe the severe strains that had developed between the Party and the PLA by creating a balance between political and military requirements. To this end Lin pursued parallel policies. The most publicized one was designed to reassert overall political control over the armed forces, to strengthen political education, particularly at the basic levels, and to reaffirm Maoist military principles as the practical guide to all military activities. At the same time, Lin was careful not to alienate the officer corps. Under his leadership, the excesses of the anti-professional campaigns were curbed, combat readiness was emphasized, the militia was retrenched, and conventional weapons were procured on a selective and limited basis.

The abrupt withdrawal of Soviet advisers in 1960 'left the Chinese industry with half-built factories, partly completed assembly lines, blueprints without prototypes, and prototypes without blueprints'.[22] Hardest hit was the air force: spare parts and fuel were in short supply, many planes were grounded and some were cannibalized, and training and flight time was drastically cut. Other forces were also affected by shortages of fuel and spare parts, and a major programme for the reorganization of the armed forces was postponed.

The Chinese attempted to overcome these difficulties by indigenous production but their accomplishments were extremely limited. This was especially true of heavy weapons and equipment. Although they succeeded in producing aircraft (mainly MiG-17s and 19s), tanks (T-54s) and naval patrol craft, the numbers were small and the designs out of date. The cut-off of

Soviet assistance was not adequately compensated for by weapons made in China.

One reason was the great economic crisis caused by the collapse of the Great Leap Forward, which coincided with the withdrawal of Soviet assistance. But another reason, more important in the long run, was the policy of the leadership. By channelling resources to the nuclear weapons programme and by exalting the 'man over weapons' doctrine in the PLA, the leadership failed to provide the armed forces with the financial and political backing which were necessary for carrying out a continuous and comprehensive re-equipment programme. In addition to limiting the acquisition of conventional weapons, the leadership's policy effectively neutralized officers who desired to improve professional standards, because it made them vulnerable to charges of propagating a 'purely military viewpoint' and neglecting political considerations. This effect was perhaps more serious than the slowing down of weapons development. While there was some progress in the production of weapons, there were no concomitant advances in doctrine and operational methods essential to all-round modernization. On the contrary, in these areas the PLA entered a state of stagnation from which it did not emerge until after the end of the Maoist era.

In the improvement of political and ideological standards the PLA was a shining success. Three years of concerted efforts by Lin Biao transformed it from a hotbed of professional deviations into the chief national repository of Maoist military dogma and revolutionary ethics. Its revolutionary spirit contrasted sharply with the bureaucratism and sluggishness of the Party apparatus in the wake of the Great Leap disaster. By this reversal of roles the PLA was drawn into the political arena in a new capacity – not, as previously, to carry out the policies of a united leadership, but rather to support the Maoists against other groups in an increasingly divided Party leadership. Thus began the involvement of the PLA in leadership conflicts – an involvement that soon turned into full-scale and direct intervention that dominated all its activities for a dozen years and had a disastrous effect on its internal cohesion and military posture.

Against the background of escalating American attacks on North Vietnam and deteriorating Sino-Soviet relations, the increasing politicization of the PLA and its involvement in factional conflicts sparked another struggle at the top of the military hierachy. This struggle pitted the chief of staff, Luo Ruiqing, against Lin Biao and Mao. Appointed to his post in 1959, Luo had been a public security officer who had obviously been brought into the PLA to enforce political control. But in the course of performing his duties, Luo had become the spokesman for the professional military. From his vantage point, the possibility of a military clash loomed on the horizon and Luo advocated urgent measures to prepare for this eventuality. These consisted of giving priority to the PLA's military role, building up its forces for a positional defence, accelerating the production of conventional weapons, and improving relations with the Soviet Union in order to obtain the most needed equipment.

Luo's proposals were rejected by Lin and Mao, who remained committed to a strategy of 'people's war' as the ultimate defence against the threat of invasion, and to a cautious and unprovocative foreign policy as a way of reducing such a threat. At the end of 1965, Luo was removed from office (he resumed public duties in the mid-1970s but died several years later). The PLA's continuing reliance on a mass-based 'people's war' strategy was symbolically reaffirmed by the abolition of all ranks in the armed forces, which were not reinstituted until almost twenty years later.

Although Luo was dismissed, his views on the production of conventional weapons were not rejected. In 1965, defence expenditures began to rise rapidly, reaching a peak in 1971. The estimated annual growth in defence expenditures for the period of 1965–71 averaged 10 per cent. Aside from the nuclear programme, these expenditures were translated into the expanded production of conventional weapons systems – mainly aircraft, air defences, patrol craft and submarines.

These improvements in the PLA's force posture were, however, completely inundated by the tidal waves that swept over the country as the Cultural Revolution got underway. As the PLA became more and more involved in the great upheaval, its military role became increasingly subordinated to current political needs. Despite advances in the weapons of the general purpose forces, the overall combat capabilities of the PLA declined drastically.

The PLA in the Cultural Revolution: The Politics and Effects of Intervention

The Cultural Revolution was a great disaster for the PLA.[23] It entangled the army in bruising factional fights and deeply divided the military leadership at all levels of the chain of command. It forced military commanders throughout the PLA to focus their concerns on political manoeuvring rather than on military manoeuvres. It diverted troops from routine tasks and severely strained their discipline. It threw the organization and regular procedures of the PLA into disarray. The Cultural Revolution, in short, effectively transformed the PLA from a professional military into a political force.

These effects were not foreseen by any of the principal participants in the Cultural Revolution, because the deepening political involvement of the PLA resulted from the escalation of the Cultural Revolution, which occurred in response to unexpected developments. This escalation began when the

Maoists were stymied in their efforts to purge Party organizations by using the newly formed Red Guards. Thwarted by the unexpectedly forceful resistance of the Party bureaucracy and faced with mounting chaos, the Maoists decided that the only alternative to terminating the Cultural Revolution was to commit their last remaining asset – the PLA – in support of the 'revolutionary' forces. After the Maoist leadership removed PLA leaders opposed to such a momentous move, they ordered the PLA to intervene directly in the factional struggles raging throughout China in order to 'support the Left'.

This decision subjected the PLA to intolerable strains, which became apparent from the outset of its entry into the volatile political arena in January 1967. Confronted with contradictory directives to maintain order and to support the Left, regional military commanders generally opted for stability rather than revolution. To fill the vacuum created by the paralysis of Party and administrative organs, military commanders, in co-ordination with moderate leaders in Beijing, established Revolutionary Committees, which the PLA dominated. Where such Committees were not set up, the PLA ruled directly through Military Control Committees.

The army's preference for order and for working with old-time cadres aroused the opposition of revolutionary activists, to which the army responded in accordance with shifts in the balance of power among the radical and moderate wings of the Beijing leadership. As the balance shifted, the behaviour of the PLA alternated between repression and restraint. Eventually, the proponents of a hard line toward anarchic 'revolutionary' elements, who plunged China's main cities into total turmoil, gained the upper hand. By the time the Cultural Revolution was terminated in April 1969, the Red Guard organizations had been largely broken up, and the power of their mentors in Peking appreciably diminished. As the Party organizations were still in disarray or were defunct, the PLA became the supreme political and administrative authority in the provinces and, largely as a result of this, a central force in Beijing politics. At the height of the upheaval, some two million troops were assigned to political duties.

But the PLA was also severely split as a result of the terrible stresses caused by its intrusion into the political struggles. The main rift was between Lin Biao and some of his colleagues in the high command, who had favoured intervention and had become identified with the radical Left, on the one hand, and, on the other hand, most regional commanders and professional military leaders, who had to bear the bitter consequences of leftist policies, and who were allied with the moderate wing of the Maoist leadership. Not only had Lin failed to protect his regional commanders from Red Guard assaults, but he had dispatched main force units to support radical organizations which the military commanders in the regions were trying to suppress, thereby exacerbating intra-army rivalries. These rivalries isolated the Lin Biao group within the military establishment and undercut Lin's power base in national politics, even as the PLA gained supreme political authority. The effect of these splits on Lin's position became apparent in the immediate aftermath of the Cultural Revolution.

When the upheaval ended, the army did not return to the barracks. On the contrary, the military continued to consolidate its power in the political sphere by directing the process of Party reconstruction which got under way after the turmoil. Since the reconstituted Party Committees were to be superior to the army-dominated Revolutionary Committees, the Party leadership viewed the process of reconstruction as a way of getting the military out of politics and of reasserting civilian control over the army. The military, however, did not co-operate. Instead of stepping aside in favour of civilians, the military used their political posts to ensure that their representatives would be appointed to leading positions in the new Party Committees. China's political system thus became military-dominated.

The military refused to withdraw from the political arena not simply because power, once acquired whatever the initial impetus, is not easily given up. They refused to withdraw primarily because of the hostility of most military commanders to the radical Left. Consequently, the military were determined to block radical representatives from gaining positions of power, and as long as this possibility existed, they were not prepared to surrender their political posts and expose China again to the threat of disorder.

Internal PLA rivalries produced by the Cultural Revolution also contributed to its continued hold on political power. In order to strengthen the PLA as his power base in national politics, Lin Biao sought not only to consolidate its political position, but also to replace regional officers who had 'accounts to settle' with him and his supporters during the reconstruction of the Party. These attempts strengthened the determination of regional commanders to hold on to their positions. Rival PLA groups thus had different motives for remaining in the political arena, but the result was a failure to return power to the civilians.

This failure united the radical and moderate wings of the Beijing leadership in a coalition against Lin Biao, who was held responsible for the continued domination of the military. Crucial to this coalition was the support or acquiescence of Lin's opponents among the regional commanders and professional military leaders at the Centre, as evidenced by the ability of Mao and Zhou Enlai to isolate Lin and his close colleagues with relative ease. As a result of his isolation, Lin and his supporters acted in desperation, and Lin was reportedly killed in a plane crash when he fled to the Soviet Union after allegedly attempting to assassinate Mao.

After the defeat of the Lin Biao group, the coalition that had brought it about became unstuck, and the Maoist leadership again split into radical and moderate wings. Consequently, the remaining years of the Maoist era were dominated by constant conflict between these groups and their supporters throughout the power structure. In this conflict, policy differences were inextricably intertwined with power struggles. The radicals – stigmatized after their downfall as the 'gang of four' – wanted to perpetuate the mass-oriented and ideologically inspired practices of the Cultural Revolution in order to preserve the revolutionary character of Chinese society at all costs; the moderates, however, wanted to discard or dilute these practices and give priority to material development. As the prerequisite to the acceptance of its approach, each group tried to fill leadership positions at all echelons of the political pyramid with its supporters, generating a continuous contest for power. Adding force and urgency to this contest was Mao's declining physical condition and the imminent prospect of a great succession struggle.

Capitalizing on their success in curbing radical excesses in the final stages of the Cultural Revolution and after its termination, moderate leaders took the initiative in policy-making and in reinstating veteran cadres, who had been disgraced and dismissed during the Cultural Revolution. The radicals, however, did not remain passive in the face of this threat to their position. Utilizing their domination of the mass media and their access to Mao, they repeatedly launched attacks on moderate leaders and their policies. As a result, the twilight years of the Maoist era were marked by political instability and uncertainty.

In these unpropitious circumstances, PLA leaders tried to repair the damage done to the armed forces during the Cultural Revolution, and to return them to a more regular track. The obstacles were enormous. One was the continued, if substantially reduced, involvement of PLA commanders and troops in political and administrative affairs. More important, the PLA became a prime target of attacks by radical leaders, who mistrusted the bulk of the PLA leadership for political and ideological reasons. As a conservative political force, the PLA was suspect because it had taken the lead in cracking down on marauding Red Guards during the Cultural Revolution, and continued, with few exceptions, to co-operate with moderate leaders in the capital and the localities. The radicals, therefore, tried to undermine the PLA by meddling in its internal affairs, by discrediting its veteran leaders and traditions, and by attempting to bring some PLA elements into their camp.[24]

The radicals also looked with suspicion on the attempts of PLA leaders to improve its military capabilities and professional competence. For one thing, they presumably figured that the more the PLA strengthened its professional attitudes, the less it would be amenable to their influence. They obviously preferred the army to be highly politicized, so that its internal cohesion would not be cemented by common professional views. Furthermore, the radicals looked upon the PLA as a breeding ground of views that were 'purely military'

22

and were incompatible with Maoist values. The PLA was, therefore, a prime objective of radical attacks, which were aimed at any manifestation of military professionalism. Such attacks obstructed the development of the PLA's equipment and the improvement of its professional skills.

Nowhere was such obstruction more evident than in the aftermath of the highly important mid-1975 meeting of the Military Affairs Committee, at which Deng Xiaoping, who had been appointed chief of staff shortly before the meeting, outlined an ambitious programme for the modernization and consolidation of the armed forces. The programme, however, never got off the ground during the Maoist period because the radicals subverted its implementation.[25] This is how two post-Mao reports, the substance of which there is no reason to doubt, described what happened after the meeting:

> The 1975 enlarged meeting of the Military Commission laid down a series of principles, policies, and measures for accelerating the building of our army along revolutionary and modern lines ....The "gang of four" smeared this as the "bourgeois military line". When we went in for training and studying techniques and other professional matters, they said we opposed putting politics in command and that ours was "purely a military viewpoint". When we undertook scientific research and armament, they said we opposed the concept of "people's war" and embraced the "theory that weapons decide everything"....[26]

> In his speech Vice-Chairman Deng mentioned that fighting a battle requires steel and non-ferrous metal and that fighting a battle to boost steel production, like a tough battle fought by the army, is not an easy task in industry. By sleight of hand, the gang of four changed the statement into "fighting a battle is fighting a battle for steel" and then attacked the statement as being an "exponent of the theory that weapons decide everything"....[27]

In this state of affairs, the PLA could hardly pursue regular and long-term programmes of re-equipment, training and reorganization, and the damage done to it in the preceding years was not repaired. Although the production of weapons systems begun in the 1960s was expanded in the 1970s, particularly of aircraft and naval vessels, it remained isolated from other areas of the army's activities. Thus, while weapons were developed selectively, professional standards declined totally. And this decline could not be reversed as long as the radicals held power. Small wonder then that their downfall was greeted by the military paper with what seemed like a sigh of relief: 'The smashing of the "gang of four" ', it said, 'has swept away the biggest obstacle to army building.'[28]

2

Leadership Politics and Perceptions

The previously quoted comment of the army paper that the downfall of the radical leaders had 'swept away the biggest obstacle to army building' only highlighted the intimate link between leadership politics and the fortunes of the military. This link remains strong as ever in the post-Mao years. Whatever the influence of the military as an institution on national decision-making, it is ultimately the top Party leadership that determines policy for the defence establishment. In the Maoist period, its policy retarded the progress of the PLA; since then, leadership policy has provided the essential impetus for the drive to military modernization. A brief discussion of leadership politics is, therefore, necessary for understanding military policy.

The Political Setting

Although Maoist military policy was ultimately responsible for the deterioration of the PLA, the policy could not be changed in isolation from other sectors of society. This was because Maoist military policy was only one aspect of an all-encompassing revolutionary blueprint which Mao sought to impose on Chinese society, and the PLA was only one institution which bore the consequences of the Maoist campaign. Military reforms, therefore, had to be preceded by leadership changes which would lead to the abandonment of Maoist ideology as the guide to China's development.

Rooted in the revolutionary struggle of the Chinese Communists, this ideology was populist, voluntaristic and anti-bureaucratic. Increasingly fearful from the late 1950s that the gains of the revolution were jeopardized by the by-products of material modernization, Mao revived the ideology of the past to safeguard these gains in the present. Positing it as a source of Party policy, Mao sought to wage a permanent 'class struggle' against bourgeois ideas and the forces to which such ideas gave rise. Convinced that bourgeois 'class enemies' continued to exist even after the Communists seized power, Mao called for constant inculcation of revolutionary values to ensure that material development would not dilute the egalitarian goals of the revolution. He insisted on the implementation of policy through campaigns of mass mobilization to keep society in permanent turmoil and to prevent bureaucratic domination. And he tried to isolate the Chinese people as much as possible from foreign influences.

Despite his commitment to this ideology, Mao was not intrinsically opposed to material modernization. As much as other leaders, he strove to develop China as fast as possible to create national wealth and power. But Mao also strove to insulate the modernizing society from the corrosive consequences of modernization. In this way, he hoped to achieve a society that was both 'modern' and 'revolutionary', and to nurture an all-round individual who was both 'red' and 'expert'. However, the intractable realities of development demonstrated that these two goals could not be attained at the same time. Forced to choose, Mao was prepared to subordinate material progress to the preservation of revolutionary values.

This choice was unacceptable to most of Mao's colleagues. Although committed to socialist objectives, they were not prepared to sacrifice economic progress for Maoist ideology. Never a monolithic group, they were united in their readiness to compromise Maoist revolutionary values for economic development by adopting methods that were pragmatic, bureaucratic and materialistic. Although many of them had supported Mao in the launching of the Great Leap Forward, they were profoundly shocked by its catastrophic consequences and were determined to abandon the ideology and methods on which it was based.

To Mao this meant abandoning the revolution, and after the failure of the Great Leap Forward he waged a relentless crusade to prevent this happening. This was why Mao remained committed to the principles of the Greap Leap even after it collapsed, and looked with disdain upon the policies of retreat which followed it. This was why in 1962 he demanded an end to the retreat, and became increasingly furious at the Party leadership and its apparatus for failing to implement his directives. This was why he launched the Cultural Revolution to shake up the Party and escalated the upheaval several times rather than call it off when he encountered resistance. And this was why he elevated radical leaders to the summit of power and sanctioned their activities as a counter-force to the moderate leaders and their policies.

The parting of the way between Mao and his colleagues shattered the political consensus of the first decade and polarized the leaders in increasingly brutal struggles for power, policies and survival. Although these struggles also took a heavy toll of Mao's political authority, the Chairman remained the ultimate arbiter of Chinese politics. Relying on his charisma, personal stature and political acumen, Mao was able to intervene at critical junctures in the political process to block the formal adoption of policies which diverged from his social blueprint. He intervened in this way, for example, at the famous Tenth Plenum of the Central Committee in order to reverse the drift away from revolutionary policies that followed the disaster of the Great Leap Forward. Although such intervention did not prevent various power-holders from quietly contradicting central directives, these trans-gressions did not amount to a change of direction. Such change could not take place in Mao's lifetime.

After Mao, breathtaking change became the watchword of the new regime.[1] By the end of the 1970s, a titanic effort to reform the Chinese social and political system was under way. Six years later the nation was in the throes of what Deng Xiaoping aptly called a 'second revolution', as stunning reforms swept away the Maoist legacy and sought to rebuild the Chinese system in a bold new mould.

Facilitating this revolution have been far-reaching changes in the make-up and thinking of the ruling elite. By far the most important change has been the restoration since 1979 of a consensus concerning China's basic political and economic objectives. This ended a twenty-year rift over the relative signific-ance of material progress and revolutionary purity in the development of the country. Although consensus has not precluded policy conflicts, they have been contained within a broader commitment to common national goals. Consequently, in sharp contrast to the Maoist period, conflicts have not polarized the leadership and paralysed the decision-making process. On the contrary, it is the absence of irreconcilable ideological differences at the top of the power structure that has largely accounted for the dynamism of the post-Mao development drive. When differences have cropped up, they have been devoid of ideological content, and their effect has been to slow down but not alter the policy course.

Within the framework of this consensus, disparate groups of leaders which came together to topple the 'gang of four' have jockeyed for power and clashed over policy. Several large groups can be identified, although this division simplifies reality because it takes no account of subtler shades of opinion and political alliances. Foremost is the group headed by Deng Xiaoping, which consists mainly of veteran Party officials and administrators who had largely been purged during the Cultural Revolution. After several years of sinuous manoeuvring, the Deng group eliminated its major rivals and emerged as the paramount force at the top of China's power structure. It then mounted a determined effort to project its influence into the lower reaches of the ruling hierarchy. Secure in their dominant political position, Deng and his colleagues raised the banner of radical reform and have led the nation on its dramatic dash to modernization.

Their principal opponents were neo-Maoist leaders headed by Mao's designated successor, Hua Guofeng. Hua came to power during the Cultural Revolution and had co-operated with the radical leaders, but turned against them after Mao's death. Although favouring modernization, Hua and his supporters highlighted their link with the Maoist legacy, which undergirded their power, and tended to invoke Maoist slogans to legitimize their policies. For this reason they were branded the 'whatever' group by their opponents on the grounds that they wanted to abide by whatever Mao had said.

Hua Guofeng and his group crumbled quickly under the weight of Deng Xiaoping's power plays. Not only did they lack a solid power base, but Hua was a lacklustre figure, whose main claim to authority was his dubious anointment by Mao and his hopeless attempt to cast himself in the Chairman's image. Also working against them was their invocation of Maoist slogans, which was sharply out of step with the post-Maoist political mood. It did not take Deng long after returning to political activity in mid-1977 to undercut Hua's position. Deng's tactic was to appoint a great number of rehabilitated victims of the Cultural Revolution to pivotal leadership positions in the provinces and localities. Since Hua's main grass-roots support came from cadres appointed during the Cultural Revolution, this tactic critically weakened his position. By the time the landmark Third Plenum of the 11th Central Committee was convened in December 1978, the balance of power had shifted decisively in favour of Deng's forces.

The Third Plenum has rightly been viewed by the Deng leadership as a crucial turning point in China's post-Mao history. The Plenum rehabilitated Deng's purged colleagues, appointed his key allies to the Politburo and criticized the neo-Maoists. It also reversed verdicts on important episodes, such as the Tiananmen Incident of 1976, after which Deng was dismissed from office by a coalition in which Hua and his allies played a central role. The Plenum also brought about the termination of 'class struggle' and adopted Deng's programme of 'socialist modernization' which gave precedence to economic development. Encapsulated in the pragmatic slogan 'taking practice as the sole criterion of truth', which Deng inscribed on his banner, this programme completely changed the course of China's development.

After the Plenum, Deng kept up relentless pressure on the hapless Hua and his supporters. One line of attack was further to chip away at Hua's image by criticizing his slogans and discrediting him personally. Prominent in this campaign were the sensational show trials of the 'gang of four' and Lin Biao's associates, which began at the end of 1980, and which by implication were also directed at personalities like Hua and his associates, who had been important in the Cultural Revolution and its aftermath.

A more significant line of attack was directed at deposing Hua's allies from positions of power at the centre and replacing them with Deng's associates.

This was done over the next two years at a series of Party meetings. The ultimate victim of these moves was Hua himself. At the National People's Congress in September 1980, Hua resigned as premier in favour of Zhao Ziyang, and two months later stepped down as Party chairman and chairman of the Military Affairs Commission, although this act was not announced until the Sixth Plenum of the 11th Central Committee in June 1981.

This was another landmark Plenum. After months of internal discussions and debates, the Central Committee repudiated a critical part of the Maoist legacy by blaming the Chairman directly for the catastrophe of the Cultural Revolution. It also criticized Hua's performance, and announced his replacement as Party chairman by Hu Yaobang. The *coup de grâce* to Hua and his allies was administered by Deng at the 12th Party Congress in September 1982, when Hua Guofeng was removed from the Politburo and demoted to the Central Committee, while his remaining supporters lost their positions in the ruling organs. Hua and his group were thus a fleeting force in Chinese politics.

Another group that Deng had to contend with consisted of veteran 'old guard' Party leaders, who survived the Cultural Revolution despite intense hostility between them and the 'gang of four', and who played a critical role in the downfall of the radicals. The group's most prominent member was the late defence minister Ye Jianying and it included such prestigious figures as Li Xiannian. Members of this group protected Deng after his fall from power in 1976 and pushed for his reinstatement in 1977. However, they were more conservative than Deng, and opposed him over the extent to which Mao's legacy should be repudiated in the pronouncements and policies of the new leadership. Their attachment to this legacy derived both from the integral link between their personal stature and the past symbolized by Mao, and from their belief that the legacy was essential for the legitimacy of the post-Mao rulers, as well as for the unity and stability of the country.

Deng's relations with Ye and his colleagues were much more complex than with the Hua group. First, members of the Deng and Ye coalitions shared ties of friendship and co-operation that went back many years and they treated each other with respect and restraint. Second, the 'old guard' commands great prestige in China and its views had to be taken into account. Most important, Ye and his close circle of allies were not contenders for power, and their activities were aimed at influencing policy rather than capturing positions.

For these reasons, Ye and his colleagues did not pose a threat to Deng, though they undoubtedly exercised a restraining influence. To accommodate their views, Deng presumably had to make marginal concessions and tactical retreats, most notably perhaps in toning down the denunciation of Mao. However, the 'old guard' did not divert the Deng leadership from the main lines of its policy. While still a force to be reckoned with when Deng consolidated his power and launched his reforms, the influence of the 'old guard' was already on the decline. Although they did not respond to Deng's prodding to relinquish their official positions at the 12th Party Congress in 1982, many 'old guard' leaders were old and infirm, and at a special Party conference in September 1985 they 'resigned' en masse from their posts. Most prominent among those who retired were the old marshals Ye Jianying, Nie Rongzhen and Xu Xiangqian. Ye died in October 1986.

Much more problematic for Deng has been the opposition to his policies from senior members of the Politburo, foremost among whom have been Chen Yun and Peng Zhen. Although also 'old guard' figures, they differ from members of the Ye group in important respects. First, they had been purged during the Cultural Revolution (Peng Zhen was the first senior victim, although Chen Yun had fallen from grace several years earlier and was denounced during the Cultural Revolution), and their personal stature is not dependent on maintaining a link with the Maoist legacy. Second, although advanced in age (in 1985 Peng Zhen was eighty-two and Chen Yun in his mid-eighties) they were active in policy-making during the high tide of the reform campaign. Third, their criticism has not been aimed at broad ideological issues but at specific reform policies.

Chen Yun's main concern has been finding the right balance between central planning and market forces. He has likened the relationship between a planned economy and a market economy to a cage and a bird. The plan is the cage and the bird is the market. If the cage is too tight, the bird cannot move about and develop. If the cage is too loose, the bird will fly about excessively and cause problems, such as inflation. If there is no cage, the bird will fly away, that is, the economy will run out of control. His criticism of Deng's policies was that the reformers were unleashing market forces which were in danger of getting out of control, and he advocated a tighter cage, i.e. more central planning and less dependence on supply and demand. Peng Zhen has reportedly been primarily concerned with law and order, advocating social discipline and greater efforts against the decline of moral standards.

What impact men like Chen and Peng have had on national policy cannot be determined since the policy-making process is hidden from outside observers. There is no doubt that Deng has had to take their views into account, especially Chen's criticism of economic policy. Chen, in particular, has apparently had a restraining influence on the economic reforms, and is presumably one of the main leaders responsible for the periodic pull-backs. However, the differences between Deng and his critics are a matter of degree, not principle. In principle, China's post-Mao leaders have remained united on the desirability of modernization and its direction. And this unity is the critical motive force behind the reform drive.

What impact the differences at the top have had on officials at lower levels of the ruling hierachy is not known, but some suppositions can be made. One is that a large number of the Party's forty-four million members are hold-overs from the Cultural Revolution and some of them are doubtless unrepentant Maoists. They must look with disdain at the abandonment of Maoist tenets, but have to lie low. Another supposition is that many officials, particularly at higher levels, are not necessarily Maoists, but seem to be more politically authoritarian and ideologically orthodox than the Deng leadership. These officials have opposed Deng's relatively liberal policies and have pounced on opportunities to reverse the trend. Such was the case in 1983, when officials tried to redirect and broaden Deng's campaign against 'spiritual pollution' with such zest that it had to be called off. A third supposition is that many officials oppose Deng's reforms simply because a looser economy and a more permissive society have seriously reduced their power and the benefits that go with it.

The disaffected officials could conceivably constitute a formidable opposition – especially if they joined forces – that could obstruct Deng's reforms in the course of implementation. However, several factors militate against this. First, these officials belong to disparate groups with different interests. Second, the Deng leadership has not remained idle in the face of dissent but has launched periodic rectification campaigns to weed out officials who harbour 'leftist' ideas. The most significant long-range campaign was launched in October 1983, and was aimed at inculcating Party members with Deng's reform ideology and ousting those who dissented from it. Most important, the top leaders have not only remained united enough to produce a common programme, they have also been determined enough to push it through. And this cohesion at the top has been the strongest force against resistance from below.

While leadership unity is the essential prerequisite for the success of modernization, it is not enough. Policy formulated by the leadership has to be implemented and how this is done depends decisively on the bureaucracy.[2] The present leaders know well from their own experience that the Chinese bureaucracy can vigorously carry out the leadership's directives, as it did in the 1950s, but also can subtly block such directives, as it did in the early 1960s, or can remain largely passive, as it did until the late 1970s.

In the view of the Deng leadership, the inherited Party and government bureaucracies were largely ill suited to carry out the modernization programme. Administrative structures were overstaffed, cumbersome and inefficient. A large number of cadres were poorly educated, incompetent and arrogant. The low educational standards jeopardized the whole modernization effort. In 1984 it was reported that only 4 per cent of the country's 44 million Party members were college graduates. Some 14 per cent were graduates of a senior middle school or a secondary technical school, while half were primary school graduates or illiterate. Another problem has been the spread of corruption, nurtured by unprecedented opportunities for personal enrichment.

To overcome these obstacles to modernization, Deng launched a series of administrative reforms designed to revamp China's administrative structures and to upgrade the quality of personnel. One objective has been to simplify and rationalize organizations by reducing overstaffing, abolishing super-fluous positions, merging departments and establishing clear lines of responsibility. Another objective has been to raise the standards of bureau-crats and to reform their style of work. One means to this end has been the recruitment and promotion of cadres who are 'younger, more professional and more knowledgeable' – a campaign which Deng has pursued with relentless resolve. This campaign has been coupled with an equally vigorous effort to bring about the retirement of old and incompetent cadres. At the same time, the leadership has taken steps to stamp out corruption and nepotism.

The efforts to reform the bureaucracy have run into resistance, which is hardly surprising. These reforms endanger the vested interests of entrenched officials throughout the bureaucracy, and these officials have dragged their feet. Retirement has been a particularly vexatious problem. To cope with it, the leadership has instituted a regular retirement system designed to ensure that by 1984 old cadres below the rank of minister or provincial governor would have retired. The aim is to replace them with officials in their forties and fifties, the so-called 'third echelon' leaders, who are not only younger but also better educated and much more fit to handle the complex tasks of a modernizing society.

Many hurdles thus stand in the way of Deng's grand design for China after Mao. Some of these hurdles have undoubtedly slowed the pace of reform, others have diluted its content. Given the colossal undertaking which Deng and his colleagues have taken upon themselves, this is hardly remarkable. What is remarkable is their dedication to radical change despite the pitfalls and difficulties, and the results which they have achieved by the middle of the 1980s.

These results indeed add up to a 'second revolution'. Deng and his colleagues have dismantled the Maoist legacy, but have not fallen back on the Soviet-style system that had preceded it. They have cut China off from past experiences and set it on a daring new course. They have done this by overturning the central institutions and practices of Chinese society and replacing them with untried alternatives.

Deng's revolution began in the countryside in 1979, when the Chinese started to introduce the 'responsibility system'. Under this system, the collective enters into contracts with individual households which receive a portion of the land and pay an agreed rent. The household undertakes to sell a fixed quota of production to the state. All surplus produce can either be sold to the state at higher prices than the fixed quota or sold on the free market. By 1984 the contract system was in effect in over 90 per cent of the Chinese countryside. Households are also permitted to engage in a variety of other profit-making activities. By 1984 an estimated 100 million peasants, almost 30 per cent of the rural labour force, were reportedly engaged in non-agricultural activities, such as industry, handicrafts, mining, construction, transport and services. In 1984 the 'responsibility system' was institutionalized on a long-term basis when it was announced that contracts between the collective and individual households could be concluded for fifteen years or more and could be transferred to other families. In five years the system of collective agriculture had been swept away.

The effects of decollectivization have been dramatic. In contrast to the period 1953 to 1978, when agricultural output grew at an average rate of 3.2 per cent per year, average annual growth in the years 1979–83 was between 7 and 8 per cent.[3] Rural incomes also rose rapidly. In the period 1955–77, per-capita rural income grew from an estimated 103 yuan to only 113 yuan – an increase of only $3.50 in twenty-two years. From 1978 to 1983, according to official sample surveys, per-capita income more than doubled from 134 yuan in 1978 to 310 yuan in 1983 – an increase of over 18 per cent per year.[4] The results – in the form of new houses, television sets, refrigerators, tractors and trucks – while far from widespread, have become a growing feature in the countryside.

The urban industrial sector was the next target of reform. After taking partial measures – which, among other changes, did away with Maoist egalitarian practices and put professional managers in charge of industrial enterprises – the leadership accelerated and expanded the restructuring of the urban economy. One step was the opening in April 1984 of fourteen coastal cities to foreign investment on the pattern of the Special Economic Zones established in 1979. This decision permitted foreigners to operate factories and businesses in the opened cities and gave them preferential tax treatment.

The high point was the Central Committee's decision on economic reform adopted in October 1984. Mandatory planning, with the exception of major products, was to give way to guidance directives and market forces. State control of enterprises was to be relaxed, and firms would be allowed to seek materials, court customers, handle profits and losses, and set wages. Prices were to be adjusted in accordance with market forces. And wages were to be linked with actual work. The departure both from the Maoist scheme and from the Soviet-style system is stunning.

The significance of the rural and urban reforms can hardly be exaggerated.

They represent a venture – bold to some, brazen to others – unknown in communist countries, except possibly to a smaller extent in Hungary. While China is not going capitalist, Deng and his associates have certainly turned it in that direction in order to achieve rapid progress. If Mao's approach could be summed up as revolution before modernization, Deng's is modernization by means of a 'second revolution'. And Deng's revolution – like Mao's – has had profound implications for the development of the PLA.

The 'Second Revolution' and the Military

While Mao's effort to perpetuate the Communist revolution was largely responsible for the deterioration of the PLA, Deng's effort to undo the Maoist legacy has provided the vital thrust to its modernization. The replacement of the Maoist blueprint by a grand design for rapid development created the essential conditions for reforms in all sectors of society. The defence establishment has been one of the main beneficiaries of this change. Designated as one area of the nation's 'four modernizations', the PLA has been brought into the mainstream of China's 'second revolution'. Backed by leadership consensus on the need for military modernization, and unencumbered by concepts inimical to military needs, the PLA high command embarked on the long-delayed and much-needed renovation of the armed forces.

Other circumstances have reinforced Deng's desire for military modernization. One has been the political importance of the military. In the brief succession struggle that erupted after Mao's death, the PLA high command performed a vital function in toppling the radical leaders. During the period of transition to the ascendance of Deng Xiaoping, the military enjoyed great power and prestige as the main prop of the new leadership. Although Deng has radically reduced the political role of the PLA, its generals remain an important source of support. This support was particularly important for Deng in the early stages of the reform drive. Lacking Mao's stature and political capital, Deng had to operate through coalitions, and the backing of the military was crucial to the effective functioning of any coalition. And lacking Mao's standing among the veteran military leaders, Deng could not assume, as Mao could, that their support would be ultimately forthcoming, whatever differences may have existed over specific issues. Deng, therefore, had to be sympathetic toward the needs of the military, if only to ensure their goodwill and support.

However, this attitude has not been rooted in need alone. Far from it. As the godfather of China's modernization, Deng has been in the forefront of the effort to extend it to the military. Although he has rejected military demands

33

for more resources, this has been out of overriding economic considerations only. In areas not subject to economic limitations, Deng has personally pioneered and pushed the campaign to make the PLA more professional and proficient. Deng and the professional military thus agree on the basic needs of the PLA, even if not always on the order of economic priorities.

This agreement was strengthened by the common concern over the weaknesses of the PLA at the end of the Maoist period. Deng and other leaders appear to have been genuinely worried that the armed forces were incapable of fulfilling their basic functions. In 1975, it was Deng who drew up a programme for the comprehensive modernization of the PLA, but the programme was sabotaged by the radical leaders. In 1977, he voiced his concern about the army's capability to a high-level military meeting: 'comrades worry whether, following the long-term destruction caused by Lin Biao and the "gang of four", the armed forces will be able to fight in case of enemy attack unless consolidation is carried out rapidly. These worries are by no means groundless.'[5] China's post-Mao leaders, to be sure, never perceived a threat of an imminent 'enemy attack', and by the mid-1980s whatever threat had existed in their perception had receded. However, this does not detract from their desire to have a standing army capable of defending China and acting as a credible deterrent against an attack. Having rejected Mao's belief in the superiority of the 'human factor' and 'people's war' as the all-inclusive answer to China's defence needs, Deng and his colleagues know very well that the PLA's capabilities can be improved only by military modernization.

This was strongly brought home to the Chinese leadership by their Vietnam venture in 1979. Setting out to 'teach Vietnam a lesson', the Chinese learned one instead. Although the results of the war were inconclusive, teaching the Vietnamese a lesson required a swift and decisive victory. This the Chinese patently did not achieve. Instead they learned how hamstrung the PLA was by its obsolete military equipment and antiquated procedures against a much smaller but better equipped army. The affront to China's national dignity and Deng's personal prestige was considerable. This experience presumably provided part of the rationale for China's decision to do nothing when Vietnam destroyed the Chinese-supported Kampuchean bases of the anti-Vietnam coalition in the spring of 1985. Although the PLA had made substantial progress since 1979, the Chinese may have been reluctant to put it to the test. Since the need to respond to future Vietnamese actions cannot be ruled out by the Chinese leaders, and since China's long-term regional objectives in any case require credible capability to project military power to the outlying areas, the importance of military modernization is further underscored.

Military modernization is also dictated by the long-term aspirations of the Chinese leaders. Whatever protestations they may make to the contrary,

China's leaders share an elemental ambition to make China a great power, commanding respect and influence in global politics, and playing a major role in the strategic balance between the superpowers. Since Deng and his associates have jettisoned Mao's vision of realizing this ambition by pursuing a revolutionary policy in the international arena, they know that advancing China's world status requires military power far beyond what was sufficient for defensive purposes under the Maoist doctrine. At the very least, they have to increase the PLA's capability to defend China without risking mass destruction so as to decrease their vulnerability to military threats. In the next stage, they will have to acquire a sea and air reach of considerable proportions. Although Chinese leaders do not anticipate a significant narrowing of the gap between their global aspirations and military capabilities in the near future, their world outlook has set the course for the long-range development of the PLA.

In sum, the PLA after Mao has benefited both from the national modernization crusade and from more parochial calculations. There are, however, strict limits to the modernization of military hardware and equipment. These derive mainly from the leadership's ambitious economic development plans. Because resources are few and demands many, the defence establishment has been given low priority – lowest among the 'four modernizations'. The military budget has remained more or less constant since the start of the decade and its share of national expenditure dropped considerably by the mid-1980s.

The leadership's decision severely to limit short-term weapons modern-ization stemmed from its belief that economic and technological develop-ment should come first. Its readiness to take such a decision – and the military's concurrence with minimal opposition – can be attributed largely to the common perception of external threat shared by the Chinese political and military leaders.

Threat Perception and Military Policy

Military policy is shaped by a variety of considerations but it is the leadership's perception of threat that is paramount. The nature of the threat and the response to it are decisive in determining the doctrine of the armed forces and their development. For this reason, there always was a connection between threat perception and military policy in Chinese strategic planning. However, this connection has become closer and more complex in the post-Mao period, because of the changes that have occurred in the leadership's perception of threat.

Previously, the Maoists were tied to one all-embracing doctrine – the doctrine of 'people's war' – which was supposed to provide the answer to all major conventional threats. In this situation, the perception of external threat was much less significant than in the post-Mao period. First, because for the Maoists the nature of the threat did not have a crucial bearing on military preparedness of the armed forces, since they assumed that even an ill-equipped PLA was capable of coping with any invasion by employing a strategy of 'people's war'. In contrast, the post-Mao leaders have rejected this stategy as a blanket response to all threats and are, therefore, much more concerned about the combat capability of the PLA. Second, the Maoists tended to refrain from differentiating between nuclear and conventional threats. This was because of their need to claim that a ground invasion would inevitably follow a nuclear strike, since it was only against such an invasion that the Chinese supposedly possessed advantages which made them virtually unconquerable. In contrast, the post-Mao leaders have abandoned the 'people's war' strategy as the sole response to all possible types of invasion and, hence, have no compelling need to maintain the link between nuclear and conventional war. They are, therefore, able to make a more pragmatic differentiation between various types of threat and to relate them to the requirements of the PLA.

What then are the threat perceptions of the post-Mao leadership and how have they affected its military policies? No attempt to answer this question can claim to be accurate because the Chinese are hardly in the habit of publicly discussing contingency plans in detail. However, by inferring from their statements, policies and practices it is possible to speculate on the types of threat the Chinese may have considered and, by a process of elimination, to determine which threat they view as most likely.[6] Since no realistic leadership can hope to prepare the armed forces for all possible threats, the one it views as most conceivable is the threat that will decisively shape its military policy and the building of the armed forces.

It can be assumed by inference that the Chinese leadership of the 1970s and 1980s must have taken into account at least five types of military threat. Four of these were direct and one indirect, and all were posed by the Soviet Union. They are discussed in what seems to be the reverse order of probability from the standpoint of the Chinese.

The first and most severe, albeit also the most unlikely, is the threat of an all-out nuclear strike on China's population centres. Since military planners have to consider an Armageddon scenario when faced by an adversary possessing awesome nuclear might, the Chinese must have taken this possibility into account. However, they do not seem perturbed by such a threat and it has no meaningful role in their calculations. The reason is obvious: it is virtually impossible to conceive of circumstances which would induce the Soviets to launch an attack of this magnitude. The scenarios which could lead to such an attack lie outside the realm of reasonable speculation. In one scenario, the Soviets would be intolerably provoked by reckless Chinese behaviour over a lengthy period. However, both such behaviour and the response are inconceivable. Even during the Cultural Revolution, which the present leaders have vowed will not recur, events never approached a point at which the Soviets contemplated the nuclear destruction of China. And at that time, China had no second-strike capability and no influential friends in the international community. Even if a future Chinese leadership changes the current course of Chinese foreign policy, it is hard to imagine that it will under any circumstances behave in a blatantly provocative fashion over a prolonged period. The next generation of Chinese leaders looks likely to be much less revolutionary than its predecessors and the spectacle of Maoist days, when China managed to alienate most countries, is not likely to be repeated. Even if the Chinese act provocatively towards the Soviet Union, or towards the United States for that matter, the superpowers can take a variety of actions in response short of an all-out nuclear attack.

Another hypothetical scenario envisages the Soviets launching a general nuclear attack as a result of escalation. This scenario has to assume several previous and lower levels of conflict, including a nuclear exchange. However, given the record of caution in military matters exhibited by both Russia and China even in the periods of high tension, such a possibility also stretches the imagination beyond reasonable limits. Also beyond reasonable limits is the apocalyptic scenario occasionally drawn up by observers which sees China growing so strong and menacing that Russia will be moved to deal it a crippling blow. Given the enormous technological chasm that separates the two countries, the possibility of China reaching a level of development where such considerations might even come into play is generations away. And as China grows stronger, so does its retaliatory capability. Moreover, even as China grows stronger it will not necessarily become more dangerous. Quite the opposite is equally, if not more, likely.

The second type of threat – a general ground invasion of China – is as improbable as the first. Observers point to the Japanese invasion of the 1930s as a precedent for a similar move by the Soviets. This analogy is completely misleading. First, the circumstances are totally different: in the 1930s China was weak and divided, some Chinese leaders co-operated with the Japanese, and there was no threat of escalation into nuclear war. Second, despite their overwhelming superiority, the Japanese were able to hold only limited areas and never subjugated China. If anything, the lessons of that invasion constitute a potent argument against its repetition. This is especially so since it is difficult to understand what realistic purpose such an invasion could serve, even though several scenarios have been constructed.

One scenario suggested by analysts is that the Soviets would invade China to install a regime favourable to them after toppling an unstable Chinese government. Such a scenario is extremely implausible. First, it is difficult to imagine circumstances which would lead to the collapse of the Chinese government. Even at the height of the terrible turmoil caused by the Cultural Revolution, the weaknesses of the regime (entirely self-inflicted) never endangered its existence. Even assuming a collapse, the force of modern Chinese nationalism would rule out the possibility of a leadership group allying with a Soviet invader, or, indeed, of Soviet forces taking effective control of the country, as the Japanese learned in the 1930s and 1940s. Another scenario assumes that a ground invasion might come as a mopping-up operation after an all-out nuclear attack. However, this scenario rests on two improbable assumptions. First, that there would be a nuclear attack of this magnitude; and, second, that the Soviets would consider it practical to invade such a devastated area.

The most compelling argument against the possibility of a conventional invasion is that military strategists who take a good look at China's territory, size and military capability, however limited by comparison with the superpowers, would have to take total leave of their senses to advocate such an invasion. In any case, it is precisely against a general conventional attack that a strategy of 'people's war' would be most effective, and the Chinese view it – not unreasonably – as the main deterrent against such an attempt. This is the one practical and significant reason, as distinguished from other non-military constraints, why the Chinese have not completely abandoned the 'people's war' doctrine in the post-Maoist period.

The third threat is that of a limited nuclear strike and it is undoubtedly taken far more seriously by the Chinese than the first two. The reason is that the Chinese already had the traumatic experience of being subjected to such a threat by the Soviets, and what happened once makes the possibility of it happening again more acute. The Chinese had this experience after the border clashes of 1969, which came as a climax to steadily mounting tensions in Sino-Soviet relations. These tensions were caused by China's belligerent behaviour during the height of the Cultural Revolution and the consequent Soviet build-up of military forces along their common border, to which the Chinese responded by increasing their own presence. The Soviet threat was effectively impressed upon the Chinese by signals and steps which strongly suggested that the Soviets were seriously considering the possibility of launching an attack – most probably nuclear – against Chinese military installations and centres. In retrospect, there seems almost no doubt that the Soviets were waging intense psychological warfare to intimidate the Chinese, and were not seriously considering a surgical strike on China.

If so, they were successful. Given China's political isolation and military inferiority, its leaders could not but take the threat seriously. There was nowhere the Chinese could turn for support as a counterweight to the Soviets. Although the United States strongly disapproved of a Soviet attack, the rapprochement between China and the United States was not yet under way. There was also little the Chinese could do in the way of 'quick fixes' to deter the Soviets. Not only had the Cultural Revolution isolated the Chinese from potential West European suppliers of military equipment, but whatever hardware they could obtain on a crash basis would have been of marginal value to their retarded armed forces.

The Chinese were, therefore, compelled to back down from their provocative position: they agreed to hold border talks with the Soviets and toned down their anti-Soviet propaganda. This was a sobering experience. It demonstrated to the Chinese the futility of their 'dual adversary' policy, which alienated them from both superpowers, and left them dangerously isolated in a crisis of major proportions. It turned them into an outcast among smaller powers, which in other circumstances could support China against Soviet threats. And, most importantly, it exposed China's vulnerability to nuclear blackmail. As a consequence, the Chinese were jolted into action that was intended to avert a similar threat.

The first line of action was to accelerate the development of their nuclear capability so as to provide China with a minimal deterrent. In 1970, the Chinese started to deploy nuclear missiles and by 1971 they had a force of some twenty medium-range ballistic missiles with a range of 600 nautical miles and undoubtedly aimed at targets in the Soviet Union. In 1970–1, they completed the production of a Chinese-made TU-16 medium bomber with an operational range of about 1,500 miles which was capable of delivering nuclear bombs.[7] Even though this bomber was extremely vulnerable to advanced air defences, the possibility that one or more bombers might penetrate the defences must have added an element of uncertainty to Soviet calculations and enhanced China's nascent nuclear deterrent. In the following years, the Chinese enlarged and refined their nuclear capability, as will be detailed further on, and acquired what is generally deemed to be a small but credible deterrent.

The second line of action was to improve China's relations with the United States, so as to create a counterweight to Soviet power. Abandoning their 'dual adversary' policy, the Chinese decided that the Soviet Union was more dangerous to them than the United States, and that they should co-operate with the United States against the Soviet Union. Such co-operation relieved the Chinese of a simultaneous threat from both superpowers and eliminated the advantage which the Soviets had enjoyed of assuming that they faced an isolated China on the eastern front. An added benefit to China of the rapprochement with the United States was that it paved the way for the establishment or widening of ties with a host of other countries, thus further improving China's political position in the international arena.

These developments significantly strengthened China's strategic posture vis-à-vis the Soviet Union. Although the enormous gap in total military power remains, the military and political efforts of the Chinese have substantially reduced the threat of a limited nuclear attack by the Soviets. Their nuclear weapons constitute a small but assured second-strike capability, which restrains the Soviets from issuing credible threats with impunity. Their political stature as a respected and active member of the international community further narrows Soviet opportunities for nuclear harassment. Thus, while the Chinese certainly must take the threat of a limited nuclear attack into account, it is no longer omnipresent. Barring extremely aggressive actions on their part, in which the Chinese are hardly likely to engage, this threat is also remote and improbable.

The fourth among the direct military threats – also improbable but the least implausible – is that of a limited ground attack. Such an attack carries the lowest risk of escalation and is least likely to cause a major international crisis. It could come about if political and military tensions boil over into armed hostilities, like the attack the Soviets launched on a very limited and localized scale after the first border clash in 1969. A similar attack on a larger scale could be mounted in order to relieve Chinese pressure elsewhere, for example in Vietnam, although the Soviets did not do this during China's short invasion in 1979. It could be initiated to teach the Chinese a lesson for some hostile act, very much like what the Chinese tried to do to the Vietnamese in 1979. It could occur due to an escalation of border clashes. Whatever the cause, the most likely objective would presumably be Soviet capture or destruction of China's industrial heartland in the northeast, either to exert pressure on the Chinese or to punish them. Another objective could be the conquest of territory in the barren northwest, an objective that would be easier to accomplish but would have a smaller impact.

The threat of a limited ground invasion, like that of a limited nuclear strike, is not totally hypothetical for the Chinese. They had perceived such a threat in 1965, due to the escalation of American involvement in Vietnam. At that time the leadership disagreed on the gravity of the threat and on the response. Most concerned was Luo Ruiqing, then chief of staff, who presumably reflected the views of the professional military, and who evidently considered the possibility of an American attack on China to be far more serious than did the political leaders. To counter this threat, Luo advocated a linear defence by the PLA, including a possible pre-emptive strike beyond China's borders, instead of the Maoist strategy of 'luring the enemy in deep'. Luo warned that the PLA was unprepared for such a defence and called for a crash programme of weapons updating, primarily by turning to the Soviet Union.

Luo's proposals were rejected by Mao and Lin Biao, who were less apprehensive about the threat. They felt that a policy of supporting revolutionary movements without committing Chinese troops would tie down the United States in local conflicts, but would not provoke it to invade China. They also ruled out reconciliation with the Soviet Union under any circumstances. But the main reason for their calmer attitude was the belief that even should China be invaded by the United States, the Chinese could repel an invasion by a strategy of 'people's war', which would offset their weapons inferiority.

Unlike the Maoists, the post-Mao leaders do not believe in 'people's war' as the catch-all response to all threats. Both their statements and military manoeuvres in recent years indicate that the Chinese envisage 'meeting the enemy at the gate' in certain circumstances rather than withdrawing into the interior in the first phase of a ground invasion. This means that the Chinese will adopt a positional strategy to defend key cities and military installations, a strategy which requires reasonably well-equipped forces. Had China's new leaders perceived a direct threat to China's security, it is reasonable to assume that they would have initiated a crash programme of weapons acquisition to plug the most gaping holes in China's defences. And since China cannot produce such weapons in the short run, the new leaders, uninhibited by doctrinal constraints, would undoubtedly have resorted to the import of the most urgently needed items.

As it turned out, the Chinese leaders were not stampeded into a buying spree of military wherewithal, despite some pressures from the military. Since the reason has been neither their belief in 'people's war' nor the unavailability of arms markets, it can only be this: China's leaders do not perceive a threat to security that justifies the taking of extreme measures.

It is not, of course, that the Chinese have been unconcerned about the Soviet military threat. The presence of more than forty Soviet divisions, even if not at full strength, on the Sino-Soviet border, and the sophisticated infrastructure which the Soviets have built up, are doubtless a source of disquiet. This was why the Chinese designated a Soviet pull-back as one condition for the improvement of relations, although it is not known to what extent they will insist strictly on this condition. However, the Chinese clearly do not view these divisions as poised for an immediate attack. Furthermore, the threat of such an attack recedes in Chinese perceptions as relations between the two countries improve.

This Chinese attitude, which became more sanguine towards the Soviet threat after the turn of the decade, goes a long way towards providing the rationale for the leadership's military policy. Because the Chinese have not perceived an emergency military situation, they felt confident that they could avoid adopting a programme of hasty weapons acquisition which, in their judgement, is extremely expensive in the short term and counter-productive in the long run. Instead they decided on a policy of gradual military

41

modernization, which encompasses incremental renewal of hardware and gradual improvement of the entire military infrastructure.

The fifth possible threat facing the Chinese is indirect – the threat of encirclement stemming from the world-wide surge of Soviet power. This threat deeply worried the Chinese until the end of the 1970s. Attributing it to the British retreat from east of Suez and the decline of American power, the Chinese perceived the Soviets as trying to dominate a sea route that extended from the Black Sea – through the Mediterranean, the Red Sea, the Indian Ocean and the Western Pacific – to the Sea of Japan.

This worry intensified as tensions rose between China and Vietnam after 1975, while the Soviets acquired influence and naval and air bases in Vietnam and Kampuchea. It reached a high point after the Soviet invasion of Afghanistan, which only confirmed China's worst fears of the 1970s – that the Soviets were bent on global hegemony and were extending their power closer and closer to home. In the early 1980s Chinese perceptions began to change, and by the middle of the decade they had greatly relaxed their view of the Soviet threat. However, even at the height of their anxieties, the Chinese did not view the Soviets as posing an immediate military danger and did not see themselves as the only target of Soviet expansionism, nor the main one. In China's outlook, the main Soviet threat was to Western Europe.

This view began to take hold in the early 1970s, when the Chinese felt that the danger of a limited Soviet nuclear strike had been deterred by their nascent nuclear capability and their strategic alignment with the United States. It was given high-level sanction by Zhou Enlai at the Tenth Congress of the Chinese Communist Party in 1973. 'China', Zhou said, 'is an attractive piece of meat coveted by all. But this piece of meat is very tough, and for years no one has been able to bite into it.' The Soviets, Zhou continued, 'were making a feint to the East while attacking in the West, and stepping up their contention in Europe and their expansion in the Mediterranean, the Indian Ocean, and every place their hands can reach'.[8]

This thesis received extensive elaboration in subsequent years, as the Chinese railed against what they deemed to be a global Soviet drive for hegemony, and sought to rally 'anti-hegemonistic' forces around the world to contain it. The thesis was challenged by radical leaders, who saw a direct Soviet threat as more probable than Zhou did.[9] This led them to advocate stronger political mobilization at home and a more militant revolutionary policy – against both superpowers – abroad. After the downfall of the radicals, the initial consensus among China's leaders was, despite some vague reservations from the military, that although the Soviet Union harboured aggressive long-range designs on China, Western Europe remained the main focus of its aims.

According to the Chinese, the reason derived from 'the position Europe occupies in the overall strategy of the two superpowers', for 'whoever controls Europe has the world in its grasp'. Since 'the Soviet Union runs tremendous risks if it wants to take Europe by force', it resorted to the concept of 'seizing Europe by stratagem'. This concept envisioned the exertion of direct pressure on Europe, on the one hand, and indirect pressure through its 'backdoor' (the Middle East and Africa) and its 'soft underbelly' (the Persian Gulf and the Indian Ocean), on the other hand.[10]

In this scheme of things, the Chinese did not see a direct danger to themselves. According to one analysis, of course, 'the Chinese people know that Soviet revisionism is bent on destroying them and that they must be properly prepared against a war of aggression'. However, there was no urgency about this because 'the contest between the Soviet Union and the United States is focused on Europe'. From this vantage point, even the Soviet troops on China's border were not seen as a major menace, as they had been several years earlier, despite their growing strength. The bulk of Soviet forces, the Chinese said, were deployed in Europe, and while 'some of them are in the Far East, they are directed chiefly against the United States and, second, Japan'. Naturally, these forces were also a threat to China, but China was not alone; other Asian countries were threatened as well, because the threat was 'dictated by the Soviet strategy for world hegemony'.[11]

This view of the Soviet threat to China became less reassuring for a brief period at the end of the decade due to increased Soviet pressure in the East. In the view of one Chinese commentator, although Europe remained the main target of Soviet global strategy, 'since the latter part of the 1970s the Soviet Union has been constantly expanding its strength in Asia and the Pacific region'. This expansion was manifested in Soviet support of the Vietnamese invasion of Kampuchea, and particularly in the Soviet invasion of Afghanistan. Its purpose was to 'close in on the Persian Gulf from both East and West and gain superiority in its overall strategy'. Another purpose was 'to encircle China' which was 'a big obstacle to Soviet expansionism in East Asia'. Since a military attack on China 'will yield no useful results', the purpose of the Soviet Union was to 'create a situation in which China is encircled and is under threat of attack from both north and south, so as to bring about an untranquil atmosphere and to undermine our programme of the four modernizations.'[12]

This, more apprehensive, view of the Soviet threat did not last long. By 1982 China's attitude towards the Soviet Union had undergone a change, which was part of a broader and more basic reassessment of China's international posture and foreign policy.[13] The new approach represented a shift away from China's fixation of the 1970s with building an anti-Soviet coalition centred on the United States in favour of a policy no longer dominated by a strategic alliance with the United States. This policy highlighted China's independence, flexibility and Third World orientation. While still looking to the West, and particularly the United States, for economic and technological support, China chose to distance itself from the superpower confrontation. Its primary objective was to secure a peaceful international environment for the great modernization effort at home.

Several trends combined to produce this change. One was China's growing disenchantment with Sino-American relations after the Reagan administration came into office. In China's view, the attitude of this administration endangered the important progress that had been made in cementing ties between the two countries in the last two years of the Carter presidency. Although marred by the Taiwan Relations Act, which provided for the continued American sale of arms to Taiwan, the Chinese viewed this progress as the successful culmination of efforts to create an anti-Soviet alignment with the United States. The new relationship was symbolized by several steps, foremost among which was the normalization of relations, which had not advanced since the Nixon visit. It was solidified by the relaxation of American restrictions on the export of military technology to China, and the reported establishment of a joint surveillance facility in China to monitor Soviet missile tests. To all intents and purposes, the Chinese had forged a strategic alignment with the United States under the Carter administration.

In their view, Reagan's policy jeopardized this alignment. The immediate source of strain was the re-emergence of the Taiwan issue in the form of Chinese opposition to continued American arms sales to the Nationalist government. Sparked by suspicion that Reagan wanted to pursue a two-China policy, the Chinese turned the issue of arms sales into a test of American intentions towards China. They felt that their importance in triangular global politics had been downgraded by the Reagan administration, and were peeved that what they deemed to be adequate economic and military advantages were not provided by the United States. In this state of pique, the Chinese inflated the arms issue, as well as other minor frictions, into cardinal questions relating to China's sovereignty, territorial integrity and national honour. Although the Reagan administration tried to placate the Chinese towards the end of its first term, by then the Chinese had already reappraised their foreign policy and had struck out in a new direction.

This direction was charted by their judgement that China had become too closely allied with the United States, which looked upon it as a junior and unimportant partner in the strategic relationship. This state of affairs was unacceptable to the Chinese. For one thing, it damaged their efforts to gain influence in Third World countries and stood in the way of their desire to become a leader of these countries. For another, it was an obstacle on the way to relaxing tensions with the Soviet Union, which the Chinese were then considering as part of their effort to create a stable external environment for their internal development. But, most importantly, it conflicted with China's self-image as a great power and with the determination of its leaders to play the balance-of-power game to China's advantage.

A redirection of China's foreign policy was possible from the standpoint of China's leaders due to the change in their perception of the Soviet threat. This crucial change resulted from a combination of several factors. One was the more relaxed and less paranoiac approach of the Chinese leaders to the outside world. Central to this approach was their assessment that the Soviet expansionist drive of the 1970s, which had been responsible for raising international tensions, had lost much of its force. On the one hand, the Soviet Union's difficulties in Afghanistan and Poland, as well as economic stagnation and prolonged succession problems at home, made the Soviet Union appear less dangerous. On the other hand, the build-up of military might under the Reagan administration seemed to blunt the surge of Soviet power and meant that the Soviets were not likely to achieve the global strategic ascendance which the Chinese had feared in the 1970s. Another factor was the progress of military modernization in China, which gave the Chinese leaders confidence that the Soviets had to be far more restrained in considering a military option against China than they might have been several years earlier. In addition, the dissipation of the ideological dimension in Sino-Soviet relations and China's abandonment of a revolutionary foreign policy drained much of the emotional content from these relations, and enabled the Chinese to look at the Soviets in a more pragmatic way. Finally, the Chinese leaders need a stable and serene external environment in order to concentrate on internal modernization, and this cannot be attained without a marked improvement in Sino-Soviet relations.

The shift in China's perceptions and policies was possibly preceded by leadership debates, which ranged over other vital issues as well. These debates may have pitted the proponents of close ties with the United States, led by Deng Xiaoping, against leaders who questioned the utility of this approach on the grounds that it compromised China's independence and provoked the Soviets. Perhaps to prove to his opponents – and to the United States – that he would not permit China's allegiance to be taken for granted, Deng agreed to a more even-handed approach to the superpowers, while retaining China's basic American orientation. Deng may also have placated critics of his foreign policy in order to assure support for his domestic programme. Though less significant than the change in strategic outlook, domestic considerations may have contributed to the formulation of a new course in China's relations with the superpowers.

By 1985 the main lines of this course were clearly and firmly established. On the one hand, China was determined to improve relations with the Soviet Union. Despite initial Chinese insistence that three obstacles – the stationing of troops and nuclear weapons at the Chinese border, Soviet occupation of

Afghanistan, and Soviet support for Vietnam's occupation of Kampuchea – had to be removed prior to any improvement in relations, they appeared ready to skirt these issues and to proceed in areas where progress was possible. On the other hand, China still looked on the United States as the most important source of economic and technological support for its modernization programme. China's perception of the superpowers thus became more varied and complex, but also more practical and cool-headed.

Implications for Military Modernization

The impact on the military of the shift in threat perception has been profound. First, by taking a more hard-headed look at the threats likely to confront China, the leadership significantly scaled down the missions of the PLA. Consequently, the PLA is no longer saddled with the vague task of preparing for all contingencies with equal intensity by falling back on 'people's war'. Since no army can undertake open-ended preparations, and since, in any case, the 'people's war' strategy did not demand urgent military modernization, the result was the decay of the PLA. The gradation of threats by the new leaders and the presumed positing of a limited conventional attack as the main, albeit remote, threat has shifted the activities of the PLA to the attainment of a much more limited and pragmatic objective. This objective has become the focus of intensive and practical preparations. As Li Desheng, political commissar of the newly established National Defence University, said: 'in making a strategic shift in the guiding idea on building the armed forces, we should switch from basing our work on the war readiness posture of "fighting an early, major and nuclear war" on to the normal track of building a regularized and modernized revolutionary army during a period of peace'.[14]

Second, by positing that even the threat of a limited invasion is remote, the leadership has removed a sense of urgency from strategic deliberations and decisions. This has enabled it to decide on a policy which accords low priority to weapons modernization in resource allocations, and attaches supreme importance to a basic and long-term overhaul of the defence establishment.

Third, the rationale underlying this policy is strengthened by the leadership's perception of the indirect threat of strategic encirclement. Although this threat greatly receded in the leadership's view by the mid-1980s, it has not disappeared and China has to take appropriate measures. However, such measures – which include, for example, the acquisition of an ocean-going capability – can only be taken very slowly and in a piecemeal fashion. Since the threat is not pressing, gradual modernization does not jeopardize China's security.

3

A New Military Policy

The commitment of China's post-Mao leaders to military modernization, tempered, as it was, from the outset by their determination to give precedence to economic sectors and by a diminished threat perception, left open several questions that had to be answered before a force-building policy could be adopted. These questions pertained to the whole range of issues facing a modernizing army, but the contentious ones boiled down to the core issue of weapons renovation. What should be the speed and scope of this renovation? What should be the PLA's share in the allocation of resources? To what extent should military technology be imported?

The attempts to resolve these questions at the start of military modernization brought to the fore two distinct viewpoints, which have remained a source of periodic leadership disagreements. Although it is not always possible to identify the personalities behind the different viewpoints, there is no doubt that the protagonists have been divided essentially along civil–military lines. On other issues — primarily those concerning reforms outside the PLA — alignments have been much more fluid, as groups in the PLA found allies among civilian leaders against coalitions of Party and PLA leaders. But when it came down to the central question of weapons procurement and budgetary allocations, military leaders have tended to unite behind a common cause — as have the civilian leaders. Such unity has not precluded tactical alliances between civilian leaders — for example, those advocating faster development of heavy industry — and the defence establishment. Nor has it precluded variations in the attitudes of civilian leaders towards the demands of the military. Nonetheless, it has been the institutional and political identification of leaders that above all else has determined their stand on the policy of weapons modernization. Conflicts are thus still very much civil–military conflicts. They are, however, entirely different from the debilitating disputes of Maoist days: they no longer centre on whether to reform the armed forces, but on how to achieve this objective.

The policy worked out by the new leadership, especially after Deng Xiaoping returned to power, has set strict limits on weapons procurement, and even stricter limits on purchases from abroad, chiefly due to the enormous cost of large-scale rearmament. At the same time, within these limits it has encouraged renewal and refinement of armaments, including small imports of vital items. In areas not constrained by cash shortages, radical reforms designed to improve the operations of the military establishment have been the order of the day.This policy has provided the guidelines for the post-Mao development of the PLA. To understand how it was arrived at and why, it is necessary to trace the process of its formulation.

Weapons Acquisition and Defence Spending

Shortly after the death of Mao and the arrest of his radical supporters, statements began to emanate from military circles demanding a swift and sweeping modernization of the Chinese armed forces — particularly its weapons and equipment. Muffled for nearly two decades, these demands now burst forth in tones that reflected long-suppressed fury. They were characterized by unprecedented frankness in describing the weaknesses of the PLA, and unheard-of forcefulness in calling for their rectification. Although couched mainly as condemnations of the despised 'gang of four', the demands of the military were also clearly intended for anyone who questioned the need for military modernization.For example, one article by a military unit — doubtless a cover for a high-level writer or writers — put its views like this:

> Whoever said a word about improving the equipment of PLA units would be accused of practising revisionism and following a bourgeois military line. Whoever called for improving the PLA units' equipment would be attacked as acting in line with the theory that weapons decide everything. Whoever wanted to develop guided missiles and nuclear weapons would be attacked through the allegation that if satellites flew in the sky, the red flag would surely fall to the ground. The gang would even say: In case of war, we can counter the enemy's weapons no matter how advanced they are and no matter how war develops .... This is out-and-out nonsense and the height of absurdity.

The authors left no doubt as to their view: 'good weapons defeat poor weapons and . . . sophisticated weapons are needed to guard against aggressors. This is the most basic fact in military affairs.'[1]

This 'fact' was reiterated in numerous military statements, which coupled calls for weapons modernization with warnings about the consequences of not taking such action. For example, one article early in the period explained the need for new weapons:

Since war goes on continuously, weapons and equipment must be improved continuously. If one should hold that we do not need to strengthen our weapons and equipment anymore because today we already have planes and artillery, one either has something up his sleeve or is ignorant. This is because we must not remain stagnant and make no advancement militarily, especially in modern warfare. Remaining stagnant and making no advancement militarily means lagging behind. Everyone knows that one who lags behind will take a beating.[2]

An article attributed to the National Defence Scientific and Technological Commission could not be more blunt in its demand for rapid modernization: 'Anyone who still thinks that in any future war against aggression it will be possible to use broadswords against guided missiles and other nuclear weapons ... is evidently not prepared to possess all the weapons and means of fighting which the enemy has or may have. This is a foolish and criminal attitude ....' The reason was crystal-clear to the authors:

We must realize that any future war ... will be a people's war under modern conditions. The suddenness of an outbreak of modern war, the complexity of co-ordinating ground, naval and air operations, the extreme flexibility of combat units and the highly centralized, unified, planned and flexible command structure − all these factors make it necessary for our army to have appropriate modern equipment.[3]

Some of the statements coming from the military linked the demand for weapons modernization with a threat perception that depicted the Soviet danger in stronger terms than those laid down by the leadership consensus. Although the leadership itself had not defined the precise nature of this threat, the consensus, as already noted, was that it was indirect. The military, however, saw the threat differently − or at least said it did. An important article in Hongqi by the theoretical group of the headquarters of the General Staff put the PLA's view this way: 'Soviet revisionism has not given up its intention of subjugating us. With the tiger and wolf in front, we shoulder heavy responsibilities. We must be prepared to fight early and in a big way, seize the time and speed, move vigorously and fast and be well prepared against a war of aggression. We must make up for the time lost ... and accelerate the pace of our army's revolutionization and modernization'.[4] Whether or not the military really viewed the Soviet threat as more serious than did their civilian counterparts, it is clear that they articulated this view as part of their campaign to gain concessions from the leadership in weapons modernization.

The most authoritative exposition of the PLA's viewpoint in the early post-Mao period was given by the minister of defence, Xu Xiangqian, in a Hongqi article [5] written to commemorate the anniversary of the Red Army − always an important occasion for programmatic statements. Xu drew an alarming picture of the Soviet Union's aggressive global designs and underlined their relevance to China's security:

> The Soviet Union has stationed a million troops along the Sino-Soviet border and in Mongolia, has employed offensive strategic weapons there, has greatly strengthened the power of its Pacific Fleet, frequently holds large-scale military exercises with the intention of invading China, and has plotted to perform surgical nuclear operations on China, posing a direct military threat to China. It has constantly intruded into China's territorial land, waters and airspace and created a series of grave incidents. . . .The Soviet Union has been desperately trying to foster pro-Soviet forces, seek military bases and peddle the 'Asian security system' in countries . . . around China in a wild attempt to strategically encircle China.

Although Xu repeated the standard line that 'all of social imperialism's acts are of course aimed against the United States and Japan', he added that the Soviet Union was 'also making increasing efforts to prepare for an aggressive war against China'.

After paying tribute to Mao's strategy of 'people's war' as the means for countering an invasion, Xu slipped in a dramatic departure from that strategy, which radically altered the PLA's defence strategy and required a new force structure. While affirming that 'actively defending and luring in deep are the basic principles of our strategy', Xu went on to say that this did 'not mean allowing the enemy to go wherever he likes; it means forcing him to move in the direction we want, organizing a strong defence with our priorities well placed, preventing the enemy from driving deep into our areas, leading him to battlefields prepared and organized in advance . . . .'

This strategy is hardly consistent with the basic principles of 'people's war'. While a 'people's war' may be eminently relevant in case of a general invasion of China, the likelihood of this occurring, as already emphasized, is simply beyond comprehension. More likely is the possibility that an enemy will head for China's critical installations and cities close to the border. This, according to Xu, is exactly what the Chinese will try to prevent by confronting the invader at an early stage with mobile warfare and positional defences. The Chinese, in short, will fight in a manner that is much closer to conventional than to 'people's' war. Such a response, however, requires forces that are much better equipped than the PLA was in the late 1970s. Small wonder, then, that Xu, after expressing confidence in the PLA's ability to overcome superior forces, emphasized that 'we will be the subject of attack if we do not have modernized and powerful national defence strength and do not master all the weapons as well as the struggle tactics and methods which the enemy already possesses or may possess'.

The demands of the military in the early post-Mao period seemed to have been virtually open-ended. At no time since the foundation of the regime did the military extend such demands and at no time were their demands presented so emphatically. A combination of reasons accounted for the new manner of the military.

One was their political status in the transition to the post-Mao era. Having played a crucial role in defeating the radicals, the PLA had become a central pillar propping up the Hua Guofeng leadership. Clearly conscious of their importance, military spokesmen could permit themselves to address this leadership in confident and insistent tones without fear of being called to order. The aggressiveness which occasionally marked military statements also surely stemmed from the exuberance felt by commanders at being freed from the fetters of the radicals, who had humiliated them for years and had forced them to suppress their professional views.

However, the most important reason behind the urgency of military demands was plainly the concern of PLA commanders about the dangerous deterioration of weapons and equipment. The consequences of this deterioration will be detailed in Chapter 5. Suffice it to say here that when the Maoist period ended, the PLA lacked the most basic items needed to defend China against a modern enemy. It lacked all-weather, night-flying inter-ceptors, equipped with sophisticated electronic gear. It lacked a modern air defence system, surface-to-air and air-to-air missiles. It lacked tanks with advanced technology and anti-tank missiles. It lacked trucks, armoured personnel carriers and transport planes. It lacked anti-submarine warfare equipment and ship-to-ship missiles. It lacked advanced communications equipment. All these items, and numerous others, it lacked in large quantities.

Whether military commanders really believed that it was possible to carry out a comprehensive modernization of the PLA's weapons in a short time is doubtful. Even the most militant commanders must have realized at this stage that the costs of refitting the armed forces just partially – aside from a host of other difficulties – were stupendous. Just how stupendous was clarified in a US Department of Defense study made in 1979. According to this study, which was leaked to the *New York Times*, the purchase by China from the United States of weapons and services deemed adequate by American experts to give China a 'confident capability' for defence against a Soviet conventional attack would cost between $41 billion and $63 billion at 1977 prices.[6] China's published defence budget for 1978 was roughly $10.5 billion. American analysts, however, believed that real expenditure was about twice the published figure, and that some 40 per cent of the defence expenditure went for the procurement of weapons and equipment.[7] If this figure is accepted, it meant that in 1978 about $8.5 billion was earmarked for weapons procurement, but expenditure for conventional weapons was still lower since a portion of this sum was absorbed by nuclear weapons. The conclusion was clear: a rapid refitting of the PLA with modern weapons, even though still on a limited scale, would have cost somewhere in the region of up to ten times the annual budget for weapons procurement. This was a sum that the Chinese leadership plainly would not even begin to contemplate, especially since it did not perceive a threat to security that necessitated urgent action.

Senior military leaders could hardly have been unaware of these calculations. Although it is quite possible that many high-ranking military men did not fully appreciate the staggering cost of new conventional weapons and the complexity involved in absorbing them, they must have understood that open-ended demands for technological modernization could not be met. In view of this, the extreme demands made by the military in the early days of the new period should be attributed more to psychological exhilaration, and even more to political posturing, than to a realistic expectation that they would be fulfilled. By highlighting the deficiencies of the PLA, and even displaying them to prominent foreign visitors – such as US Defense Secretary James Schlesinger, whose party was in China at the time of Mao's death, and the *New York Times* military correspondent Drew Middleton, who visited China a few months later – the military were probably staking out a bargaining position in internal debates on national policies and resource allocations.

If some officers nonetheless harboured high hopes for rapid weapons renewal they were quickly set straight by the new leaders about the limits of defence modernization. Statements by these leaders, though less assertive than some military pronouncements, were no less adamant in delineating a different standpoint. Its essence was simple: economic development must take precedence over weapons modernization in the short term because a solid economic and industrial foundation is essential for sound advances in the defence sector. Weapons procurement, therefore, was placed last among the 'four modernizations' – behind agriculture, industry, and science and technology. This standpoint has withstood subsequent leadership changes and policy shifts, and has remained the wellspring of the regime's weapons development strategy.

An elaborate exposition of the leadership's position was provided by a Radio Beijing broadcast that discussed Mao's stand on the relationship between economic and military development.[8] It began by underlining the interdependence of the two sectors: 'Stepping up economic construction means strengthening the material foundation of national defence construction. National defence construction is the reliable guarantee that economic construction can be carried out.' It then laid down the order of priorities: 'Our principle is that ... we should strengthen national defence construction on the basis of the development of economic construction.' The broadcast then explained the reason for this order:

Why is it necessary first of all to step up economic construction in order to strengthen national defence? . . . It is well known that the people must first be fed and clothed in order to strengthen national defence and to be able to fight. Therefore, agricultural development has a great bearing on strengthening national defence . . . .

The development of heavy industry in particular is of the utmost importance for national defence construction. To . . . strengthen national defence, it is necessary to produce planes, guns, tanks, warships, rifles, ammunition, and other weapons and equipment . . . . if we are not to be bullied by foreign enemies we should also have atom and hydrogen bombs, modern communications equipment, transport means, and so forth. All these cannot be obtained without the development of . . . basic industries. Only by developing such industries rapidly can we lay a solid material foundation for strengthening national defence.

Finally, the broadcast spelled out the choices facing the nation. One was to reduce expenditure in the economic sector so as to step up the development of national defence. This way, it said, was wrong. The other alternative was to reduce military expenditure and divert the funds to economic construction. This, said the broadcast, was the correct way because it would facilitate the strengthening of national defence. How should this alternative be implemented? Quoting Mao, the broadcast said that defence expenditure should be reduced to about 20 per cent of all spending. However, it also indicated that while this proportion should be maintained as the standard, there may be an increase in the absolute level of defence spending as a result of economic development.

However, even during the brief period of Hua Guofeng's ascendance, the defence budget was kept below 20 per cent of national expenditure despite Hua's need for PLA support. More important, the defence budget decreased as a percentage of the total budget. In 1977 the military budget amounted to 14.9 billion yuan, or 17.6 per cent of total state expenditures. In 1978 it rose to 16.7 billion yuan but dropped to 15.11 per cent of the total budget.

Hua's readiness to subordinate military to economic considerations must have sprung from a complex of calculations. The overriding one was undoubtedly his precarious political position and his desire to consolidate his power. Although dependent on the goodwill of the military, Hua was even more dependent on the support of civilian leaders and officials who formed a much larger constituency than the military, and who carried greater weight in organs that would determine his fate. Hua had to appeal to this constituency, and no appeal could be stronger than the prospect of all-out economic development, which had been stifled for so long by Maoist policies, and for the advocating of which many officials had paid so dearly.

Hua was also aware that the extreme demands for military modernization did not reflect the views of all senior PLA leaders, and that the rejection of these demands was not likely to hurt him seriously. Above all, Hua presumably counted on the support of Ye Jianying, who had been instrumental in masterminding the arrest of the 'gang of four' and who had emerged as one of the top leaders of the new regime. In this capacity, Ye had interests and influence which far transcended his institutional identification. One of his interests was the maintenance of a link with the Maoist period, which Ye had survived and with which he was not prepared to make a decisive break, despite his condemnation of its excesses. Hua was the personification of this link. At the same time, Ye could be expected to back Hua's modernization programme because he took a broader view of national needs than his younger and more professionally oriented colleagues. His pronouncements did not evince the sense of urgency that characterized other military statements, and did not include calls for rapid and massive modernization of weapons.[9] Hua, in short, had to curry favour with leaders determined to develop China in a non-Maoist way while living up to his role as Mao's chosen successor.

The grand programme for China's modernization unveiled by Hua in early 1978 reflected this balancing act. In ambition and ambience, the Ten-Year Plan of development for the period 1976–85 submitted by Hua evoked memories of the Great Leap Forward. Hua's outlook was that 'by the end of this century, the planned output of major agricultural products per acre is expected to reach or surpass that of advanced nations of the world, and the output of major industrial products to approach, equal or outstrip that of the most developed capitalist countries'.[10] To achieve these extraordinary aims, the Ten-Year Plan stipulated that the country would produce 400 million tons of grains and 60 million tons of steel, compared with the 272 million tons and 20 million tons produced in 1976. The value of agricultural output was to rise by 4 to 5 per cent annually, twice the average increase since 1953. Industrial output was to increase at a 10 per cent annual rate. State investments in capital construction were slated to equal the total for the past twenty-eight years.[11]

Although the Plan gave high priority to agriculture, the largest share of state investment was to go for the expansion of basic industries and the transportation infrastructure. In eight years the regime planned to build 120 'large-scale projects', with primary emphasis on major heavy industries. Foremost among these was the steel industry, which was to benefit from the construction of ten large complexes.[12]

If the tone of the Ten-Year Plan was reminiscent of the Great Leap, the policies pursued by the Hua leadership went against Mao's most sacrosanct tenets of development. These policies stressed stability and discipline rather than revolution, personal material gain and higher living standards rather than egalitarianism and austerity, and professional competence rather than political qualifications.[13] Maoist methods, in short, were rejected in favour of pragmatic policies designed to achieve sustained economic growth.

The attainment of such growth meant that strict limits had to be put on military modernization. The scarcity of resources and the massive increase of projected investment in economic sectors ruled out a substantial rise in the military's share of national funds. This was indicated by Hua Guofeng, when he presented the new modernization programme and mentioned military modernization only in passing. 'We must', he said, 'take steel as the key link, strengthen the basic industries and exert a special effort to step up the development of the power, fuel and raw and semi-finished materials industries and transport and communications. Only thus can we give strong support to agriculture, rapidly expand light industry and substantially strengthen the national defence industries.[14]

Despite this, Hua may have held out the prospect of increased funds for the military in the near future. Engaged at this time in a rearguard power struggle with Deng and his allies, Hua may have been reluctant overly to antagonize potential supporters in the defence establishment. Hua, furthermore, probably believed his own forecast about the economy, and expected rapid returns which would facilitate the satisfaction of some military demands. Even if no specific understanding between Hua and the military was reached, PLA leaders, like their civilian counterparts, may have been carried away by the rhetoric that surrounded the launching of the modernization programme and looked forward to benefiting quickly from the anticipated economic advance.

This anticipation may largely explain the extraordinary surge of visits by Chinese military or military-related delegations to many countries in the early years of the post-Mao period. According to a US government source, from 1976 to 1978 about 600 delegations consisting of 4,000–5,000 people visited Western Europe and the United States.[15] The Chinese surveyed a wide range of military technologies and displayed an interest in making purchases, arousing widespread expectations for substantial deals. Such expectations were fuelled by hints from the Chinese. For example, a senior Chinese officer, Wu Xiuquan, deputy chief of the General Staff, who was described as being in charge of the PLA's equipment and holding an important position directly responsible for the defence modernization programme, said in an interview on Tokyo television that China had adopted a policy of introducing foreign military technology to modernize its armed forces, and that studies were being carried out on jet fighters such as the Harriers and Mirages, on West German, Swedish and American tanks, on anti-aircraft weapons, helicopters and communications equipment.[16] Small wonder then that *Strategic Survey*, published by the International Institute for Strategic Studies, said in its review of 1978: 'The prospect was that limited sales to China of weapons that could be clearly labelled as defensive would be completed in 1979.'[17] The prospect, however, did not materialize. What happened?

What happened was that the grandiose plans and high hopes of China's new leaders fell victim to intractable economic realities. The modernization programme, as it quickly turned out, was the product of yearning rather than learning: in drawing it up, the leadership had failed to make hard-headed economic projections. This frame of mind can be attributed to the exhilaration which resulted from the downfall of the radicals, and to the release of pent-up desires for rapid modernization. But it could not be a basis for a realistic economic programme. And, indeed, shortly after the implementation of the programme got under way, it ran into serious difficulties.

The launching of the Ten-Year Plan was followed by a flurry of activity. In the first year of the Plan, more than 100,000 construction projects of different sizes were initiated, but due to shortages of material and financial resources many had to be abandoned. The concentration of investment in heavy industry hampered the growth of agriculture and light industry, the two main sources of capital accumulation. In heavy industry, the development of the coal, electric power, petroleum, transportation and building material industries failed to keep pace with the growth of the metallurgical, machine-building and processing industries. Fuel became scarce and, due to a shortage of electric power, industrial capacity was severely under-utilized.[18]

As such problems emerged, the leadership reassessed its plans and decided on a drastic change of course. At the Third Plenum of the 11th Central Committee in December 1978, China's leaders called for basic revision of the original development plan, and particularly for a shifting of focus from capital construction to agriculture. Following the Plenum, the leadership convened a series of conferences to discuss changes in economic programmes. At the same time, the press began to warn against rashness and to speak of the need for a slower growth rate. In the spring, some major projects were shelved, and negotiations for many large-scale imports of plants and machinery were suspended. These steps were translated into a major decision at the second session of the Fifth National People's Congress held in June 1979. Presented as a policy of 'readjusting, restructuring, consolidating and improving the economy', the decision lowered most of the targets of the Ten-Year Plan and shifted the emphasis of development from heavy industry to agriculture, light industry (consumer goods), housing and transportation.[19]

What the economic retrenchment meant for the military establishment was not specified in the leadership's decision, but its immediate implications were obvious. First, the slowdown in the growth rate reduced the prospects for an increase in allocations to the PLA in line with the advance of the economy. Second, the curtailment of heavy industry, and particularly steel, meant that less materials would be available for military industries. Third, the suspension of large-scale imports suggested that if the leadership was prepared to take this step with respect to high-priority sectors, there was little hope that it would sanction substantial imports for the military establishment.

The decision to retrench was reached when, and partially because, the political balance of power had shifted decisively in favour of Deng Xiaoping and his allies. This shift greatly strengthened the hand of civilian leaders in the dialogue with the military. Deng had extensive networks of supporters in the Party and government hierarchies and was far less dependent on military backing than Hua had been. Deng, moreover, was a known advocate of military modernization and could count on the co-operation of the professional officers, even if some of his policies went against their desires. Deng, in short, was in a much stronger position to withstand military demands for more money. This quickly became apparent in the defence budget.

Although the 1979 defence expenditure of 22.3 billion yuan exceeded the budgeted figure by 2.9 billion, this was due to the costs incurred by the Vietnam War. In the military budget for 1980 this overrun was subtracted so that the budget equalled that of 1979 – minus the outlay for the war. In subsequent years, the defence budget remained steady until 1986 at 17 to 18 billion yuan, but dropped almost every year as a proportion of the national budget. In 1985, the military budget rose slightly to about 18.7 yuan, but fell sharply as a share of national expenditure – from 16.3 per cent in 1980 to 11.9 in 1985. Thus, under Deng's leadership the expected increase in the military's share of national spending did not materialize although the economy grew rapidly.

The reductions in military expenditure that began in 1980 were implemented despite the poor performance of the PLA in the Vietnam War, and despite pleas from the military, which obliquely invoked the lessons of this performance, for rapid weapons renewal. According to foreign analysts, the PLA in Vietnam was hampered by the shortage of armoured personnel carriers, trucks, transport planes and sophisticated surface-to-air missiles, which limited the advance of Chinese troops for fear of exposing them to Vietnamese fighter bombers. It was also hampered by inadequate logistics and primitive communications. A document reportedly circulated among high Chinese officials admitted that the PLA had 'not been able to conduct a modern war'. And the main reason lay not in the quality of the PLA's soldiers but in the state of their weapons and equipment.[20]

A cogent case for correcting this situation was made by an editorial in the army paper, which was published on Army Day in 1979. The editorial reached into the past to recall the Korean War, but the analogy with Vietnam was unmistakable. 'Raising our army's combat capabilities to the modern level', the editorial said, 'is something for which a large number of our army's comrades have long yearned day and night.' The experience of the Korean War, the editorial went on, demonstrated that a modern war cannot be won if the armed forces are not adequately modernized. Although much progress had been made since the war, it was, the editorial stressed, 'far from enough'. The editorial then appealed to the leadership: 'Considering the gap between our scientific level and advanced world levels ... we should have a stronger sense of urgency and responsibility as regards the modernization of our army.'[21]

The military's case for weapons modernization was repeated in a wide-ranging survey of its desires and demands published by the defence minister, Xu Xianqian, in the journal *Hongqi* on the occasion of the thirtieth anniversary of the founding of the People's Republic of China.[22] 'The fast development and extensive application of modern science and technology have caused tremendous changes in weaponry,' Xu said. Therefore, 'the modernization of weaponry has become an integral part of national defence modernization'. Xu underlined the importance of conventional weapons and acknowledged implicitly that their development had been neglected in relation to nuclear weapons: 'We must develop our weaponry with stress on the main points and in a planned way. Take conventional weapons and special weapons. We are developing nuclear weapons to break down the nuclear monopoly. We use them in defence. We do not base our victory in war on nuclear weapons.' He then called for the early updating of conventional weapons: 'We must actively design and manufacture new-type weapons. We must strive to equip our army with new weaponry in a considerably short period, improve our weapons step by step and make it attain the advanced world level.' This task encompassed a variety of weapons systems: 'Our country has vast territories with a large population and varied natural conditions. This invariably imposes different demands on national defence.'

Xu's insistence on re-equipment 'in a considerably short period' must have been only the public manifestation of intense behind-the-scenes efforts by the military to modify the leadership's attitude towards arms acquisition, particularly as reflected in the decision to cut the budget after the Vietnam War. However, the leadership did not budge from its stand. The policy of weapons modernization, which began to crystallize under Hua Guofeng's leadership, was confirmed and clarified after Deng Xiaoping rose to power. Whatever uncertainty still existed about the military's share of resources was thus removed. This was presumably one reason for Deng's readiness to relinquish his post as PLA chief of staff, to which he could not have devoted more than fleeting attention, but which he held apparently for several years in order to restrain the military. His replacement, appointed in early 1980, was Yang Dezhi, a professional soldier who could be counted on to carry out Deng's policy. In his first important speech, delivered to a session of the National People's Congress in September 1980,[23] Yang both voiced the disappointment of the military at the rejection of their demands and explained the rationale for the rejection:

The broad masses of commanders and soldiers . . . are longing for rapidly changing our economic backwardness and the backwardness of our military technique and equipment, and for greatly improving the material and cultural life of our people and armed forces. Such feelings are completely understandable. However . . . it is not yet possible to bring about very speedy development of our national economy. Therefore, it will also not be possible to achieve very great progress in the modernization of our national defence.

The new commander then appealed to his troops: 'Comrades in the armed services must make full allowances for the difficulties being experienced by the state, adopt an overall point of view, and correctly handle the relations between national defence construction and economic construction. Should our demands exceed the capacity of our economy, they will badly affect the speed of our economic construction.' He also appealed to the political leaders: 'it is also hoped that the state can increase national defence modernization'. Yang then set out the army's tasks in the light of the financial situation: 'we should . . . do a good job of streamlining our administrative structure and reorganizing our troops, make an earnest effort to practise economy and put our limited material and financial resources to the best possible use so that we can save money for new equipment'.

The essence of the leadership's weapons development policy as enunciated by Yang – gradual updating as the economy advances, improvement of existing equipment, and savings to finance procurement – has not changed in subsequent years, although by the mid-1980s the emphasis had shifted from economic development to economizing in the armed forces as the main means for increasing funds. This policy has been accepted by the military, but not without misgivings, which have undoubtedly been deepened by the decline in the PLA's share of national spending, despite the rapid growth of the economy in the first half of the 1980s. The attitude of the defence establishment has been reflected in periodic pronouncements which, as a rule, have both justified the leadership's policy and highlighted the continuing need for weapons modernization.

An important statement in this vein appeared in the November 1982 issue of *Hongqi*.[24] Although the author, Shao Huaze, was not identified as a military man, it can be safely assumed that the article expressed the views of the defence chiefs. After expressing pride in China's strategic weapons, the author went on to say that 'generally speaking, our weapons and equipment are relatively backward; they are restricted chiefly by the levels of economic development of our country. Modernization of national defence can only be a gradual process.' He then explained the dilemma of military modernization: on the one hand, national defence cannot be separated from 'the central link of economic construction', because this will impede economic development as well as national defence; on the other hand, 'with the daily development of the economy . . . national defence should be modernized continuously'. This meant, the writer emphasized, that national defence 'should be supplied with increasingly better material and technical conditions and with ever better weapons and equipment . . .'. At the same time, 'the scale and speed of building up national defence should . . . not go beyond the limits of our national financial and material capacities and should not affect the speed of economic construction'. The army, therefore, 'must continuously improve its weapons and equipment and make full use of the existing ones so as to win victory with the available weapons and equipment'. In the end, the writer made clear that the military's acceptance of the leadership's policy did not imply acquiescence in downgrading weapons modernization: 'we must always adhere to . . . taking economic construction as the basis', he said, but at the same time 'we must guard against the misunderstanding of the comrades who seem to think that national defence construction is no longer so important'.

A forceful presentation of the military's viewpoint that also upheld the Party's policy was made by Zhang Aiping in March 1983, in his first important statement[25] after his appointment as defence minister several months earlier. This appointment in itself was a concession to the military, since Zhang replaced Geng Biao, whose assignment to that post less than two years previously was doubtless resented by the defence establishment. A foreign service officer for most of his post-1949 career, Geng had served as ambassador to several countries and as vice-minister for foreign affairs before being named director of the Party's international liaison department. The reasons for his elevation to defence minister remain unclear, except that perhaps this was Deng's way of impressing upon the PLA chiefs their subordination to civilian authority. In any case, Geng was a lacklustre defence minister who made no major statement during his brief tenure, and left no visible mark on the military establishment. In contrast, Zhang was very much a military man. He had been deputy chief of staff for many years before being made chairman of the National Defence Science and Technological Commission in 1975. This important post, which Zhang held until his appointment as defence minister, put him in the forefront of the efforts to develop China's military technology. In Zhang, the military had an eminent spokesman for their views on weapons modernization, while the civilian leadership had a defence minister whose word carried great weight in the military establishment.

Zhang's regard for military and civilian viewpoints was evident in his article. 'Our Party', he said, 'has always attached great importance to the role of weapons in wars. . . . In order to achieve modernization of national defence, our first task is to develop and produce sophisticated military equipment.' Zhang then came to the crux of the problem. 'Modernization of our national defence', he emphasized, 'must be based on our national economic construction.' In allocating resources the government had to give priority to other sectors and this was 'an entirely correct decision'. The military had to take the needs of other sectors into account and to 'carry out ... strict budgeting within the scope allowed by the limited amount of funds ... practise thrift and organize development of the most important and most urgently needed equipment'. Zhang ended on an upbeat note, intended both to appeal to the civilian leadership and to allay the anxieties of the military:

> From now on, with the development of the country's economic construction and the flourishing of science and education, more favourable conditions will be created in turn for national defence modernization. This means not only that funds for building national defence will be increased but that more fine scientific and technological results will also be shifted to ... promote ... national defence modernization.

Writing in Hongqi[26] to greet two important occasions – the anniversary of the founding of the Red Army and of the People's Republic – Yang Shangkun, secretary of the Military Affairs Commission, began by praising the progress made under Deng's leadership: 'especially since Comrade Deng Xiaoping took charge of the work of the Military Commission, we have brought order out of chaos and carried out reforms to do away with outdated things and develop new things so that a new, vigorous situation has emerged in the building of the Army. As a result, there have been new improvements in the military and administrative areas and in the equipment of our troops.' However, much remained to be done. 'We should develop the most urgently needed new types of weapons and equipment as soon as possible .... In future wars against aggression ... under no circumstances should we neglect the important role of weapons.... We should ... strive to change the backwardness of our weapons and equipment.' But, Yang stressed, this would be a slow process. 'The modernization of our Army', he said, 'must be suited to the development of the national economy. We have a large population, a poor foundation and limited funds. Therefore we should not incur huge military expenditures as the superpowers do.'

Yang then restated the essentials of the weapons modernization policy but, unlike earlier statements, did not hold out the prospect of increased funds as a result of economic growth. 'First of all,' he said, 'we should ... concentrate ... on developing the most urgently needed defensive weapons and equipment. Second, we should update the equipment in an orderly way and step by step, allowing the coexistence of outmoded and modern equipment .... In order to stress the main points, we should give up some things of secondary importance.' Finally, while 'we should import some necessary and advanced technological equipment', modernization has to 'rely on our strength to develop weapons and equipment'.

If Yang Shangkun did not specify where money for weapons acquisition would come from, Yang Dezhi, the chief of staff, did so in an article published in *Hongqi* in August 1985[27] to celebrate the fifty-eighth anniversary of the PLA's founding. Writing when the great structural reforms in the PLA initiated earlier in the year were under way, Yang made clear that the leadership viewed the savings generated by these reforms as the main source of increased funds for the armed forces. He first reiterated the subordination of military to economic development:

> The state's economic construction is of overall importance and the Army should serve it and act within the framework of economic construction . . . . If the state's economic construction is ignored in carrying out Army building, this will hinder the state's economic construction and cause the Army's modernization programme to be like water without a source or a tree without roots . . . .

The chief of staff then again highlighted the PLA's need for technological updating: 'the modernization of weaponry is an important indicator of Army modernization. If an Army does not have modern weapons, it cannot become a modern Army. In recent years our Army's weapons have been improved to some extent, but the level of modernization is still relatively low and there is still a wide gap compared with the requirements of modern warfare.' However, Yang clearly implied that even as the economy develops, the PLA cannot expect major benefits: 'Fundamentally speaking, we should rely on the development of the national economy and science and technology to change the backwardness of our weaponry. At present China's economy is still relatively backward. The state should concentrate human, financial and material resources on economic construction. Therefore it is not in a position to put more money into the development of national defence.' Only by cutting costs in the defence establishment will money become available for weapons procurement: 'via reform and streamlining, we should decrease the number of our soldiers, eliminate obsolete and backward equipment, reduce expenses for food, clothing and daily expenses of personnel as well as for the maintenance of equipment. We should spend more money on the development of urgently needed weapons . . . .'

The policy of weapons development, as it had evolved by the mid-1980s, was thus more stringent on allocating money from the national budget to the PLA than had been hinted by the civilian leaders and expected by the military several years earlier. Nonetheless, within the limits set by this policy, as will be detailed in Chapter 5, the Chinese have made substantial improvements in military hardware. This has been done primarily by refining rather than replacing existing equipment. Extensive replacement of weapons over the short haul would have required large-scale imports of military technology. This alternative, however, was ruled out by the leadership in the early phases of the post-Mao military modernization campaign.

Weapons Import Policy

A source of ongoing, and occasionally heated, debates and deliberations among the Chinese leaders has been the question to what degree should China open its doors to foreign technology in its modernization drive. This issue is particularly pertinent to the military. The reason is plain: since China is unable to produce a vast array of modern weapons in the short run, the only way it can rapidly re-equip the armed forces is by importing such weapons. Consequently, military leaders who advocated the immediate rearming of the PLA with new weapons also advocated the purchase of some weapons abroad. To be sure, even officers who were most ardently in favour of this course must have realized at the outset that extensive refitting of the PLA with modern arms was out of the question. Nevertheless, in the heady atmosphere of the late 1970s, they may still have argued for some purchases of completed weapons systems to rectify the most dangerous deficiencies in China's defences. In a radical departure from the previous policy of 'self-reliance', Xu Xiangqian, the defence minister, made the case for arms imports in 1979:

> The current international conditions for modernizing our country are greatly different from those in the past . . . . We should see that science and technology have no class nature. Conducting economic exchanges with and importing technology from other countries is an important way to promote a country's . . . development. We must, under the premise of maintaining independence, keeping the initiative in our own hands and relying on our own efforts, learn the good things of foreign countries and selectively import advanced technologies which we urgently need.[28]

The range of the military's quest for 'advanced technologies' was indicated by the many Chinese delegations which descended on Western Europe and the United States in the late 1970s. These delegations familiarized themselves with several dozen weapons systems and expressed interest in buying numerous items. But interest did not lead to deals. The initial enthusiasm of the Chinese for new weapons soon gave way to extreme reluctance to make purchases.

A prime example of this shift was the prolonged but ultimately fruitless process of negotiations for the purchase by China of Britain's Harrier vertical take-off and landing aircraft.[29] The Chinese first expressed interest in buying over a hundred Harrier jets in 1972, but subsequent talks were suspended towards the end of the Maoist period as a result of political uncertainty in China. At the end of 1977 the Chinese reaffirmed their intent to buy the aircraft, and in the course of 1978 many Chinese delegations examined its parts and performance. But although the Chinese seemed eager to move towards concluding the deal, the Callaghan government delayed its approval and attempted to tie the sale of the Harriers to a larger trade package. Just when the British government decided to sign a formal letter of intent, China invaded Vietnam and the signing was postponed. In 1979, Chinese interest in the sale waned; while in 1978 they had expressed readiness to buy seventy to a hundred Harriers immediately, by 1979 they were talking about twenty to forty-five, and their complaints about British prices increased. At the end of 1979, the new government under Thatcher dropped the condition that tied the Harrier to civilian trade, but by then the Chinese had lost interest entirely. Despite subsequent British efforts to revive the deal, by the spring of 1980 it was clear that the Chinese were not buying.

Whether or not the Chinese would have actually signed the deal in 1978 or 1979, whatever their professed intent, is not certain. What seems certain is that at that time they had not yet reached a firm decision on the scope of weapons imports. In 1978 the options were still open. A year later they began to move away from the possibility of big deals, and by early 1980 had decided against large-scale import of weapons. The immediate reason was the economic reassessment which the Chinese carried out in 1979, and the drastic retrenchment which this reassessment forced upon them. Since retrenchment necessitated the suspension or slowing down of negotiations for the import of technology and equipment, it was natural that defence would be one of the main sectors affected. However, the rationale underlying the policy on the import of weapons had more profound sources.

The paramount consideration was strategic. Resort to 'quick fixes' would have made sense only if there had been a dire danger to the nation's security, and if the rapid acquisition of new weapons would have significantly reduced this danger. On both counts, there was little reason for the Chinese to take this course. First, Chinese leaders perceived no immediate military threat which required urgent action to strengthen China's defence, and even the military, after several vague outbursts, did not invoke the spectre of an imminent attack to support their demands. Second, China's military needs were so vast and varied that acquisition of several state of the art weapons would have made slight difference to its overall defence posture.

Why, then, were the Chinese interested, genuinely as it seemed, in purchasing the Harrier? The most plausible explanation is that this impression was created by Chinese officials before the leadership had fully weighed the implications of the transaction, and before it had arrived at a policy of weapons acquisition. The Chinese, it will be recalled, first showed interest in the Harrier in 1972 – at a time when a Soviet military threat still loomed large in their view. The strategic build-up and diplomatic campaign which they launched in the wake of the 1969 border clashes to reduce this threat were only beginning to bear fruit, and the possibility of further military engagements along the frontier could not be ruled out. In these circumstances the Chinese presumably wanted the close-support aircraft to enhance ground force protection against a Soviet conventional assault. They probably assumed that, despite their overall inferiority, the rectification of even one major deficiency would raise their defensive capability. If China was under threat, a 'quick fix' may have seemed better than no 'fix'.

This was no longer the case in the late 1970s. By then, Chinese fears of a Soviet attack had greatly receded and there was little sense in resorting to stop-gap measures. Nevertheless, the Chinese resumed negotiations for a Harrier deal. This step, however, was presumably the product of bureaucratic momentum and of the post-Mao infatuation with foreign technology rather than of cool-headed calculations. When the euphoria dissipated and the leadership was forced to make hard choices, it concluded that there were no compelling military reasons for large imports of weapons.

There were, however, compelling economic reasons against such imports. Due to the appalling backwardness of the armed forces, their needs were so great and all-encompassing that the cost of meeting them by buying abroad would have been tremendous. A US Department of Defense study estimated that in order to defend itself against a Soviet attack China would need at least 3,000 to 8,600 medium tanks, 8,000 to 10,000 armoured personnel carriers, 16,000 to 24,800 heavy-duty trucks, 6,000 air-to-air missiles, 720 mobile surface-to-air missile launchers, 200 air superiority fighters and 240 fighter bombers.[30] The cost of such an acquisition programme would, as already mentioned, run between $41 billion and $63 billion. It has furthermore been estimated that for every dollar the Chinese spent on the purchase of weapons from abroad, they would have had to invest three dollars in the infrastructure needed to absorb these weapons.[31]

According to another analysis, China's minimal defence requirements included modern anti-armour capabilities, battlefield air defences, inshore naval defence capabilities, especially anti-submarine, and territorial air defences. Even the first steps towards meeting these requirements would have cost an enormous sum. For example, the initial acquisition costs of tanks would have run to between $5 billion and $7 billion. The addition of mechanized infantry, mobile artillery as well as service and combat support investment costs would have more than doubled this figure. The initial acquisition costs of battlefield air defences would have been in the order of $1 billion, while ground equipment for air defence would have cost at least $500 million. The acquisition of a minimum number – about 400 – of the cheapest type of interceptors capable of dealing with Soviet aircraft would have cost at least $3 billion with only minimal provision for maintenance gear and spare parts.[32] These estimates pale by comparison with one report which put the overall cost of a major modernization programme for the PLA at the astronomical figure of $300 billion.[33] Whatever the precise costs of re-equipping the PLA, two conclusions were inescapable. First, its colossal needs could be effectively satisfied only by an across-the-board modern-

ization programme because 'quick fixes' were completely inadequate,
Second, such a programme of big weapons imports could not be undertaken
because the enormous costs of completed weapons were way beyond China's
means.

While the crushing costs of new weapons were enough to rule out
substantial purchases, there were additional considerations. 'Even if we
could buy them,' said a textbook on national defence, 'it is not certain that
others would be willing to sell . . . .'[34] Such doubts were well founded. Despite
the rapprochement with China, successive US administrations displayed a
marked reluctance to lift restrictions on arms sales to China.[35] By the late
1970s the Chinese felt that the informal 'strategic partnership' which they had
forged with the United States should have resulted in American readiness to
provide them with up-to-date weapons and technology. However, American
policy on the nature of military ties with China fell short of Chinese
expectations. Throughout the decade, American policy-makers were divided
over this issue, which was part of a broader division over the role of China in
United States global strategy towards the Soviet Union – the so-called 'China
card'.

Following the Soviet invasion of Afghanistan, the Carter administration – in
a move designed to punish the Soviets – agreed to sell selected items of non-
lethal military equipment to China, as well as a wide range of 'dual use'
technology, but the Chinese viewed this only as a step to further concessions.
Whether they would have actually bought large amounts of finished hardware
if offered is doubtful, but they may have wanted broad access to American
defence technology through licensing and co-production arrangements. In
any case, what they seemed to want most was a United States commitment to
the transfer of weapons to China, which the Chinese viewed as a symbolic
pointer to their importance in American strategy. This they did not get. In 1981
the Reagan administration went further by proposing to consider specific
Chinese requests for the purchase of weapons on a case-by-case basis.
However, the Chinese viewed this decision as a bribe to buy off their
opposition to continued American arms sales to Taiwan. This was unacceptable to them. At any rate, by then the Chinese had already decided on a policy
of defence modernization that gave only a very limited role to the import of
military technology.

The West Europeans also proved to be less than enthusiastic about selling
arms to China. Fearful of antagonizing the Soviets, the Germans pulled back
from contacts with the Chinese when the Soviet Union protested. The British
and French continued to negotiate but tried to portray possible arms sales as
purely commercial ventures devoid of strategic significance. The British, in
particular, acted during the Harrier talks as if they were doing the Chinese a
favour, and for a time tried to play down the military dimension of the

prospective deal by linking it with the concurrent purchase by China of civilian goods.[36] The Chinese, in short, had good reason to write off both the United States and West European governments as responsive and reliable arms suppliers.

Apart from budgetary constraints and the unreliability of suppliers, there were additional reasons for the reluctance of the Chinese to tie themselves to huge weapons imports. For one thing, the Chinese were apprehensive of becoming dependent on suppliers for knowhow and spare parts, which could make them vulnerable to political pressures or sudden cut-offs. These dangers were not an abstraction to them. The modernization of the PLA in the 1950s was, as already noted, carried out with massive imports of weapons and equipment from the Soviet Union. When the international interests of China and the Soviet Union began to diverge toward the end of the decade and the Chinese caustically criticized Soviet leadership of the Communist bloc, the Soviets abruptly terminated all assistance to China in 1960. Whether they did this to pressure the Chinese to fall into line or, as seemed more likely, to punish them for their intransigence, the effect on the PLA was devastating. Most affected was the Chinese air force. For several years, there were shortages of spare parts, fuel and new equipment. Many planes were grounded, some were cannibalized, and training flight time was drastically cut. The damage to the ground forces was likewise substantial. The military budget for 1961 was reduced, new equipment did not arrive, and a programme for re-equipping the armed forces was postponed.[37] This experience left the Chinese determined, as the defence minister phrased it, not to be put in 'the possible state of being controlled by others'.[38]

It also convinced them that copying imported weapons was not a sensible long-term solution to the PLA's technological backwardness. As Defence Minister Zhang Aiping made clear, while in the initial stages of modernization it is necessary to 'model some weaponry on that of others', this cannot be a permanent policy. 'If we are content with copying,' he said, 'we will only be crawling behind others and still be unable to attain our anticipated goal.'[39] The defence minister was speaking from first-hand knowledge. In establishing China's defence industry during the 1950s, the Soviets naturally set up production lines based on their designs. When they pulled out of China in 1960, the Chinese made a major effort to develop new weapons, but were unable to break out of the Soviet mould except in select cases. They had to limit their efforts to a few projects such as the modification of the MiG-19 and the development of missiles. Total reliance on Soviet models in the 1950s thus became a major reason for the backwardness of the Chinese armed forces in the 1960s and 1970s. The leadership, therefore, decided 'to modernize our national defence through developing military equipment by relying on our own scientific and technological strength'.[40]

Even if the Chinese were to import prototypes and production techniques rather than completed weapons, as is clearly their preference, they would still face difficulties in absorbing and using sophisticated military technology. In this regard, the Sino-British jet engine agreement[41] must have been sobering. Concluded in 1975, the agreement provided for the supply by Rolls-Royce to China of fifty supersonic Spey jet engines, for a licence to manufacture these engines in China, and for the provision by Rolls-Royce of facilities and expertise for engine testing and maintenance. Suitable for installation on small airframes (such as the British version of the F-4 Phantom), the Spey engine was believed to have been purchased by the Chinese for a new interceptor – a modified version of the MiG-23 – which they were developing. This deal was expected to advance Chinese jet-engine technology by six to ten years, and to provide China with the ability to produce and service such engines independently by the early mid-1980s.

This expectation did not materialize. Although more than 700 Chinese engineers and technicians received training in advanced techniques at Rolls-Royce in Britain, the project ran into difficulties. According to one report, by early 1981 the Chinese had tested four engines but were unable to meet their objective in various areas. The major problem was apparently that they did not have an airframe for the Spey engine. According to another account, by mid-1981 the Chinese had been able to procure only three engines and the British-built factory in Xian was idle. Whatever the precise details, the Chinese must have learned from this project that they would have to tread with great caution before coming to similar arrangements in the future.

Given all these considerations, it is hardly surprising that when the Chinese leaders had to decide on the scope of weapons imports, they adopted a policy which precluded large-scale purchases of arms from other countries. As Zhang Aiping said in his first major statement as defence minister, 'it is not realistic or possible for us to buy national defence modernization from abroad'.[42] By 1980, this policy was already in force. Big arms deals, such as that for the Harrier, were rejected. Visits by Chinese military delegations abroad tapered off dramatically after the initial surge. And China's subsequent purchases, as will be seen in Chapter 5, were extremely limited and made with great circumspection. The Chinese, in short, have been acting according to the precept that in the drive to military modernization 'the fundamental way is to rely on ourselves'.[43]

This, however, was in no way tantamount to 'self-reliance' in the Maoist mould. China's military leaders are well aware that the prolonged isolation of the PLA from advances in weapons technology was one of the prime reasons for its stagnation. The effects of this isolation were doubtless dramatically impressed upon many Chinese officers who were exposed to new weapons during their visits abroad in the late 1970s. The Chinese, therefore, did not intend to shut off their military establishment from foreign technology, but aimed to use such technology in a limited and selective fashion. 'Our national defence construction', they said, 'cannot be in isolation .... we need to get outside help, and we particularly need to study all advanced things of foreign countries that would be beneficial to us ....Therefore, we should uphold the policy of making self-reliance primary, and on this premise selectively and vigorously import some advanced technologies that we urgently need.'[44]

Implications of the New Policy

The military policy which emerged towards the turn of the decade had two main implications for the PLA. One pertained to weapons renewal. Although civilian and military leaders were not divided over the need for such renewal, they differed on the speed and scope of its implementation. These differences were resolved by a compromise – incremental modernization of weapons and limited use of foreign technology – which gave greater weight to the priorities of civilian leaders and fell short of satisfying the desires of many professional officers. Despite the limits, however, the policy provided considerable scope for the improvement of weapons, as the Chinese demonstrated in subsequent years.

The second aspect pertained to modernization in other, non-technological areas of military activity. Here no compromise was needed because the leaders agreed on both the problem and the remedy. The problem was bluntly summed up by the defence minister: 'we should admit that our army cannot meet with the demands of a modern war'. This was because 'there are many questions concerning the use of modern weapons, the organization of joint operations and bringing the various armed services into full play. We should also see that our armymen's scientific and cultural level is not high and that any army cannot be modernized if its men do not have modern scientific and cultural knowledge'.[45] The remedy, as the Chinese have repeatedly stressed, was to undertake reforms that would transform the PLA. As a senior commander put it: 'What is referred to as reform is to do away with all rules, regulations and work style that do not conform to the needs of modernization; study new situations; solve new problems; sum up new experiences; and establish new rules and regulations.'[46] The point of departure for the transformation of the PLA into a modern army was a reassessment of Maoist military doctrine.

4

'People's War Under Modern Conditions':Military Doctrine in Flux

The defence policy of the Deng leadership set the framework within which PLA planners had to reassess and revise Maoist military doctrine. This task put the military in a quandary – a quandary which paralleled and reflected the broader dilemma faced by the Party leadership in formulating defence policy. Just as the leadership was aware of the need to modernize the armed forces, so the army high command was aware of the need radically to revise Maoist military doctrine. The reason is that this doctrine is unsuitable both to the type of warfare the Chinese are likely to wage in the future, and to the modernization of the PLA which is taking place in the present. However, just as the Party leadership is unable to allocate large-scale resources to the military, so army leaders are unable to make a complete and explicit break with Maoist doctrine. The reason is that – pending vast technological advances in the PLA – this doctrine has to remain the final counterweight to the inferiority of the armed forces in weapons and equipment and the ultimate deterrent to a general invasion of China.

As a way out of this quandary the Chinese have devised the formula of 'people's war under modern conditions'. This is a transitional defence doctrine designed to guide the PLA as it moves slowly along the long road to modernization. Although the Chinese have not provided a systematic exposition of 'people's war under modern conditions', their pronouncements and practices indicate that the two parts of the formula do not carry equal weight in the minds of military leaders. While some central components of 'people's war' have been retained for pragmatic reasons, the adaptation of the PLA to 'modern conditions' is the main concern of its leaders. Thus, the doctrine of the Chinese armed forces in the post-Mao period, like their weapons and equipment, contain both old and new elements, but the trend is unmistakably in favour of the new. In order to assess this trend, it is necessary to recapitulate the chief features of Maoist military doctrine.

Maoist Military Doctrine[1]

The Maoist doctrine of 'people's war', which dominated the development of the PLA for nearly two decades, was essentially the same doctrine which Mao had formulated for the Red Army during its revolutionary struggle. It began to take shape in the late 1920s in the Jinggang Mountains, to which Mao had led remnants of the routed Red Army, and matured in the late 1930s in Yan'an, from which Mao and the Chinese Communist high command directed the operations of the Red Army against the Japanese. The product of expedience and experience, Maoist military doctrine evolved as a pragmatic response to the circumstances which confronted the Chinese Communists in their revolutionary struggle. The paramount and permanent feature of these circumstances was the overwhelming material inferiority of the Red Army in relation to opposing forces, be they the Nationalists, the Japanese or even warlord armies. The problem of the leadership was how to offset this inferiority by capitalizing on the assets which the Chinese Communists had at their disposal: China's vast territory and difficult terrain, highly motivated soldiers and the support of the population. By providing guidelines for fighting and army-building in conditions of material adversity, the 'people's war' doctrine proved to be a singularly successful answer to this problem.

After the Chinese Communists came to power in 1949, the doctrine of 'people's war' became largely irrelevant to their immediate requirements. First, the Sino-Soviet Treaty of 1950 gave the Chinese leadership assurance that the United States was deterred from attacking China, and obviated the need for urgent preparations to defend the mainland against an impending invasion by a greatly superior force. Second, since the leadership was committed to the modernization of the PLA, it saw little utility in retaining principles and practices which were designed to counterbalance technological inferiority.

This attitude was strengthened by the experience of the Chinese in the Korean War. On the strategic level, the doctrine was inapplicable, because the Chinese did not wage a defensive war in their homeland. Nonetheless, they entered the war in the expectation that reliance on Maoist tactical and organization principles would counteract the inferiority of the Chinese forces in weapons and equipment. Consequently, the Chinese operated in accordance with time-tested methods of force concentration, close combat, night fighting and political indoctrination. However, as has been seen, after initial

71

successes, these methods proved to be ineffective in the face of greatly superior firepower and equipment, and the Chinese forces suffered intolerable casualties and hardships. The lesson learned by PLA commanders was that Maoist doctrine was no substitute for modern weapons and organization.

This lesson was a major motive force behind the great modern transformation of the PLA in the 1950s, which was led by the newly formed Chinese professional officer corps. Impelled by the needs of a modern army and influenced by Soviet advisers, Chinese officers quickly assimilated modes of thinking and operation which departed drastically from Maoist norms. As a result, during this period little was heard of Maoist military doctrine.

The modernization of the PLA, it will be recalled, was disrupted in the late 1950s due to a combination of several factors. The far-reaching professionalization of the armed forces provoked a reaction from Party and military leaders who were concerned by the growing gap between the PLA's revolutionary traditions and its Soviet-inspired practices. This reaction was radicalized by developments outside the armed forces. One was the deterioration of Sino-Soviet relations, which convinced the Chinese that they would have to acquire a nuclear capability by themselves, and raised doubts about the credibility of Soviet protection against the military threat from the United States. The second was the adoption of radical development policies, which highlighted mass mobilization and created a national climate of anti-professionalism.

Just as the Maoist leadership found inspiration in its revolutionary past for its policies of national development, so it resurrected and reasserted the revolutionary doctrine of 'people's war' in the armed forces. And just as Maoist ideology was supposed to turn China towards a revolutionary path of development, so Maoist military doctrine was supposed to redirect the development of the armed forces to the Maoist military model. However, the revival of the doctrine also had several aims which were specific to the military establishment. The first was to provide the PLA with the strategy and tactics necessary to cope with the possibility of invasion by a vastly superior enemy at a time when China had no nuclear deterrent at all, but was particularly vulnerable to a preventive attack as it moved towards the acquisition of strategic weapons. Another was to facilitate a drastic reduction of expenditure on conventional forces, which would largely freeze their progress, in order to channel resources to the nuclear sector. The third was to reorient the development of the PLA towards a primary reliance on the 'human element' in order to prepare it for waging a 'people's war' from a position of technological inferiority. Directed first at the United States and later at the Soviet Union, the declared doctrine remained unchanged until Mao's death, although even before that implicit changes were evidently introduced.

The cornerstone of Mao's military doctrine is the concept of 'man over weapons'. Without belittling the importance of weapons in war, Mao insisted implacably that the outcome is ultimately determined by the 'human factor' – properly mobilized and politically motivated soldiers, fighting in accordance with the correct strategy and tactics. As propagated by Mao, this concept differed from the banal notion that the quality of manpower operating weapons is a crucial element in war. Its uniqueness lay in the belief that the 'human factor' can act as a substitute for both the quantity and quality of the opponent's weapons. In Mao's view, the primacy of the 'human factor' was not altered by the passage of time and the progress of technology. Therefore, it provided the underpinning for China's doctrine of defence against the superpowers in the nuclear era.

This doctrine was based on several related assumptions. The first was that until China developed a credible nuclear deterrent it could do very little militarily to prevent a nuclear attack upon it, although it could take measures – such as civil defence and dispersal, concealment and protection of key installations – to reduce the destructive effects of such an attack. The second assumption was that if an attack were unleashed, it would wreak havoc on China's industrial centres, but – and this was the crux of the entire doctrine – it could not destroy rural China. Since China was predominantly a rural country it could not, therefore, be subjugated by nuclear strikes. From this followed the third assumption – that an enemy bent on total victory would have to follow up nuclear strikes with a ground invasion of the mainland, otherwise the nuclear attack would be of little long-term benefit to the attacker. And against a conventional ground attack the Chinese held advantages which made them virtually unconquerable. These advantages derived from China's territory, terrain and population, but foremost among them was its ability to exploit the 'human factor'. Thus, in the second and conventional phase of the war, China's strengths would give it overall superiority despite its technological weaknesses.

This phase was envisaged by the Chinese as a protracted war of attrition. China's strategy would be based on a defence in depth, and its primary objective would be to destroy enemy forces rather than to hold territory. This strategy had several stages. First, the Chinese army would abandon urban centres and border areas and would withdraw into the interior, trading space for time. The enemy would be drawn deep into Chinese territory and would be forced to fight in unfamiliar conditions and hostile terrain, to extend his lines of supply and communications, and to divide his forces. In the meantime, the entire able-bodied population, and especially the trained 'people's militia', would be mobilized to wage a 'people's war' alongside the regular army. Enjoying all the advantages of fighting on home ground, the Chinese would then attack the enemy's divided units by concentrating their own forces to create tactical superiority in battles of their own choosing. In fighting these battles, Chinese troops would use long-standing methods which stressed mobility, night fighting, deception, surprise and superior intelligence. In this way, the Chinese would gradually overcome the enemy's material superiority and, by destroying his forces piecemeal, would erode his strength in a long process of attrition. In the final stage, the Chinese army would switch from a strategic defence to a strategic offence aimed at repulsing the weakened invading forces.

As long as the Chinese had no nuclear capability they had little choice but to fall back upon the 'people's war' doctrine as a universal response to all major military threats. However, their reliance on this doctrine was based on extremely dubious premises, of which the Chinese themselves were doubtless aware. The first was that an enemy would launch an all-out nuclear attack on China as a prelude to a ground invasion of the mainland. The second, and even more unrealistic, premise was that a massive ground invasion to conquer China would follow a nuclear strike. Also highly questionable was China's professed readiness to abandon densely populated centres to an invader in order to 'lure the enemy in deep'.[2] Although in the 1960s Chinese leaders did not rule out an unprovoked surprise attack, first by the United States and later by the Soviet Union, they could not have realistically expected to wage a war according to Maoist strategy in its entirety.

Despite this, propagation of the 'people's war' doctrine had several purposes. It was meant to deter enemy leaders from launching an attack on China by impressing upon them the futility of such an act. It was intended to instil confidence in the population at a time when both superpowers were hostile towards China. It was aimed at strengthening the morale of the troops by persuading them of China's invincibility despite its technological inferiority. But whatever its precise aims, the greatest impact of the 'people's war' doctrine was on the development of the PLA, because the doctrine – like all doctrines – not only laid down guidelines for waging a war, it also shaped the building of the armed forces for this kind of war.

As already observed, this impact was felt by the PLA in several ways. Expenditure on conventional forces was reduced by the need to produce nuclear weapons, and rationalized by reliance on the strategy of 'people's war'. To compensate for the resultant technological retardation, the centrality of the 'human factor' in the development of the PLA was vigorously reasserted. Consequently, political and ideological needs were placed above military considerations, egalitarian practices dating back to revolutionary times were restored, and political controls were tightened. The militia was revived and accorded a central role in defence strategy. The cumulative effect of these measures, it should be emphasized again, was a sharp decline in the professional standards of the PLA.

This decline was most pronounced during the last decade of the Maoist period, when radical leaders gained power and, for political reasons, used Maoist military doctrine as a sanction for imposing extreme leftist policies in the armed forces. Just how extreme these policies were is evident from accusations levelled against radical leaders after their demise. Even allowing for the gross exaggerations which characterize such accusations, there can be little doubt that the damage done to the military capabilities of the armed forces was severe. A few examples will illustrate the extent of this damage.

The former defence minister, Lin Biao, allegedly perpetrated several 'fallacies' in the armed forces. One was that 'ideology can substitute for materials', which led his supporters to claim that 'as long as people's ideology is grasped well, torpedoes can be fired by pushing them out of tubes with men's heads when proper launching equipment is not available'. Another 'fallacy' regarded 'politics as magic', so that "whoever said politics should be applied to vocational work was regarded as a revisionist and vehemently criticized".[3]

The 'gang of four' was similarly condemned for undermining the combat readiness of the armed forces. 'They smeared our efforts to study and analyse the enemy situation and conduct education on preparedness against war as gestures purposely to scare people.' In response to arguments for defence modernization 'the gang of four said slanderously: "you are following a bourgeois military line and practising the theory that weapons decide everything". Releasing a stream of poison,' the radicals 'sabotaged both mental and material preparation'. Whoever disagreed with them was branded as opposing the revolution:

> Whoever grasped preparedness against war would be labelled by them as using preparedness against war to suppress revolution. Whoever conducted military training would be described by them as holding a purely military viewpoint. Whoever wanted to build national defence projects or people's defence projects would be described . . . as harassing the people and wasting money and as making passive defence. Whoever wanted to strengthen armaments industrial production would be described . . . as making a fetish of weapons and as feverish advocates of the armaments industry.[4]

The intervention of radical leaders in military affairs extended to the PLA's internal activities. They subverted discipline by encouraging people 'to regard revolution and discipline as opposed to each other', and by claiming that 'to observe discipline was to practise slavishness'. They reportedly told the soldiers that 'an ordinary fighter can oppose his squad leader, squad leaders can oppose platoon leaders, and platoon leaders can oppose company commanders'.[5] And they undermined stability by advocating the notion that 'failure to arouse the masses to express their views freely, write big-character posters and hold great debates in PLA units meant suppression of democracy'.[6]

The radicals also disrupted training on the pretext that concentration on training meant that 'politics are swept aside' and that troops should give priority to political study. 'Their main stick and label was that grasping military training means advocating the purely military viewpoint.' They also claimed that training did not require rigorous efforts, which was another version of 'the fallacy that when a good job is done in revolution, production will go up naturally. . .'. They refused to accept that, while 'grasping revolution can promote military training', it 'cannot serve as a substitute'.[7]

No less serious were the attempts of the radicals to counterpose the militia to the PLA. In order to create the 'so-called second armed forces', the radicals spread the 'fallacy' that the PLA was not 'as good as the militia' and that it was not 'reliable'. Invoking Mao's injunction about the importance of the militia, they tried to turn it into an armed force under their control: 'Chairman Mao always stressed that the militia should play a support and supplementary role to the armed forces. But the gang of four . . . said it was fine to build two armed forces – the regular armed forces and the militia . . . .'[8]

The doctrine of 'people's war' and its associated practices were periodically criticized by senior military leaders as dated and detrimental to the armed forces. As has been seen, Defence Minister Peng Dehuai and Chief of Staff Luo Ruiqing were dismissed for their dissent, while Deng Xiaoping was attacked by radical leaders for advocating large-scale military modernization. However, such efforts did not dislodge Maoist military doctrine from its position of supremacy. By equating fidelity to the doctrine with political loyalty, the Maoists managed to suppress opposing views and to silence professional officers. A senior military leader, Su Yu, described this state of affairs in the following words:

> For a long time, Lin Biao and the gang of four freely used such labels and sticks as 'pushing politics aside', 'purely military viewpoint', 'opposing Mao Zedong thought' and 'the theory that weapons decide everything' to suppress and attack people everywhere. This seriously shackled our minds in the field of military science, and there was hardly a true democratic environment. As a result, some people confused academic questions with political and ideological questions.[9]

Another senior military leader, Xiao Ke, described how this state of affairs stifled the development of doctrine:

> In the past, Lin Biao and the 'gang of four' pushed an ultra-Left line and set up many forbidden areas in the teaching and learning of military affairs. These forbidden areas may be summarized in two sentences: What was written in books must not be changed or expanded; and what was not written in books must not be said or thought of. The result was nothing of the past could be changed and everything had

to be done in the same way it was done in the past. Whoever failed to do so was labelled as having 'pulled down the banner'. In writing articles and making speeches, people used a lot of quotations and copied and imitated a lot.[10]

In this situation the professional officers could do little but sulk and wait for the day when they would be able to break their silence.

'People's War Under Modern Conditions'

When the military did break their silence, pronouncements on questions of doctrine were at first highly cautious. Although these pronouncements went hand in hand with fervent calls for military modernization, they were far more subtle and restrained. Tampering with Mao's military doctrine was a highly sensitive matter because it was inextricably linked to the broader issue of how to treat Mao's ideological legacy. Until this issue was resolved by the leadership, the military were extremely wary in their comments on 'people's war'.

This wariness was conspicuous in their early statements on the subject. An article by a military unit, for example, reaffirmed the Maoist notion that 'it is people, not guns, that constitute the decisive factor in winning a war'. But then it went on to say that 'we should also fully affirm the role of weapons, which in no way means backing the theory that weapons decide everything'.[11] Another article also first condemned this theory, but then noted that 'we have never negated weapons as an important factor in war'.[12]

The most striking example of doctrinal tightrope-walking in the early post-Mao period was an article by Su Yu, which introduced the term 'people's war under modern conditions'.[13] Although ostensibly an exposition of 'people's war', the ulterior motive of the article was clearly to stress the need for modern strategy and tactics. To this end, Su selected for discussion large-scale campaigns in which the regular army had played the central role. He highlighted the importance of 'mobile warfare', 'offensive campaigns', 'quick and decisive battles' and 'positional warfare', and gave only passing mention to 'guerrilla warfare'. Nothing was said about protracted war or mobilization of the population. In the end, Su came to the main point of the article:

> Our method of fighting should vary in different wars or in different stages of a war, in different times and places, with different enemies or with different weaponry or equipment. It is necessary to ... change tactics, and study and master the latest tactics developed along with new technology and equipment.[14]

The need for circumspection in discussing doctrinal matters was greatly reduced after Deng Xiaoping's important speech to the army political conference in June 1978. In this speech Deng came to grips with the dilemma facing the post-Mao leadership: the need to retain the link to Maoist ideology for reasons of legitimacy while departing from it for practical purposes. Deng's ingenious way out of the dilemma was to declare that Mao himself had sanctioned such departure by stressing the necessity to 'seek truth from facts'. Therefore, Deng said, 'we must at no time violate' Maoist principles, 'but we must integrate them with reality, analyse and study actual conditions and solve practical problems'.[15] Deng thus sanctioned the revision of Maoist doctrine without repudiating Mao, a sanction which gained added force after he consolidated his supremacy at the Third Plenum of the llth Central Committee in December 1978.

The change in the pronouncements coming from the military was dramatic. Su Yu, who in mid-1977 had wrapped his views in layers of hints, spoke out forthrightly in a speech to the Military Academy in January 1979.[16] While Mao's military thought is a 'valuable asset', Su said, 'this by no means implies that Mao Zedong's military thought needs no further development'. The essence of Mao's thought is that 'we need realistically to analyse specific wars and realistically to study wars and their guiding laws'. Some of Mao's principles, Su went on, 'no longer fit the actual conditions of future wars, and we should have the courage to break through them'. As to problems of which Mao was not aware, 'we must have the courage to break new paths and make new developments'. Su then gave specific examples of the need for change:

> Although we still don't know much about future wars, we have fought for several decades and we do have plenty of elementary understanding about wars in general. For example, we can no longer cope with a concentrated enemy attack with rifles, machine-guns, hand-grenades and dynamite charges. We must have sufficient anti-tank artillery and guided missiles. For another example, if we are to fight a large-scale mobile war with an enemy on the plains, we must solve the problem of gaining local air supremacy.[17]

Speaking to the Military Academy, Xiao Ke said that in order to prepare officers for commanding modern combat operations, it was first necessary to 'emancipate the mind'. Mao's thought was 'born from practice and must be tested through practice and constantly be improved and developed. We cannot rigidly adhere to conclusions that no longer conform with the new conditions.'[18] Xiang Zhonghua, political commissar of the military region from which China's attack on Vietnam was launched in 1979, said that discussions on taking 'practice as the sole criterion for testing truth' should be carried on in the light of China's experience in the war. Reality, he said, should be the guide 'in building our PLA units and the need to adapt ourselves to modern warfare . . .'.[19]

A forceful argument for doctrinal innovation was put forward by Defence Minister Xu Xiangqian in a *Hongqi* article in October 1979.[20] 'We must', Xu said bluntly, 'equip ourselves with advanced military thinking to meet the needs of modernizing our national defence and the needs in a future war.' To do this, Xu continued, it was necessary to combine Mao's thought with 'the practice of modern warfare' and to 'solve problems realistically'. Modern science and technology, Xu emphasized, were 'developing with each passing day .... These changes will surely cause corresponding changes in the method of fighting.'

Xu then implicitly but unmistakably made a case for a break with the 'people's war' doctrine. 'War', he said, 'is now conducted in a way different from that in the past. Take our future war against aggression for example. The target of attack, the scale of war and even the method of fighting are new to us.' Therefore, 'our military thinking must tally with changing conditions'. If this is not done, Xu left no doubt as to the consequences: 'if we treat and command a modern war in the way we commanded a war during the 1930s and 1940s, we are bound to meet with a big rebuff and suffer a serious defeat'. Xu pressed his case by citing a European example, but the relevance to China was crystal-clear:

> We have seen many incidents in the history of war in which an army was defeated . . . because its commander had backward military thinking and directed operations in the wrong way. During World War II, the French Army was not inferior to the German Army in strength and weaponry. Nevertheless it was defeated in a short period by the German Army. An important reason . . . was that France's military thinking at that time remained at the state of World War I and lagged twenty years behind . . . .We must learn from this historical lesson.[21]

In concluding his discussion of doctrine, Xu laid out the tasks facing the Chinese military:

> In particular, we must . . . study the enemy, take the actual conditions of the enemy and ourselves into consideration and find out the laws for directing a people's war under present-day conditions. We must whip up a hightide of studying military science with emphasis on the strategy, tactics, science and technology of modern warfare.[22]

This theme was taken up by the military press. An editorial in the army paper, which called for large-scale modernization of the armed forces, emphasized that such an effort 'first requires us to change our thinking'. Officers, it said, should 'study the new situations and problems, be brave in creativeness and smash the rigid or semi-rigid way of thinking. When our thinking progresses there will be great progress in our modernization.' [23] Another article noted that 'modern warfare is vastly different from that of the past; therefore our minds should never become rigid and by no means should we stick to outmoded conventions'. But this, noted the army paper, was no easy matter: 'the achievements won in ideological emancipation are still not quite enough when compared to the needs of modernization'. The thinking of 'some comrades', it said, was still 'ossified' and they were 'accustomed to following the beaten path and acting in accordance with old conventions'.[24]

However, a more serious problem appeared to be uncertainty regarding the nature of doctrinal change. 'The question remains', said the commander of the Nanjing units, 'as to how to understand and apply correctly Chairman Mao's military thinking and strategies and tactics under current conditions'.[25] This question was elaborated by the army paper: 'Which of the series of army-building principles and policies, strategies, tactics and revolutionary traditions are still playing a guiding role in today's army-building and in the conduct of future warfare? Which ones should be continued and developed in consonance with the new conditions, and which ones are partially or completely outmoded and should be partially or completely abandoned?' Its answer hardly dispelled the uncertainty: 'we must distinguish among them according to the principle of seeking truth from facts and by proceeding from current conditions'.[26]

This uncertainty was dispelled to a large extent after the Sixth Plenum of the 11th Central Committee adopted the long-awaited resolution on the history of the People's Republic since 1949 – the Deng leadership's appraisal of the Maoist period. By criticizing Mao's mistakes while affirming his achievements, the resolution removed the shield of invincibility which had protected Maoist dogma from change and put the Party's imprimatur on far-reaching innovation. How this applied to the military was made clear in an important article by Song Shilun,[27] commandant of the Academy of Military Sciences, who went much further than his predecessors in specifying the revisions which the Chinese made in Maoist military doctrine.

After paying homage to this doctrine, Song underlined the one basic principle which the Chinese have retained in the post-Mao period: in case of a full-scale invasion of the mainland, the Chinese will 'rely on people's war to defeat the enemy . . . '. Song then said that it was necessary to 'supplement' Maoist principles 'in accordance with new situations'. This meant that 'in upholding . . . people's war, we must add modern conditions to it. Under modern conditions, there are many aspects . . . which differ from the people's war in our army's history'. What are these 'aspects'?

First, if attacked, the Chinese will not abandon territory automatically in order to draw the enemy into the interior, but will try to block his advance by positional warfare, and then go on the offensive. The Maoist strategy of abandoning cities and key installations will thus not be 'wholly applicable to future wars'. Garrison and reserve forces will bear the brunt of an attack while mobile and guerrilla warfare will play a supporting role in eroding the enemy's strength. This change requires new methods in preparing the army for a new type of warfare.

Second, in contrast to traditional 'people's war', 'it is obviously very insufficient to rely on the infantry alone'. In future wars, China will employ 'ground forces' – which means combined arms – and methods of fighting will have to change 'because of development in weapons and technical equipment'. Third, the whole concept of logistics is new, because the notion that 'our army's sources of manpower and material are mainly at the front is no longer applicable in future wars'. In these wars, fighting 'without a rear is unimaginable in a modernized army'.

Fourth, the army can no longer be a combat force and a civic force. Given the division of labour between the civil and military authorities, the main mission of the army is to prepare for fighting. 'Naturally, it is still indispensable to do some tasks of a work team and production team when necessary . . . but they are subordinate to that of forming a fighting force.' Finally, the development of the army 'should be subordinated to the needs of battle' and not to political and ideological concerns, as had been the case when Lin Biao and the radicals held power. For example, while leadership of the Party is a basic principle, this does not mean that Party committees should make decisions in wartime. Under conditions of modern warfare, commanders should not be hampered by procedures but should act 'at their own discretion'.

The innovations in China's military doctrine are thus basic and significant.[28] To restate briefly, operational continuity with Maoist doctrine will be maintained only if China is attacked along a broad front by a massive army bent on subjugating the country. In this extreme contingency, the Chinese will resort to a Maoist strategy of 'people's war': they will draw the enemy deep into China's hinterland, mobilize the population for total war, and wage guerrilla and mobile warfare to erode the enemy's strength in a protracted war. However, short of such an attack, the Chinese will not abandon their industrial centres but will 'meet the enemy at the gate' – or close to it. Instead of resorting to defence in depth, in which guerrilla and mobile warfare are primary, the Chinese will hold their ground by putting the main emphasis on 'positional defensive warfare', waged by combined arms and supported by mobile and guerrilla warfare. This change in strategy requires other changes: a well-equipped regular army, with a substantial logistic base and high professional competence, rather than a Maoist 'people's army', living off the land and the enemy. And these changes are far more than a mere 'development' of Maoist doctrine; they amount to a wholesale departure from its central tenets.

Although Song clearly pointed to this departure, neither he nor other senior military leaders have been overly forthcoming in discussing their vision of a future war 'under modern conditions'. One reason may be their reluctance to elaborate on a war which the Chinese are still far from prepared to wage against a technologically superior enemy. Another may be the need to retain an ideological link with Maoist doctrine, which would inevitably be severed in detailed discussions of modern war. Whatever the reasons for the public reticence, there is no doubt that such discussions take place in inner circles. Periodically they surface publicly in articles which do not bear the imprint of high-level authorities, but doubtless reflect their views. One such article, published in August 1983, explained the 'characteristics of modern warfare' – characteristics which implicitly make such warfare irrelevant to Maoist doctrine.

The author listed seven such characteristics. First, in addition to large-scale ground attacks, both sides must launch 'strategic air raids' against targets deep in the enemy's rear, particularly against 'long-range weapons for surprise attacks'. Second, the initial stage in a modern war is much more important than before. Modern war breaks out suddenly, and the opening phase is shorter, its scale is much larger and it is much more destructive than before. Third, the scope of the modern battlefield is much larger and entirely different from the past. Fourth, because modern war is waged on the ground, in the air and on the seas, and because it is waged with weapons which are much more destructive than before, it is much more difficult to distinguish the front from rear areas. Fifth, there is much greater reliance on logistics, and this includes supplies, maintenance and medical facilities. Sixth, command and control are completely different from those of the past, and are crucial to the outcome. Modern command methods require computers and automatic control systems, as well as sophisticated electronic reconnaissance and communications systems. Seventh, the 'human factor' is still important, but this is because the operation of modern weapons requires advanced skills, and because the entire population is affected by modern war – not because the 'human factor' is a substitute for modern means and methods.[29]

That China's leaders have to all intents and purposes abandoned 'people's war' as an operational doctrine has been more evident from their conduct than from their commentaries. As will be detailed in later chapters, the development of the PLA has been exclusively guided by professional objectives, which the Maoists had derided as representing a 'singular military viewpoint'. Its programmes have been geared to preparations for fighting a modern war and have rejected the Maoist reliance on the 'human factor' to assure success. Its internal procedures bear little resemblance to the Maoist model, which had put 'politics in command' of military affairs. And, despite financial constraints, its weapons and equipment have been modernized and increased. In short, from the vantage point of Maoist military doctrine, the PLA has changed beyond recognition since the end of the Maoist era.

Nowhere has this change been more strikingly demonstrated than in the large-scale manoeuvres held by the PLA since the early 1980s. As described by the Chinese, the type of war simulated in these manoeuvres has nothing to do with Mao's concept of a protracted 'people's war' of attrition, and the forces waging this war are vastly different from the infantry 'people's army' of Maoist days. Commenting on these exercises, Yu Qiuli, director the General Political Department, said that 'they reflected the new fighting style of our army' and displayed its 'modernization and regularization level'. The participating units included 'motorized infantry, airborne units, artillery units, ground-to-air missiles, anti-tank missiles, engineer corps and the air service of the air force'.[30] The battlefield was complex:

> In the invisible space, electrons interfered with the enemy's radars and disturbed its command system. The enemy launched counter-interference and counter-disturbance. There were planes flying one above another in the air: fighters, bombers, attackers and armed helicopters. They gave support to the ground force at high, medium and low altitudes. On the ground, under cover of the aircraft, groups of tanks made wide-angle, front and depth attacks and similar defences one after another. Helicopters carried infantrymen to co-ordinate with tanks their attack on the 'enemy' positions. Airborne troops cut off the 'enemy's' rear and turned it into the front. Long, medium and short-range artillery and missiles formed crisscross networks of fire.[31]

Whatever the performance of the PLA in the present, its future sights are clearly set on preparing for fighting a modern war.

Nuclear War 'Under Modern Conditions'

How have the changes in the doctrine of 'people's war' affected Chinese thinking on nuclear war? This is an extremely difficult question to answer because the Chinese have divulged very little about their views on the employment of nuclear weapons. Therefore, such views have to be inferred from scattered and vague references, and particularly from the development and deployment of nuclear weapons. Within these limitations, it is possible to suggest several important modifications which the Chinese have apparently made in their concept of nuclear war.

One modification is that they no longer consider the nuclear and conventional phases of a war to be inextricably linked. As noted earlier, when the doctrine of 'people's war' reigned supreme, they did not make this distinction. Their defence strategy was based on the assumption that a nuclear attack was insufficient to subjugate China, and would have to be followed by a ground invasion. In this phase, 'people's war' would manifest its advantage over a technologically superior enemy. However, in recent years the possibility of a limited war not preceded by a massive nuclear attack has replaced the concept of total 'people's war' as the most likely war the Chinese will have to wage. As a result, they seem to have severed the link between the nuclear and conventional phases of a war.

Several signs point in this direction. For one thing, the Chinese have simply dropped the formula tying these phases from major statements on military affairs. For another, senior military leaders have spoken of the need to prepare for different types of war. Xu Xiangqian, then minister of defence, wrote in 1979 that 'the armed forces in different areas have different combat tasks and different targets of attack. We must design and manufacture weapons useful in different conditions'.[32] Han Huaizhi, assistant to the chief of the General Staff, said in an interview: 'we must prepare to fight both a conventional and a nuclear war'.[33] Yang Shangkun spoke of 'being able to deal with a partial war . . .'.[34]

Most important, however, have been the training programmes and manoeuvres of the PLA. These, as already observed, have been oriented towards fighting a limited war. Reports on exercises carried out by the PLA do not suggest a post-nuclear attack scenario, in which Chinese troops have to cope with the effects of a nuclear strike. Furthermore, civic defence measures, which had figured prominently in China's preparations for war a decade earlier, have hardly received any attention in recent years.

Another change in the approach of the Chinese to nuclear war has been in their concept of deterrence. From the time of their first nuclear detonation the Chinese have repeatedly maintained that they are developing nuclear weapons solely for defence, and that they will not be the first to use nuclear weapons. In order to deter an attack, the Chinese have relied on a combination of denial and retaliation, although the relative weight of these elements has shifted with changing circumstances. Until the Chinese acquired an operational capability, they sought to deter an enemy from attacking China by denying him victory. Denial was to be achieved by absorbing a nuclear strike and then defeating an invasion by 'people's war'. China's preparations for such a war were publicized in particular by the construction of an extensive network of underground shelters in large cities, which first began in the autumn of 1969. By demonstrating their determination to fight by all means and at all costs, the Chinese sought to persuade the Soviets that an attack on China was bound to end in failure.

The relative importance of retaliation in the strategy of deterrence increased after China acquired a nuclear capability. This capability consisted of medium- and intermediate-range missiles as well as bombers. However, their ability to survive a Soviet first strike, especially in the early years, was uncertain, particularly due to the high vulnerability of liquid-fuelled missiles. Nonetheless, missiles could be dispersed, moved or located in caves or hardened sites, while aircraft could be shifted around different airfields. This was doubtless enough to create uncertainty in the minds of Soviet strategists as to the survivability of China's nuclear weapons. And such uncertainty, in turn, was enough to endow China with a capability to deter by threat of retaliation, though such a threat was not explicitly made by the Chinese. It was, however, noted by others. As General George C. Brown, chairman of the United States Joint Chiefs of Staff, said in early 1976: 'P.R.C. strategic forces are a result of a small, but carefully conceived, strategic program. A modest, but credible nuclear retaliatory capability against the USSR has been achieved . . . .'[35] Although this was undoubtedly a crucial element in Chinese assessments of the Soviet threat and of their capability to deter it, their public declarations until the late 1970s reflected a continued commitment to 'people's war' and an implicit reliance on a strategy of deterrence by denial.

However, following the downgrading of 'people's war' in their calculations, the Chinese seem to have shifted towards greater reliance on retaliation in their strategy of deterrence. One indication has been the absence of statements highlighting China's invincibility in a total war on the mainland. More important have been specific and novel Chinese references to their strategic capability. An article in *Hongqi* said that China's 'sophisticated strategic weapons for self-defence' were 'something to be proud of. This is an important factor deterring the imperialists from launching a large-scale invasion against us'.[36] Defence Minister Zhang Aiping noted that 'we have . . . established certain defensive capability in terms of strategic weapons'.[37] And a *Renmin Ribao* editor's note appended to a report on the PLA strategic missiles unit underlined that the unit 'now has the combat capability to counter a surprise attack and to launch a nuclear counter-offensive'.[38] Although such remarks are rare, they obviously reflect a line of thinking at the highest levels which was not given public expression several years earlier.

The most convincing evidence of the importance which the Chinese attach to their retaliatory capability lies in their sustained effort to improve this capability. Significant strides have been made in this area since the turn of the decade In 1980 China tested its first full-range ICBM; it began deployment a year or so later. In 1981, the Chinese tested a potential MIRV. In 1982, they successfully fired an SLBM which promises to add a particularly important dimension to their deterrent by increasing its chances of remaining intact after a first strike. In 1984, the Chinese tested their first geostationery satellite which is crucial for modern C3I (command, control, communications and intelligence). Although the groundwork for these achievements was doubtless laid during the Maoist period, credit for the effort has been attributed by Zhang Aiping to the new leadership. As he said in an interview: 'After Comrade Deng Xiaoping began presiding over the work in 1975, we began reorganization and proposed developing intercontinental missiles, submarine-launched missiles, and geosynchronous satellites.'[39]

Perhaps the most significant change in Chinese nuclear doctrine has been the simulated employment and possible future deployment of tactical nuclear weapons. The fact that China had no tactical nuclear weapons had always put the Chinese at a disadvantage. In the early 1970s, at least two Soviet divisions armed with tactical nuclear weapons were reportedly based near the border, while Soviet bombers had been prepared for delivering tactical nuclear weapons. The Chinese obviously could not rely on countering the use of tactical weapons by resorting to their strategic capability, since this would invite nuclear devastation. Perhaps Maoist strategists downgraded the possibility of the enemy using tactical weapons because of their strategy of 'drawing him in deep', or downplayed the effect of such weapons because of the wide dispersal of forces, the vast territories over which war would be waged and the Chinese tactic of 'hugging' the enemy. In any case, whatever their thinking on this subject, it did filter out to the public.

The changes in the PLA's doctrine and posture have made the issue of tactical nuclear weapons much more acute and urgent. The issue boils down to this: what happens if China's determination to meet an invader head-on causes him to use tactical nuclear weapons to break through the PLA's defences? This question has clearly been the subject of debate in inner circles, but the curtain on the different views was raised only very slightly in an unusual article in the army paper.[40]

According to the author, one school of thought argued that 'since the enemy enjoys absolute superiority in conventional weapons, he is unlikely to use nuclear weapons in the initial stages of a war'. The implication was that there was no pressing need for the PLA to possess tactical nuclear weapons. This argument was forcefully rejected by another school of thought, represented by the author. The view of the first school, he said, was 'wishful thinking'. He then explained the reason:

> Once the enemy launched an aggressive war . . . the will to fight on both sides and the scope and intensity of the war would be unprecedented . . . .The enemy's strategy rests on a sudden, extensive and overpowering attack to achieve his predatory objectives within the shortest possible time. However, as soon as enemy forces entered our territory, they would face a hostile population, unfamiliar topography and fierce counter-attacks, especially at our major defence centres. Our stiff resistance and repeated counter-attacks could make the enemy so frustrated that he might resort to tactical nuclear weapons to spring a shock attack.[41]

The author's conclusion did not mince any words:

> We must be prepared . . . for the use by our enemy of tactical nuclear weapons in the initial stages of a future war. If we are so prepared emotionally and materially, we will be able to cope with any complex situations. On the other hand, if we believe a nuclear war is 'unlikely to occur', pay very little attention to the study of nuclear war, do not include nuclear war in training and do not base combat planning on the possibility of tactical nuclear attack but go by subjective, wishy-washy concepts, the consequences will be unthinkable in case the enemy actually uses nuclear weapons.[42]

86

This conclusion apparently prevailed. Subsequent exercises by the PLA have simulated the use of tactical nuclear weapons. At first it was only the enemy who employed such weapons,[43] but in a major manoeuvre held in mid-1982 it was reported that the PLA's 'nuclear strike capability zeroed in on the targets, took the enemy by surprise and dealt his artillery positions and reserve forces a crushing blow'.[44] Such manoeuvres presumably point to China's intention to develop nuclear weapons for battlefield use.

This intention may partly account for the announcement in early 1984 that the PLA had 'established a strategic missile wing'.[45] The new outfit has probably incorporated the existing missile units known as the Second Artillery Corps. One reason for the reorganization may be the addition of new responsibilities stemming from the projected use of tactical nuclear weapons. Since the Chinese are not likely at present to relinquish central command and control over such weapons, it is logical for this unit to assume responsibility for their use. In fact, the report on its establishment implied that the missions of the strategic wing were not limited to strategic strikes: 'rapid advances in military technology had made it necessary for the PLA to raise its combined attacking ability. Only in this way would it be able to win battles in the coming anti-aggressive war . . . .'[46]

If the Chinese decide to deploy tactical nuclear weapons, they will have to delegate authority to field units. Such a move will have to be preceded by major advances in command, control and communications systems. It will have to be preceded by organizational streamlining and the simplification of command lines. And it will have to be preceded by the promotion to senior field positions of officers familiar with modern warfare. Reforms in these areas, as will be seen, are high on the leadership's list of priorities.

Doctrinal Change and the Militia

The departure from Maoist doctrine has also been demonstrated by changes in the role of the militia, which had vital functions in a 'people's war'. Together with the field armies and the local forces, the militia formed the 'three-in-one' military system on which the strategy of 'people's war' was based. After the enemy had been drawn in deep into China's hinterland in accordance with this strategy, it was the task of the militia, in co-operation with other forces, to harass and wear him down, as well as to supply services, intelligence and manpower to the army. The mass-based militia, moreover, was regarded by the Maoists as a symbol *par excellence* of reliance on the 'human element' and as the antithesis of intolerable professional tendencies which afflicted the PLA. The professional leadership of the PLA, on its part, tended to take a dim view of the militia on the grounds that it was largely useless in a modern war and a drain on valuable resources. Changes in the role of the militia, therefore, have been inversely tied to fluctuations in the status of the professional military.

As already noted, during the period of Soviet-inspired military modern-ization, which began towards the end of the Korean War, the militia fell into oblivion. There it remained until the late 1950s, when the resurrection of the 'people's war' doctrine and the denigration of military professionalism catapulted the militia on to the national scene with much force and fanfare. To prepare the masses for a 'people's war' and to mobilize them for the Great Leap Forward, a vast movement to make 'everyone a soldier' engulfed the country. Although the importance of the militia declined after the collapse of the Great Leap Forward and the discovery of defects in its operations, it remained prominent throughout the Lin Biao period and the domination of his 'politics first' approach to defence matters.

In the early 1970s the militia acquired a sinister political significance, as it became a prime pawn in the shadowy power struggle between Maoist radicals, on the one hand, and the coalition of moderate and military leaders, on the other. Unable to make inroads into the professional officer corps, which mostly supported the moderate coalition, radical leaders tried to set up urban militias – 'a second armed force' – patterned on the model of the vaunted Shanghai militia and responsive to them. With this in mind, they attempted to detach control of the militia from the PLA and to create separate commands under their supervision.[47] That they were unsuccessful was illustrated by the failure of the militia, even in Shanghai, to rise in their support when the radicals were deposed.

Behind the power struggle over the militia lurked the continuing conflict over defence strategy and the character of the armed forces. Deng and the PLA leaders, it will be recalled, tried to launch a military modernization drive in 1975 but were briefly thwarted by the radicals, who clung to Mao's 'people's war' strategy and the militia's central role in it. Mao's death and the downfall of the radical leaders paved the way for the decline of the militia.

The decline went hand in hand with the drift away from Maoist doctrine. Unsure how to handle the Maoist legacy, military leaders, as already seen, moved cautiously at first. This caution was reflected in their treatment of the militia. For example, writing in Hongqi in 1978, then Defence Minister Xu Xiangqian emphasized the principle of allowing the enemy to come into China, albeit in a controlled manner, and played up the role of the militia in the war.[48] However, his article in the same journal a year later was a ringing manifesto for military modernization, which emphasized the need for changing Maoist doctrine and made no mention of the militia.[49] In subsequent years, although lip-service was paid to the militia, its role was circumscribed. For example, an article by the director of the political department of the Shanxi Provincial Military District started out by saying that the militia was 'the solid foundation for waging people's war'. However, he then explained that this was so because the militia was the reserve force for the standing army. Its additional tasks as an 'assistant' to the armed forces were to man 'blockhouse areas', to delay the advance of the enemy, to carry out anti-air-raid and anti-airborne defences, and to conduct guerrilla operations behind enemy lines.[50]

The *coup de grâce* to the militia, as it had existed under the 'three-in-one' system, was delivered by the Military Service Law of 1984. It abolished the militia as a separate organization and transformed it into a reserve force of the PLA. According to the Military Law, male citizens aged eighteen to thirty-five, who meet the requirements for active military service but are not drafted, are to be organized into militia organizations as reserves. The militia is divided into primary and general units. The primary units consist of soldiers retired from active service and those who have received military training and are aged under twenty-eight. The general militia units consist of male citizens aged eighteen to thirty-five who are fit for military service but were not drafted.[51] The rationale for this step was given by a *Renmin Ribao* editorial on the new Law: 'By combining the militia's service with a reserve service, we can reduce the number of troops in peacetime but can also mobilize a great number of troops in wartime. This is beneficial to both national defence and economic development.'[52] Speaking to the Second Session of the Sixth National People's Congress, which adopted the new Military Service Law, Chief of Staff Yang Dezhi explained that 'in the event of war, we will be able to use the PLA as the backbone and the militia and reserves as the broad base for forming new units and expanding existing ones at the highest possible speed . . . '.[53] Thus, the primary, if not the only, military function of the militia is to provide manpower for the PLA but not to fight beside it, as it had been designated to do under the doctrine of 'people's war'.

Doctrinal Change Goes to Sea[54]

Although the doctrine of 'people's war' was formulated for the ground forces, its predominance as a guide to the development of the armed forces inevitably affected China's sea strategy and naval affairs. In the 1950s and 1960s China's military and civilian leaders generally took a dubious view of the navy's contribution to China's security. Even professional officers, with the exception of officers involved in developing the navy, downplayed the importance of the navy and were reluctant to provide it with resources, even though they strongly advocated military modernization. The navy was regarded as a coastal extension of the ground forces.

This attitude was hardly surprising. Emerging from more than two decades of revolutionary struggle in China's vast and isolated hinterland, the new leaders were complete strangers to naval matters. After the establishment of the Communist regime they continued to think in terms of ground warfare. Their strategy was to 'open the gates' to an invader and lure him into the country's heartland, not to meet him on the high seas. The main purpose of the navy, therefore, was not to stop a massive invasion from the sea but to protect the coast against incursions.

This attitude was reinforced by Soviet influence – transmitted through Soviet advisers in China and Chinese officers sent to study in the Soviet Union. This influence was anchored in the so-called 'Young School' of Soviet naval strategy, which dominated Soviet naval development until the early 1960s. Rejecting the need for a blue-water navy as an expensive and in-effective product of imperialist ambitions, this school advocated the maintenance of a coastal navy composed of submarines and small surface vessels, supported by shore-based naval aircraft.

Propagating greater recognition for the role of the navy were senior officers who took charge of naval affairs in the early 1950s and, despite their background as ground force commanders, reorientated their thinking in line with their new responsibilities. Foremost among such officers was Zhang Aiping, who was appointed minister of defence in 1983, but who in the early 1950s dealt with naval matters in the East China Military Region, and from 1975 to 1982, as chairman of the National Defence Scientific and Techno-logical Commission, played a key role in the development of China's nuclear-powered ballistic missile submarine. These officers tried to protect their turf and pushed for its expansion. Although a minority, they were primarily responsible for the creation and growth of the Chinese navy within the limits imposed by the majority of their colleagues.

After China had recovered from the most acute ravages of the Great Leap Forward, the navy embarked on an expanded construction programme, which continued throughout the Cultural Revolution. This programme, however, was still shaped by the doctrine of coastal defence, and shipbuilding focused on small coastal vessels while large surface ships were accorded low priority. Forward-looking professional officers who disagreed with this doctrine were purged during the Cultural Revolution or maintained a discreet silence.

After the Cultural Revolution, maritime strategy was reassessed, pre-sumably under the influence of purged officers who had returned to active duty. In 1975 the naval leadership submitted a plan for the modernization of the navy which was endorsed by Mao. The plan envisioned the development of an ocean-going navy, as well as the continued expansion of coastal defence capabilities. A combination of several reasons presumably lay behind the proposal and adoption of this programme. First was the growing Soviet naval threat close to China's shores, exemplified by the massive worldwide Soviet naval exercise, known in the West as 'Okean 75', which clearly unnerved the Chinese. The second reason was the rapid development of China's merchant marine and the consequent need to protect sea lanes. The third was China's growing interest in offshore oil resources and its claims over disputed islands and ocean spaces – interests which could not be backed by a coastal defence navy. The fourth reason was the ascendance, fleeting as it turned out, of moderate leaders in China's power structure who recognized the need for military modernization and building up the navy. However, the naval modernization programme was obstructed by radical leaders who were subsequently accused of pursuing a 'continentalist strategy', which prevented China from constructing a powerful navy. Such construction had to await the removal of the radicals from the political scene.

The almost complete abandonment of Mao's military doctrine produced changes in naval strategy. These changes have received special impetus from the foreign policy of the Deng leadership, which has encouraged increased contacts with the outside world and has asserted China's international role as an independent power of the first rank. A powerful ocean-going navy is both an essential status symbol of such a role and a vital instrument for performing it. For this reason, the new naval strategy, as extrapolated from the missions envisaged for the navy, contains elements which are characteristic of modern large-scale navies: 'sea denial, sea control, projection of power ashore, presence and strategic deterrence'.[55] The naval force posture, as will be seen, is still lagging far behind the missions contemplated for the navy, but it is these missions that serve as a pointer to current and future naval development.

Strategic Doctrine and Arms Control

The changes in China's strategic doctrine may have contributed to the stirrings of a new approach to arms control. China's long-standing policy has been to denounce arms control as a ploy by the United States and the Soviet Union to perpetuate their nuclear superiority, and as an ineffective barrier to the arms race. Maintaining that only complete disarmament was a viable alternative to the arms race, the Chinese stood aloof from all efforts at arms control.

A slight shift from this rigid stand could be discerned in the mid-1980s. From total negation of arms control efforts, China began to regard them as the beginning of a process of disarmament. Concrete indications of this shift have been China's joining the International Atomic Energy Agency and ratification of the Outer Space Treaty in 1984, as well as its participation in the United

Nations disarmament meetings in Geneva. The main reason behind it is doubtless China's desire to be regarded as a leading member of the international community, equal in status to the superpowers and involved in shaping the state of the world.[56] But a contributing reason may be connected with China's new strategic doctrine. Confident of their ability to deter a nuclear attack with their small nuclear force, the Chinese may feel that they are entitled to membership in the nuclear powers' club, which they had hitherto derided, and implicitly want to be recognized as such a member.

Chinese concern about their nuclear deterrent certainly underlies their critical attitude towards the Strategic Defence Initiative. After sniping at it indirectly and in low key, the Chinese formally censured the 'Star Wars' programme in mid-1985. Deng Xiaoping condemned it as adding a dangerous dimension to the superpowers' arms race.[57] Behind this lofty posture, however, there doubtless lurked real apprehension that the Strategic Defence Initiative will weaken China's new strategic doctrine. This doctrine, it will be remembered, is based on the assumption that China's nuclear forces are sufficient to deter a nuclear attack, because even if such an attack devastates China, some surviving missiles will hit the attacker. And this, in the Chinese view, is enough to deter an unprovoked nuclear attack on China. This deterrent is jeopardized by the Strategic Defence Initiative. The Chinese know that the 'Star Wars' programme will spur Soviet efforts to develop anti-missile defences in space. These efforts may be ineffective against the great number of sophisticated missiles likely to be unleashed by the United States. But even a partial defence may cast doubt on China's chances of delivering a few retaliatory missiles.

'People's War' or 'Modern Conditions'?

Although the Chinese claim to have fused 'people's war' with 'modern conditions', both their commentaries on the doctrine and their conduct indicate that it is 'modern conditions' that dominate their strategic thinking. Their commentaries, to be sure, have been guarded because of inhibitions against breaking too explicitly with Maoist dogma, and because of the need to fall back upon 'people's war' as a last resort in the unlikely event of a full-scale invasion of China. Their conduct, however, indicates unambiguously that they do not envisage fighting a 'people's war' in the Maoist mould nor are they preparing their armed forces for it.

This view is not shared by some analysts of Chinese military affairs, who argue that the Chinese have not dismantled the doctrine of 'people's war'. Their argument is that 'people's war' has always been broad and flexible enough to encompass various applications, and that post-Mao practice is simply the extension of the doctrine to new circumstances. The argument rests on the notion that 'people's war' does not dictate a specific strategy, but is a doctrine for mass mobilization in a total war.

This argument is flawed. First, the function of a military doctrine is to provide guidelines for the conduct of a war the armed forces are most likely to wage – not to take account of any conflict that can be subsumed under the rubric of total war. The Maoist doctrine of 'people's war' envisaged a specific scenario in which the enemy would be lured into China's interior, the rural population would be mobilized to resist him, and the war would be fought by both regular and irregular forces. The post-Mao strategy is very different. Except in the event of a massive ground invasion which the Chinese really do not expect, the enemy will not be allowed to penetrate deep into China's heartland, the entire population will not have to be mobilized to take part in the hostilities, and the war will be fought mainly by the regular army.

Second, a military doctrine also has to determine the organizational structure, the weapons procurement policy and the internal practices of the armed forces in line with the kind of war they are expected to fight. The Maoist doctrine was based on the assumption the 'human element' was more important than weapons, because by employing a 'people's war' strategy, the superior quality and quantity of the Chinese troops would outweigh their technological inferiority. This assumption shaped the building, arming and training of the PLA. However, the development of the PLA in the post-Mao period has unequivocally abandoned this assumption, as illustrated by the priority accorded to modernization and professionalism.

The Chinese claim, for ideological and political reasons, that military doctrine after Mao is a direct descendant of 'people's war'. However, in practice they themselves have undermined this claim. As an operational guide to fighting and force building, Maoist doctrine has not been developed by China's post-Mao leaders; it has been almost completely abandoned.

5

Weapons and Equipment: Backward but Better

Of all the tasks facing the PLA on its march to modernization, the upgrading of weapons is foremost. To be sure, the post-Mao leadership is fully aware that enhancing the PLA's combat capability requires much more than betterment of military wherewithal. It requires basic reforms in organizational and operational procedures – reforms which, as the next chapter will show, the military high command has pursued with great vigour. Nonetheless, the leadership is also aware that such reforms supplement but cannot substitute for the modernization of weapons. All the leaders accept as axiomatic that without such modernization there can be no significant increase in the PLA's ability to fight. This consensus is anchored in the universal recognition that by the end of the Maoist era the PLA lacked the weapons and equipment essential to performing the roles envisaged by the post-Mao leadership.

The reasons for this decline have already been discussed. However, in order to appreciate the magnitude of the problems it caused, as well as to evaluate progress, it is necessary to sketch briefly the general state of the PLA in the late 1970s. But first a caveat is in order. Any assessment of the weapons and equipment of the PLA requires information which is sensitive and hard to come by. A substantial margin of error is, therefore, inevitable. Nevertheless, inadequate or inaccurate information on details does not preclude drawing up an overview which can confidently be taken as a basis for analysis.

The PLA in the Late 1970s

The general consensus among outside observers at the end of the Maoist period, subsequently confirmed by the Chinese, was that China's conventional forces, in comparison with modern armies, were inadequately

94

armed, poorly equipped, deficient in communications, lacking in logistic support and insufficiently trained for complex operations. By all Western intelligence accounts, the PLA was predominantly an infantry force – 'an army in sneakers'. The overwhelming majority of the troops were in the ground forces, which consisted chiefly of foot soldiers. The primary combat power was found in the 136 or so main force divisions. Of these, 121 were infantry, while only twelve were armoured and three airborne. The main force divisions were thought to be deficient in all types of modern weapons, other than light and medium arms and, perhaps, artillery, although most of the artillery was not self-propelled and lacked modern fire-control devices. The list of deficiencies was long and led to one conclusion: although Chinese soldiers were well fit physically and highly motivated politically, the Chinese ground forces lacked all the major attributes of a modern fighting force, such as firepower, mobility, advanced communications and logistics. The PLA, as an astute military observer put it, was an 'unarmed giant'.[1]

These shortcomings were demonstrated in China's 1979 invasion of Vietnam. The PLA's superiority in manpower was nullified by the shortage of trucks and armoured personnel carriers. Tactical communications were so primitive that orders were transmitted by foot soldiers sent from division to division. Artillery units did not have sufficient ammunition. The front did not receive food and water for days because supplies had to be transported by peasants. Food stocks – mainly noodles and bean curd – were perishable and quickly spoiled in the heat. Maps were outdated, and disintegrated in the rain. Some companies and platoons lost contact with main forces and suffered heavy casualties because they did not have proper radios. No air reconnaissance had been made of the battlefield, which increased casualties as troops discovered unexpected obstacles. In this brief but bloody engagement Chinese casualties amounted to some 26,000 men killed and 37,000 wounded. Although the war again showed the high quality of the Chinese soldier, it also showed that the PLA was not ready for a modern war. Its performance clearly fell short of the leadership's expectations.[2]

The technological backwardness of the PLA in the late 1970s was most acute in the air force. After the Soviets terminated all military aid to China in 1960, the Chinese had to produce an aircraft on their own. This was a daunting task. Having had extremely limited experience in designing aircraft, and cut off from the West, the Chinese had to lean heavily on existing models. Given the financial and technological constraints, Chinese air defence policy from the outset of 'self-reliance' was based on investment in relatively cheap and technologically unsophisticated aircraft. Low quality was to be offset to some extent by large numbers. Consequently, by the late 1970s the Chinese had the third largest air force in the world, but, compared to the advanced models employed by the Soviet Union and the United States – or, for that matter, a considerable number of other countries – the Chinese aircraft suffered from varying degrees of obsolescence. The majority of the aircraft consisted of MiG-17s and MiG-19s.

The first Chinese combat aircraft, known as the F-6, closely resembled the MiG-19. The major defect of the F-6 as the standard interceptor was its antiquated radar, which severely limited all-weather and air-to-air attack capabilities. To correct this defect without major changes in the production line of the F-6, the Chinese developed their own variant of the MiG-19, known as F-6bis. The new design of the aircraft was apparently intended to house a radar system that would give it effective all-weather attack capabilities. This aircraft first went into military service in 1962, but it is not clear whether a new radar had, in fact, been installed. Another variant of the MiG-19, known as the A-5, was developed for ground-support roles. A more modern fighter interceptor was the Chinese version of the MiG-21, which was designated F-7. However, this aircraft suffered design problems, and in the late 1960s production was halted with about sixty to eighty F-7s in service. The Chinese bomber force – consisting of Tu-16 and Tu-4 medium bombers and IL-28 and Tu-2 light bombers – was outdated and vulnerable to modern defences.

China's inability to produce a modern aircraft did not stem from lack of trying or shortage of funds. As already noted, military expenditure rose anually by about 10 per cent between 1965 and 1971, and the air force was apparently the main beneficiary of this increase. However, Chinese experts obviously could not master the sophisticated technologies associated with the production of an up-to-date fighter interceptor, particularly in relation to engine design and avionics. Antagonistic towards both the Soviet Union and the United States (until the early 1970s), and reluctant to abandon the policy of 'self-reliance', the Chinese did not look outside for help until the mid-1970s. Only in December 1975, after their air force had been falling behind modern air forces for more than fifteen years, did the Chinese sign a contract with Rolls-Royce for the licenced production of a jet engine. In the late 1970s, China was still far away from having a fighter interceptor with all-weather and night-flying capability, armed with air-to-air missiles and equipped with sophisticated electronic devices.

The deficiencies of the Chinese air force were also evident in its performance – or rather, non-performance – during the Vietnam War of 1979. Although the decision not to commit China's air power may have stemmed from a desire to limit the conflict, there were doubtless other reasons. One was probably the recognition that Chinese aircraft would be dangerously vulnerable to the effective battlefield air defence systems possessed by the Vietnamese. Another was presumably the fear that Chinese pilots were not sufficiently trained to carry out the complex operations necessary for tactical air support. Consequently, Chinese aircraft generally stayed out of range of

Vietnamese air defences and provided no support to the ground forces. In the air, Chinese fighters would have been at a disadvantage in any engagement with Vietnamese air units. Chinese bombing and attack aircraft would have been endangered by Vietnamese air defences and interceptor capabilities.[3]

The Chinese navy fared much better than the air force between the end of the 1950s and the late 1970s, but only as a coastal defence force. Like the air force, its development was severely disrupted by the withdrawal of Soviet naval assistance in 1960, but after two years of stagnation there was a resurgence in both construction and operations. Dominated by a doctrine that conceived of naval warfare as 'people's war' taken to sea, construction concentrated on craft that could employ tactics of concealment, rapid concentration of forces and combat at close quarters: submarines, missile attack boats, gun-armed coastal patrol boats and torpedo boats. Larger vessels, which were of secondary importance, included Chinese-designed guided-missile destroyers, frigates and auxiliary logistic vessels. Most of these ships could be built quickly and relatively inexpensively. The heyday of naval construction occurred during the period 1965–71, when military expenditure increased rapidly and the navy received about one fourth of all military spending, approximating that of the air force. Although the new Chinese vessels incorporated elements of Soviet technology, they were definitely of Chinese design. By 1977–8, the Chinese navy had some 85 submarines, 44 escorts (including frigates and corvettes), 920 patrol boats (746 gun- or torpedo-armed and 174 missile-armed), 24 ships for mine warfare, and more than 500 miscellaneous auxiliary vessels.

Despite its impressive development, the Chinese navy could not be classed as an open-ocean force, capable of operating at long distances from the coast. More than one-half of the fleet was made up of small patrol craft which lacked the qualities essential for operations on the high seas. The submarines were, with one exception, diesel-powered and lacked speed and endurance, though they were well suited for shallow-water coastal defence purposes. The newer missile-equipped destroyers and frigates did have the ranges for ocean-going operations, but lacked crucial air support. The minesweepers were obsolete by Western standards. The navy's capability for anti-submarine warfare was virtually non-existent. Shipborne electronics and weapons systems were deemed by outside observers effective but dated.[4]

There is little reason to question the assessment that by the late 1970s the Chinese navy probably possessed 'the largest and most efficient coastal defence force in the world. Any invader from the sea would have had great difficulty landing a force ashore and maintaining adequate combat and logistic support.'[5] However, it is most unlikely that an enemy would attempt an amphibious landing or let his surface ships lumber around Chinese coastal waters. Therefore, like the ground forces, the Chinese navy seemed to be most effectively prepared to meet a contingency that was least likely to arise.

In sum, when the Maoist period ended, China's defences suffered from critical weaknesses. As one expert summed up the situation, the ground forces did not have the weapons needed to hold the vast but sparsely populated regions adjacent to the Soviet border against an attack by Soviet armoured and mechanized forces, supported by artillery and tactical air power. The air force could not adequately defend battlefields or high-value targets for want of advanced missiles and interceptors. The navy lacked the anti-mine and submarine warfare capabilties to protect Chinese coastal shipping, and did not have the capability to counter the Soviets on the high seas.

The dimensions of the deficiencies precluded 'quick fix' solutions. For example, it was widely assumed that the acquisition by China of modern anti-tank missiles would provide an effective capability against a Soviet attack. Reality was much more complex. Infantry armed with high-quality anti-tank missiles could indeed be effective against small groups of tanks advancing without support. However, the Soviets could hardly be expected to accommodate the Chinese by sending into battle such convenient targets. Instead, it could be assumed that they would deploy large numbers of tanks supported by artillery and air power, and protected by armoured infantry. Against an attack of this magnitude, missiles alone would be of little value. To counter it, a whole array of advanced weapons (such as tanks, artillery and battlefield air defences) would be required. Similarly, missile air defences would have to be integrated with modern interceptors and sophisticated control systems.[6] In short, enhancement of the PLA's ability to fight against a modern foe demanded a colossal and co-ordinated effort to acquire a wide range of up-to-date weapons.

The Role of the Arms Industry

Whatever its needs and deficiencies, extensive re-equipment of the PLA with costly imported weapons was categorically ruled out by the Deng leadership's policy of military modernization. This policy, it will be recalled, derived from the leadership's assessment that China faced no direct military threat, and from the low priority accorded the military in resource allocation. Weapons, therefore, could only be renewed slowly and primarily by using existing models and facilities. Zhen Weishan, then commander of the Lanzhou units, succinctly summarized the dilemma facing China's defence chiefs: 'At the present level of economic development,' he said at the National People's Congress in 1983, 'it is impossible to increase military spending quickly. What is most important at present ... is to make the best use of limited funds in a planned way to increase the PLA's capability for combined operations and quick response.'[7] Within these limits, the PLA has formulated plans for weapons development which, in the words of Hong Xuezhi, director of the General Logistics Department, seek 'to combine long-range and short-range interests. On the one hand, we should pay attention to developing new equipment, and on the other strive to improve available equipment.'[8]

The successful implementation of these plans rests on the performance of the defence industry. Established in the 1950s with massive Soviet aid, the Chinese defence industry began producing a wide range of weapons based on Soviet designs. The sudden Soviet pull-out in 1960 was disastrous, but after the Chinese weathered the economic crisis they started to expand their defence industry. The number of machine-building industries was increased from two to seven, and all but one were defence oriented. Despite disruptions caused by the Cultural Revolution, defence plant capacity approximately tripled in the second half of the 1960s, especially under the shadow of the Soviet military threat. A large variety of weapons was manufactured, but almost all were based on Soviet models of the 1950s. After the downfall of Lin Biao, defence procurement was reduced severely, most drastically in the aircraft industry. Until the late 1970s defence spending rose by 1 or 2 per cent per year, as against average annual defence expenditure increases of 10 per cent for the years 1967–71. One reason for this was doubtless the weakened political position of the armed forces, but another may have been the reluctance of the military to continue producing large quantities of increasingly obsolete weapons. At any rate, much of the defence plant capacity remained idle. In 1975, despite obstruction from the radicals, the Chinese again began to expand military production facilities and to look abroad for sophisticated technology.[9]

After the purge of the radicals, expansion gathered momentum, facilitated by the prominent position of the military and fuelled by their desire for rapid development of the defence sector. An article emanating from the National Defence Industry Office early in the new period reflectd these hopes. 'Defence industry', it said, 'has considerable independence and initiative. It should be developed as fast as possible ....' The leading place envisaged for the defence sector by the authors of the article was justified by its spin-off effect on the entire economy: 'In the course of its development, the defence industry will inevitably continue to make new demands on other industries and on science and technology, thus motivating the development of the entire national economy and helping raise the levels of production, science and technology.'[10]

The hopes of the defence sector, as has been seen, did not materialize. The decision of the Deng leadership to tie the technological upgrading of the PLA to economic progress meant that the defence industry was put behind other sectors in development plans. The main features of this approach were spelled out in a *Jingji Ribao* article in May 1983. The defence industry, said the article, 'must be ... subordinated to unified arrangements for national construction. The scale ... and ... pace of development must be in line with available national resources.' At the same time, the article cautioned against 'too little investment in the defence industry' because this 'will hinder the progress of the modernization of our weapons'. Furthermore, the relationship between the defence industry and the rest of the economy is not fixed, but may change in accordance with shifts in the international situation and the availability of resources. However, in principle, 'only with the development of the national economy can we accumulate abundant construction funds for the defence industry'.[11]

The article also explained the leadership's approach to importing technology for the arms industry. Only an indigenous defence industry, it stressed, can produce the weapons required for China's peculiar conditions. 'If we pin our hopes on obtaining large-scale imports, we may as well vainly console ourselves with the imagined achievement of what we want ... .' The reasons were clear:

> This is because if we rely on purchasing whole sets of equipment and techniques from foreign countries to modernize our defence industry, then, to say nothing of our limited national means, people would be unwilling to sell us what is advanced. Even if we could afford the cost, and the sellers were willing to provide what we want, a defence industry built on such a basis would never be an independent national industry. Moreover, it would forever lag behind that of foreign countries ....[12]

However, this was not tantamount to 'promoting an isolationist policy, adhering to fixed patterns, and the blind exclusion of things foreign'. Since China's defence industry lagged far behind developed countries, 'we must, on the basis of self-reliance, strive to acquire advanced techniques and experience from foreign countries'. While doing this, 'we must also pay attention to raising ... the creativity of our scientific and technical personnel ...'. Moreover, 'we must take into consideration our solvency and our ability' to use foreign equipment.[13]

The development of the defence industry has thus been dictated by the Deng leadership's policy of gradual weapons renewal, and by its determination to maintain maximum independence from foreign suppliers. However, even gradual weapons renewal, particularly without substantial foreign assistance, has required a major effort in research, development and production on the part of the defence industry. Few details are known about this effort but the main avenues of activity can be discerned.

The first step, as Yang Shangkun pointed out, was to strengthen 'centralized and unified leadership' over the arms industries and related research organs.[14] This was essential in view of the way they had developed. When these industries were expanded in the 1960s, numerous plants of various sizes were set up throughout China, relatively independent of civilian supervision. Dispersal and decentralization were well suited to the 'people's war' strategy. Many of these plants produced light arms for foot soldiers, who were accorded the central role in this strategy. Furthermore, Maoist strategy envisaged a protracted war deep in China's interior, conducted by fairly autonomous regional commanders who required arsenals in their localities.

However, this situation did not suit the policy of the Deng leadership. The integration of defence industries into broader economic plans required tighter civilian oversight of their activities. The abandonment of the 'people's war' strategy shifted the emphasis to the production of more sophisticated weapons in larger plants. To attain greater central control, the management of the arms industries was reorganized.

In the late 1970s, all the ministers of the machine-building industries who were associated with the defence establishment were replaced by civilians.[15] In 1980, the Machine-Building Industries Commission was established, alongside the State Planning Commission and on a level just below the State Council, the highest organ of state administration. Its purpose was to tighten central supervision of the machine-building industries and to co-ordinate their production.[16] Between 1981 and 1982 all the ministries were renamed according to their functions, and two of the ministries – the seventh and eighth – were merged.[17] In 1983, a Commission in Charge of Science, Technology and Industry for National Defence was created by merging three organs: the National Defence Industry Office, which had been the main co-ordinating unit between the State Council and the arms industries; the State Scientific and Technological Commission, which had supervised defence-related research; and the Office of Science, Technology and Arms of the Central Committee of the Chinese Communist Party.[18] One important result of this move was a more rational approach to defence procurement. As Zhang Aiping, the defence minister, said at a meeting of the new commission in 1983:

> To accelerate weapons and equipment modernization, we must unify our under-standing, thinking and action in principles and policies .... we must narrow down the field, give priority to key items, concentrate on scientific research, speed up renovation, transform industrial equipment, improve technological processes, improve quality and reduce costs.[19]

Another reform has been the integration of military and civilian industries in an attempt to solve a fundamental problem of defence production, thus described by a Beijing periodical:

Everybody knows that the major characteristics of the defence industry's enterprises are as follows: they are rich in scientific and technical strengths; their technical equipment is fine; in time of war their tasks are arduous while in peacetime their capacity is under-utilized. How are we . . . going to arrange things so that in war the defence industry enterprises will be able to guarantee the needs of the forces, while in peacetime, they will be able to serve national economic construction?[20]

The leadership's response has been an innovative policy designed to maintain the production capacity of the defence industry by having it serve civilian needs when that capacity was under-utilized. Although the defence plants had always produced some civilian goods, the volume of production had been marginal. Between 1978 and 1983 the volume rose by more than 90 per cent so that production for the civilian sector amounted to about 20 per cent of the defence industry's total production. This included machine, chemical and optical products as well as mechanical and electrical goods for daily use. At the end of 1983, there were fifteen types of such products in over 300 varieties.The proportion of civilian goods in the total production of the arms industry is expected to rise to 30 per cent by the 1990s, and to 50 per cent by the year 2000.[21]

There are, according to the Chinese, several advantages to this system. First, the productive capacity and sophisticated equipment of the arms industry make it uniquely suited to the manufacture of diversified civilian products. Second, its workers are highly skilled. Third, the arms industry is well organized and is able to ensure high quality. But shortcomings are not lacking. For one thing, production schedules of civilian goods are apt to be disrupted by fluctuating military needs. For another, many plants are in remote areas and production costs are high. Moreover, military industries lack supply and marketing channels for civilian goods.[22]

The Chinese seem determined to iron out these difficulties and to develop integration of military and civilian industries under the slogan 'giving priority to military products and using civilian production to support military production'.[23] To this end, they have established a number of guidelines. The civilian goods manufactured by the defence industry must use production technologies similar to military products, and must be goods which are in short supply and have market potential. They should be produced only by tapping the unused capacity of the defence industry, since no investment for this purpose would be allowed. According to the Chinese, 'the final aim of promoting civilian products is to have the civilian support the military. Thus the development of civilian products must take economic results as the focus'.[24]

While this method of developing the defence industry has received much publicity, secrecy shrouds the role of imported technology in this sector. This much seems certain: in line with their policy of maximum 'self-reliance', the Chinese have not imported technology which would bind the development of their defence industry to foreign suppliers. Their preference has been for design technologies and the means of weapons production. The 1975 purchase of Rolls-Royce Spey jet-engine technology is an example of the sort of deal the Chinese desire. In this case, they wanted to minimize the number of Spey engines actually purchased in order to produce as many as possible in China, while the British wanted to maximize sales. In the end, the British agreed, following the purchases, to aid in modernizing a Chinese aircraft-manufacturing plant and to train the Chinese to produce a military version of the engine.[25]

Few similar instances of technology transfer are known to have been made in subsequent years. One has been a 1980 agreement with France for China to manufacture under licence Aerospatiale's Dauphin 2 helicopter.[26] Another deal under discussion since 1982 reportedly envisaged the purchase by China from France of Mirage 2000 aircraft, some of which are to be delivered as complete units and others to be built in China under licence.[27] Other agreements have reportedly been concluded with the Jeep division of the American Motors Company for the manufacture of jeeps in China; with an Austrian firm for Chinese production of 10,000 trucks, with follow-on production likely; with a Japanese company for co-operation in the modernization of China's marine diesel engine production;[28] and with Canada for the purchase of three Canadair Challenger aircraft for the Chinese air force.[29]

In April 1985, China and Italy signed an agreement for defence co-operation, according to which Italy will supply China with a variety of military items and will train Chinese military men in fields such as flight control, meteorology, computers, parachuting and alpine manoeuvres.[30] The Chinese also reportedly expressed interest in purchasing armoured vehicles, aircraft, military supplies and technology from Brazil, but no deal was known to have been concluded.[31]

China's preference for joint ventures was underlined by the Chinese representatives at a mid-1985 seminar of British defence manufacturers. In order to win contracts for selling defence equipment to China, they said, companies must be prepared to transfer technology, provide facilities for local production and be ready to re-export.[32] An agreement that meets these conditions was reached in 1985 by Vickers Defence Systems of the UK – and a Chinese defence manufacturing agency – the China North Industries Corporation (Norinco). The agreement calls for co-operation in the production of a mechanized infantry combat vehicle, probably for sale to Third World countries. Vickers will supply the vehicle's weapons systems and Norinco the chassis. The size of the project depends on market reaction to a prototype which will be constructed for overseas demonstration.[33]

For advanced military technology, China turned primarily to the United States. Several agreements and deals have been concluded. In 1984, China and the US Department of Defense reached an agreement in principle for the sale of Hughes TOW anti-tank missiles and Raytheon Improved Hawk surface-to-air missiles, including some Chinese co-production of the weapons.[34] However, subsequently the Chinese did not purchase the anti-tank missile, one possible reason being their belief that the Russians had already developed counter-measures for the TOW missile which the Americans were ready to sell.[35] They will probably want more advanced anti-tank weapons. The Chinese also signed a letter of intent with McDonnel-Douglas for co-production of twenty-five transport aircraft in China, and for co-operation in possible joint development of other advanced-technology aircraft.[36] Also in 1984 the Chinese signed an agreement for the purchase of twenty-four civilian-version Sikorsky Black Hawk helicopters. The estimated value of the transaction was $150 million. The last of the helicopters were delivered to China in December 1985, and the Chinese expressed interest in purchasing more.[37]

In 1985, China and the United States concluded a $98 million agreement to design and equip facilties in China for the production of artillery shells and other ammunition.[38] By far the most significant sale of military technology stemmed from the administration's proposal, approved by Congress in May 1986, to sell China fifty-five advanced avionics kits, at $10 million each, for China's F-8 interceptor. If the Chinese sign the agreement, their aircraft will be equipped with sophisticated head-up displays, integrated navigational and fire-control instruments, and mission data computers.[39]

The Chinese have possibly sought to modernize their defence industry in other ways as well. One may be the secret enlistment of outside aid and advice for rapid acquisition of advanced technology. Persistent reports suggest that for several years Israel has secretly supplied China with weapons and technical data, primarily for refitting Chinese tanks.[40] In addition, the Chinese may have resorted to 'reverse engineering'. In the past few years they have acquired a considerable range of high-technology weapons and equipment. Some of these items may have been dismantled for study and copying.

These are a few indications of what has clearly been a vast endeavour to modernize the defence industry. Although the Chinese have divulged few details about this endeavour, they have been somewhat more forthcoming about its results.

Modernization of Weapons

The information revealed by Chinese media reports on arms procurement is general and vague. But the overall impression conveyed by these reports is clear. It is that since 1979 the Chinese have made significant strides in providing the PLA with more advanced and higher-quality weapons and equipment. These weapons are evidently follow-on versions of old Soviet models, but substantial modifications and improvements have greatly increased their effectiveness.

For the individual soldier the Chinese have produced a 'new-type' automatic rifle which is shorter, lighter, has a higher firing rate and holds more bullets than previous models.[41] The Chinese also claim to have developed a new type of armoured personnel carrier in line with the shift in emphasis from infantry to mechanized forces.[42] The impression gained by foreign observers is that the new APC represents an early prototype and is not equal in quality to Western designs. Nevertheless, it is obviously an improvement on the older standard APC, which had difficulty operating in varied terrain, especially mountains and marshlands.[43]

In artillery, efforts have been focused on rectifying the PLA's chief weakness: the shortage of self-propelled guns. To this end, the Chinese have developed three types of self-propelled guns: howitzers, rocket launchers and cannons – all motorized and capable of firing from carriers.[44] In 1980, they purchased from British Marconi Space and Defence Systems five sets of field artillery control equipment. This computerized equipment is used in Land Rovers for aiming quickly and precisely, twenty-four guns at a time.[45] It is not known whether additional purchases were made or whether the Chinese are producing similar systems.

The Chinese reportedly made rapid developments in multiple-rocket launchers, particularly the forty-tube launcher, with which the armed forces have been equipped in recent years, and which demonstrated great effectiveness against large exposed targets during the Vietnam war. Important progress was also said to have been made in cannon research and production technology. A new method of smelting was devised which solved difficulties in producing cannon steel of great strength. In addition, a new device was installed on gun muzzles in order to reduce the effects on the operators of the blast wave caused by the firing of heavy-calibre guns. Another innovation has been a simplified type of compressed-air-controlled balancing device, which facilitates simplifying the structure of guns, reduces the period for developing new guns and enables the automation of heavy-calibre guns. New technologies in sound, light and electricity have also been applied to manufacturing guns and have greatly improved accuracy in locating, measuring and hitting targets.[46]

In line with the policy of concentrating 'limited funds and manpower on . . . weapons and equipment which have an important bearing on countering future wars of aggression',[47] the Chinese have worked fast to overcome deficiencies in anti-tank weapons. Consequently, accuracy, armour-piercing ability and range of fire of such weapons have allegedly been greatly increased. In particular, major improvement has been made in the depth, bore and penetration after-effects of armour-piercing shells.[48] By 1986 the Chinese had developed the second-generation Red Arrow 8 anti-tank guided missile.

Having belatedly discovered the importance of tanks in modern warfare – primarily, it seems, by studying recent Middle East wars[49] – the Chinese have made tank development the centrepiece of their effort to upgrade the ground forces. With the Type-59 tank – copied from the Soviet T-54 in 1959 – as the basic platform, the Chinese carried out 'some transformations in the course of imitation, and these transformations were reflected in the three major functions of the tanks – firepower, protective power and manoeuvrability.'[50] The improvements which they have made on the tank include: a protective sheet to prevent hits by armour-piercing shells from the side; a double-direction stabilizer and a ballistic computer in the fire-control system; a souped-up engine to increase manoeuvrability; and rubber-coated cater-pillars to reduce vibration and noise. The new tank is also reportedly protected against ABC (atomic, bacteriological and chemical) warfare.[51] According to foreign observers, the new tank – the Type-69 – has been refitted with an up-to-date 105mm. gun, allegedly produced in Isreal or in China with Israeli aid, and equipped with European infra-red systems.[52] Military experts consider the Type-69 to be a formidable weapon, bearing little resemblance to the obsolete T-54 from which it is derived.[53] It is a prime example of China's policy of modernizing the armed forces by improving old models and utilizing existing production lines rather than importing new weapons in large quantities.

In addition to an improved main battle tank and armoured personnel carrier, the Chinese have also produced a new-type retrieval tank, an earth mover for military purposes, a bridge-building tank and a telecommuni-cations command car.[54] Together with jeeps, trucks and armoured personnel carriers, which they have purchased or are manufacturing, these develop-ments have substantially advanced the transformation of the PLA from an infantry into a mechanized force, and have increased its ability to counter an invasion by a modern army.

Such an ability is critically contingent on vast improvements in the air force, but these have been slow in coming. Despite Chinese claims that they have produced a wide range of aircraft, including 'a new generation of high-speed fighters',[55] the PLA, according to an authoritative defence publication, 'lacks agile fighter aircraft, effective beyond-visual-range missiles, airborne early warning aircraft and close support aircraft able to deliver a first-pass attack – in short, China has virtually none of the elements of a modern air force'.[56] However, the Chinese have been making strenuous efforts to overcome these defects.

One effort has concentrated on improving the F-7 which suffered from short endurance and lack of adequate air-to-air firepower, among other deficiencies. Since the early 1980s, the Chinese have upgraded both the handling qualities and combat performance of the aircraft. Major improvements include the installation of a more powerful engine, more efficient radar, a new cockpit canopy and ejection seat, and a more effective cannon.[57]

In 1984, the Chinese revealed details of an upgraded export version of the F-7 known as the F-7M Airguard. Improvements include mainly Western-made avionics, such as a new head-up display and weapons-aiming computer system, radar with improved anti-jamming capability, an air data computer and radar altimeter, and a more secure communications radio. Other changes include a more efficient electrical system to cater to the new avionics, and an ability to carry newer and longer-range Chinese air-to-air missiles.[58] To carry out the improvements, the Chinese purchased more than $120 million worth of equipment from GEC Avionics.[59] However, according to one expert, the cockpit of the F-7M, as illustrated in a brochure advertising the aircraft, is archaic and primitive in comparison with the cockpits of modern fighter aircraft.[60]

In 1984 the Chinese also revealed that they were developing a supersonic all-weather aircraft, the F-8 (Chinese J-8). This is a delta-wing aircraft whose fuselage is larger than that of the F-7, and which has a wing span of 10 metres. It is powered by two WP-turbojets, has a maximum speed of Mach 2.3, and a range of 1,300 to 2,000 kilometres. It is said to be equipped with advanced radar and fire-control systems.[61]

According to Western observers, the F-8 has been under development for over a decade, but has been deployed only in small numbers. It is said to lack manoeuvrability and power, and will require a new engine before it is able to fulfil its role as a standard all-purpose fighter interceptor of the Chinese air force. Observers had assumed that the Rolls-Royce Spey engines produced under licence in China were destined for the F-8, but these engines were not installed in the aircraft, perhaps because they were too large for the twin-engine F-8. In the view of Western observers, it will take the Chinese at least until the late 1990s to develop an F-8 engine comparable to state-of-the-art jet engines in the West.[62]

The F-8 also needs advanced avionics. To this end the Chinese have already purchased some items from abroad. The United Kingdom has been a major supplier of equipment, led by Marconi's $95 million sale of avionics in 1980. American firms have supplied radar, navigational systems and communications equipment. In the mid-1980s, Rockwell-Coller, the major supplier of equipment for American civilian aircraft sold to China since 1972, was negotiating licenced production of military-standard radio transceivers and tactical air navigation systems in China.[63] But the most important deal is the already-mentioned projected sale of avionics equipment worth $550 million by the United States to China. Under the proposed contract, the United States will sell China avionics systems kits for fifty F-8 aircraft, plus five spares. The kits, as already noted, will include airborne radar, inertial navigation equipment, head-up display, mission and air data computers and a data bus.[64]

There have also been reports that the Chinese are developing an aircraft more advanced that the F-8 – the F-811. A model of this fighter was exhibited at the Farnborough air show in 1986. It uses the same engines as the F-8 but is a development of the earlier design and incorporates modifications requested by the Chinese air force. The aircraft was reportedly being flight-tested and was expected to go into production shortly if the tests proved successful.[65] Until the Chinese definitely overcome the problems associated with the production of an advanced fighter-interceptor, they will have to rely on older models and their air force will continue to have a major deficiency.

It will not be the only one. As far as is known, the Chinese have made no attempt to update their obsolete bomber force. Given their difficulties with propulsion and avionics, this is hardly surprising. China's bombers will remain highly vulnerable to interception by modern air defences.

In the meantime the Chinese continue to produce and deploy the F-6, F-6bis and A-5 aircraft – all derived, as already noted, from the MiG-19. According to experts, the F-6 and its derivatives can be deployed effectively against an adversary equipped with aircraft which are only marginally more advanced, but would run into difficulties against more modern and sophisticated aircraft, such as the MiG-23. This is because their performance deteriorates at high altitudes and they lack effective radar and medium-range missiles. Even if the Chinese aircraft were to have a numerical superiority, they would be unable to force more modern aircraft – possessing higher speed, altitude capability and greater detection range – into an engagement. The more advanced aircraft could hover above the effective altitude of the Chinese planes before making an attack with their more sophisticated missiles.[66]

For tactical support, the Chinese have developed the A-5, more than one hundred of which have been sold to Pakistan. (Pakistan also purchased more than one hundred F-6s.) For its production, much redesigning was done on the airframe of the F-6. As described by the Chinese, its main mission is, at low or minimal flying altitude, to make a high-speed penetration of the enemy's defences to provide close air support for ground forces. With bombs or rockets it can attack ground targets such as infantry assembly points, missile launching sites, airfields, communications centres, coastal shipping and tank formations. It is said to have great manoeuvrability, and to be armed with air-to-air missiles and guns for self-defence.[67]

Western specialists are less sanguine about the performance of the A-5.

The main shortcoming of the aircraft lies in its inadequate ability to find and hit targets. Because of limited sensors, the A-5 can only strike in a diving attack from medium altitude against a target which has already been identified on a first pass. Such an attack leaves little chance for success against modern air defences.[68] The Chinese are clearly trying to overcome this problem by purchasing and developing sophisticated radar equipment. In July 1986 they reached an agreement with Italy's Aeritalia to provide new avionics for the A-5.

The Chinese have also shown interest in purchasing equipment to cover additional areas in which they are particularly weak. One interest is in military transport planes, since their own military transport, the Y-8, has small lift capacity and outdated instruments. They have paid particular attention to heavy transports such as Boeing's CH-47. Another interest has been in long-range surveillance aircraft, such as the Boeing E-3A airborne warning and control system.[69] Finally, the Chinese seem set to acquire helicopters for a wide variety of uses. In 1984 they signed an agreement to purchase twenty-four Sikorsky S-70C-2 transport helicopters which, together with spare parts and training, is worth $140 million. The helicopters were purchased for civilian purposes, but the agreement does not exclude their being used for military missions.[70]

The Chinese navy has apparently been much more successful than the air force in procuring new weapons and equipment. For one thing, its achievements have received considerably more coverage in the media than those of the air force. For another, the tone and content of the reports suggest that the navy has not encountered the kind of problems which have held back the modernization of the air force. The impression conveyed by these reports is that Chinese leaders are confident of the navy's ability to fulfil defensive functions, and are looking towards expanding its role. 'China's navy', it is said, 'has now become a naval fighting force on a proper scale, with offensive and defensive capability.'[71] In the words of its commander, Liu Huaqing, the service has 'preliminary modern weapons and equipment systems with the capabilities to fight on the surface, under water and in the air, thereby effectively safeguarding the security of the motherland's coastal areas and territorial sea, and protecting China's maritime interests'.[72]

Reports in the Chinese media are clearly intended to substantiate these claims. Attributing the surge in naval development to Deng Xiaoping's initiative in 1979,[73] these reports provide a very general but upbeat picture of progress since then. The number of major craft increased twentyfold compared with the 1950s,[74] and the navy has developed from a major importer or copier of foreign vessels to one that designs and constructs a wide range of ships – destroyers, escorts, fast attack craft and submarines.[75] Missiles incorporating new technology are the main weapons of the vessels. Communications and navigation equipment is constantly improving.[76] New techniques of sea transfer, replenishment and maintenance are used.[77] The naval air arm and coastal defence force have likewise made progress.[78] In 1983 China reportedly had 188 missile-equipped fast attack craft, more than any other country.[79] Pilots for ship-based helicopters have been trained.[80] Two feats have been of particular pride to the navy: the 1980 voyage of a squadron to the South Pacific to participate in missile tests, which has been portrayed as demonstrating the navy's ability to conduct complex operations on the high seas; and the underwater launching of a guided missile from a nuclear submarine in 1982.[81]

Western specialists consider the satisfaction of the Chinese with naval development to be well founded. The number of ships is estimated to have increased enormously since about 1970. The conventional submarine force has tripled from thirty-five to 100 vessels; missile craft have increased tenfold from twenty vessels to more than 200; over thirty-five guided-missile destroyers and frigates have been commissioned; at least one nuclear-powered missile submarine and two nuclear-powered attack submarines have been placed in service; various auxiliary vessels, including long-range supply ships, have been built.[82]

Strong support for naval development comes from Defence Minister Zhang Aiping. His early association with the navy began in 1949 as principal organizer of the East China Fleet. More significantly, Zhang directed the PLA's first combined-arms operation in 1955 – the assault and capture of the Nationalist-held Dachen Islands. Before becoming minister of defence in 1982, Zhang had been chairman of the National Defence Scientific and Technological Commission, and in that capacity directed the development of China's nuclear-powered submarine.

Another important standard-bearer of the navy's development is its commander, Liu Huaqing. Before assuming this post in 1982, Liu had been assistant chief of staff of the PLA. Purged during the Cultural Revolution, Liu reappeared in 1977 and was identified as vice-chairman of the Commission headed by Zhang. He held this post until 1979 and presumably played a key role in the modernization of the navy.[83]

One measure of this modernization has been China's submarine force. Its importance was underlined by Liu Huaqing in a 1985 interview. 'Towering like a giant on the west of the Pacific,' China, he said, had a coastline of more than 18,000 kilometres, more than 6,000 islands and an expanse of ocean spanning 3.5 million square kilometres. To protect its coast and maritime interests, China attaches great importance to developing the navy, and this 'includes the emphatic development of its submarine force', whose essential characteristics are concealment, endurance, self-supporting capability and striking strength. In the 1960s, Liu added, submarine operations were limited to coastal waters, but now they extend to the sea areas of the western Pacific and the far-off islands. 'Of course', Liu said, 'we are soberly aware that there is still a gap between the equipment and technology of China's submarine unit and those of advanced countries .... We must acquire and absorb the advanced technology of these countries ... and borrow their experience ....'[84]

Despite substantial achievements, the Chinese navy is still backward in crucial respects. Its leaders know this full well, as is evident in statements like the one noted above, and like another one by Liu Huaqing that the navy is 'lagging behind both in scale and degree of modernization require-ments ...'.[85] It is even more evident in their search for advanced technology. As of mid-1985, this search generated more commotion than contracts. In 1983, the Chinese cancelled a £120 million contract to buy British Sea Dart missiles on the grounds that it was too expensive.[86] In early 1985, they made known their desire to buy from the United States gas turbine engines for destroyers, Mark 46 torpedos, Vulcan-Phalanx radar-controlled rapid-firing guns for use against low-flying aircraft and anti-ship missiles, and modern sonars to detect enemy submarines. Although the Americans said that the Chinese had agreed in principle to buy these items, Beijing denied that it had concluded any agreements.[87] Even if this deal goes through, it will represent a mere drop in the ocean of the navy's needs.

In the view of Western experts, these needs are vast. Several examples will illustrate this. China's missile-attack craft carry antiquated fire-control radar, and only a few have newer systems. China's most modern destroyer also has vintage fire-control and navigation radar, and lacks a combat information centre. Such a centre is also absent in Chinese frigates, as is modern radar. Sonar equipment is judged incapable of identifying and holding targets in deep-sea operations. China's major combat vessels generally lack modern ASW (anti-submarine warfare) capability. Torpedo systems aboard the older submarines are obsolescent and lack effective speed and range against fast ships. Although the Chinese have been working on reliable surface-to-air missile systems, those aboard their warships still have fire-control problems. Propulsion systems have problems which have not yet been ironed out. The naval aviation arm is not equipped for extended sea missions. Minesweepers are way out of date.[88]

Along with their efforts to upgrade conventional capability, the Chinese have worked unflaggingly to improve their nuclear weapons. The quantity of nuclear weapons, according to Western estimates, has remained more or less constant since the turn of the decade, suggesting that the Chinese consider it sufficient as a minimal deterrent and have concentrated on refining their systems rather than building new ones. The backbone of China's nuclear capability lies in land-based missiles which fall into three categories. One consists of medium-range ballistic missiles (MRBMs), of which there are perhaps fifty. These are liquid-fuelled, single-staged missiles which can be transported by road. They have a range of 1,800 kilometres, and are believed to carry a warhead with a yield of 20 kilotons. In the second category there are intermediate-range ballistic missiles (IRBMs) which may be gradually replacing the older MRBMs. Estimates of their number range from sixty-five to eighty-five. They are powered by a Chinese-designed, single-stage liquid system, have a range of 5,500 kilometres, and carry a thermonuclear warhead with a yield of 20 megatons. Finally, there is a small number of inter-continental ballistic missiles (ICBMs): two with a 13,000 kilometre range and a five-megaton warhead; and four with a 10,000 kilometre range and a three-megaton warhead.[89] In September 1985, according to Western defence experts, the Chinese successfully test-fired the CCS4 intercontinental ballistic missile for the first time with independently targeted re-entry vehicles (MIRVs).[90]

China's fledgling sea-based leg of the nuclear tripod is comprised of one nuclear-powered submarine with twelve ballistic tubes.[91] The deployment of this submarine – along with six more on order[92] – significantly enhances China's nuclear capability and largely accounts for the growing confidence of its leaders in China's ability to deter a nuclear attack by threat of retaliation.[93] This achievement is particularly important in view of the weakness of China's bomber force, which has not been measurably updated since the 1950s and is unlikely to penetrate modern air defences.

Less sensational than ballistic missiles but extremely impressive in technological feats has been China's aerospace programme. Begun in the mid-1950s, the programme reportedly absorbs almost 1 per cent of the country's gross national product. China's first earth satellite was successfully launched in 1970, followed a year later by a second and heavier artificial satellite. In 1975 China launched its first recoverable artificial satellite and this was followed by two more artificial earth satellites and two scientific experiment satellites, all of which were recovered. In 1984 the Chinese put into orbit three satellites for different scientific experiments, using a large-scale booster and indicating that they were developing a MIRV capability. In 1984 they launched their first geostationary experimental communications satellite.[94] Although used primarily for non-military purposes, the import-ance of communications satellites for improving China's C3I (command, control, communications and intelligence) capabilities is obvious.

Arms Imports and Exports

The great expectations for massive arms deals generated by China's outburst of interest in foreign weapons in the late 1970s foundered on the decision of

112

the Chinese leadership to set strict limits on the import of military technology. However, within these limits, the Chinese have steadily sought to acquire select weapons and equipment in order to advance their modernization drive. Their preference has been for technology transfer by licencing, or other forms, but their approach has been flexible. In cases where foreign suppliers refused to transfer technology, or where the Chinese urgently needed items to correct dangerous defects in their defences, they agreed to straight sales. Some items may have been purchased for study and possible copying.

In line with this policy, the Chinese have concluded a fairly broad range of deals for the purchase or co-production of military goods. To recapitulate, these goods include: jet engines; helicopters; jeeps and trucks; surface-to-air missiles; transport aircraft; marine engine technology; tank guns; radar, navigation and communications equipment; fire-control equipment; advanced avionics equipment; and, possibly in the near future, high-technology equipment for naval warfare. In addition, the Chinese have acquired items for dual use in civilian and military fields – such as computers and electronics equipment – and have received foreign help in non-ferrous mining and processing and in casting technology.[95] Where much-needed items have not been available, the Chinese have not been averse to resorting to other means: they have reportedly obtained an Exocet anti-ship missile through a third party with the intention of manufacturing copies,[96] and have allegedly been involved in trying to smuggle high-technology avionics equipment from the United States to China.[97]

Although the precise nature and scope of China's military imports is not known, it obviously amounts to a small part of total military expenditure. However, the importance of such imports to China's modernization drive cannot be measured in financial terms alone. By purchasing high-priority items and production technology, the Chinese have improved their defences in the short term and have laid the groundwork for a substantial upgrading of their arms manufacturing capability over the long haul.

If China's military imports have fallen below initial expectations, the Chinese have surprised observers by their arms exports. No military-related area better demonstrates the Deng leadership's jettisoning of Maoist principles than the volume of Chinese weapons flowing abroad and their destination. From the vantage point of military modernization, the significance of these exports is twofold: they point to the production capacity of the arms industry; and they earn large amounts of foreign currency which must be at least partly earmarked for the defence sector.

Until the beginning of the 1980s, China exported arms for several reasons, which frequently overlapped. One reason derived from the desire to strengthen China's security by providing aid to neighbouring states, such as

North Korea and North Vietnam, which were also threatened by China's enemies. Another stemmed from China's quest for political influence, either in independent states, such as Pakistan and Tanzania, or in a wide range of insurgent movements and groups. This quest became particularly acute when Sino-Soviet relations deteriorated and the Chinese tried to compete with the Russians for political influence in the Third World. A third reason was China's commitment to the promotion of world revolution in the 1960s, and its attempts to support the struggles of groups which it considered revolutionary. Throughout the Maoist period Chinese aid was given free of charge, either by direct grants or by interest-free loans. It was also modest in scope – in the eighteen years between 1963 and 1980 total Chinese arms aid amounted to slightly less than US$5 billion – and in the type of weapons provided. This was due both to the capacity of China's arms industry and to the limited needs of many of the recipients.[98]

The nature of China's arms exports was transformed by the conversion of three trends. The first was the rejection of Maoist tenets in foreign affairs and the adoption of a hard-headed approach to relations with other countries, which means that arms are sold rather than given away. The second was the enlarged production capacity of the arms industry, which resulted from the effort to upgrade the PLA's weapons and equipment. And the third was the propitious availability of new markets eager to purchase in large quantities the types of weapons which China is able to supply.

These markets emerged in the Middle East. First to conclude an arms deal with China was Egypt. Spurred by the need to replenish weapons destroyed in the Yom Kippur War in 1973, and cut off from Soviet military supplies, the Egyptians turned to China. Between 1976, when President Sadat abrogated Egypt's treaty of co-operation with the Soviets, and 1983, Egypt and China signed several agreements for the purchase of Chinese weapons. These agreements reportedly amounted to between $500 and $700 million and covered the sale of aircraft (F-6s and F-7s), submarines (Chinese-built Romeo type), surface-to-air missiles, spare parts, ammunition and knowhow.[99]

The consignments to Egypt were a pale prelude to the subsequent surge of China's arms exports to the Middle East. Brought about by the Iraq–Iran war, which broke out in 1980, this surge reportedly boosted China's military sales to $5 billion by the mid-1980s – about equal to the sum total of all China's arms transfers in the preceding two decades. In 1985 alone, China's arms sales were estimated at $2 billion.[100] According to reports in reliable publications, the Chinese have supplied Iraq with F-6 and F-7 aircraft, Type-69 main battle tanks, light arms, field artillery and huge amounts of ammunition and spare parts. Iran has apparently been the recipient of F-6 aircraft, T-59 tanks, field artillery and light arms.[101] China's readiness, though officially denied, to provide weapons to both sides in a bloody drawn-out war, which can only be prolonged by these weapons, represents a remarkable retreat from Maoist policy on arms transfers. Presented with a market made insatiable by high attrition rates, the post-Mao leadership has thrown all scruples to the winds, and has joined the ranks of countries which its predecessors had derided.

China has apparently also reaped side benefits from the Middle East arms trade, in addition to the main purpose of making money. In return for weapons received from China, both Egypt and Iraq are thought to have provided China with new models of Soviet equipment. These models are believed to have included at least two MiG-23 fighters; MiG-23 engines; an unknown number of MiG-21MF and Sukhoi Su-20 bombers; at least two types of surface-to-air missiles; at least two T-62 tanks; and anti-tank missiles. These weapons came to the Chinese with manuals and spare parts. Chinese experts, moreover, were also probably permitted to inspect other Soviet weapons on the spot. The Chinese have presumably used these models for two purposes: to study the performance of weapons they are most likely to encounter in a confrontation with the Soviets; and, more importantly, to take apart and copy them. This exercise has conceivably helped the Chinese in designing their version of the MiG-23, the F-8B, as well as in manufacturing anti-tank and surface-to-air missiles. Other weapons, most notably the Type-69 battle tank, probably incorporate components of new Soviet weapons.[102]

To promote contacts with foreign countries, the Chinese reorganized and renamed the Third through Seventh Ministries of Machine-Building, which are now known as the China Precision Machinery Import–Export Corporation (responsible for missile production); the China State Shipbuilding Trade Company Ltd; the China North Industries Corporation or Norinco (responsible for ordnance and ground forces equipment); the China Electronic Import–Export Corporation; and the China State Aerospace Technology Import–Export Corporation (aircraft and space systems). These enterprises are grouped under the management of the China Xinshidai Company, which collaborates with the General Staff on both military production and arms deals. Since 1984, the Chinese have stepped up their arms export drive. They have participated in international weapons exhibitions, and have advertised widely in Western defence journals.[103] In November 1986 the Chinese held a major arms exhibition in Beijing at which they exhibited a wide range of weapons for export.

An Assessment

An attempt to assess the significance of the post-Mao technological changes in the PLA is an uncertain undertaking. For one thing, the nature of these changes cannot be accurately ascertained due to the dearth of hard data. For another, their significance depends decisively on the missions which the Chinese leaders expect the PLA to fulfil and these, in turn, derive from threat perceptions – variables which cannot be determined with certainty and precision. Nonetheless, broad conclusions are possible.

The point of departure is that, within the limits prescribed by the policy of national modernization, the Chinese have since the turn of the decade carried out a concerted campaign to improve the weapons and equipment of the PLA. Given the base line set by the prolonged decay of conventional hardware, they have undoubtedly made steady and substantial progress. However, precisely because of this base line, their conventional forces are still at least two decades behind the technological level attained by the armies of the superpowers – or, for that matter, of other modern countries as well. Taking into account the pace of technological development and China's policy of weapons acquisition, it is unlikely that the enormous gap between the PLA and modern armies can be significantly narrowed for years.

Is the PLA, then, doomed for the foreseeable future to technological backwardness which, as suggested by some military experts,[104] renders it incapable of effectively countering a Soviet attack on China? The answer hinges heavily on two further interrelated questions: What is the significance of the improvements being made in the military equipment of the PLA? For what purpose does the Chinese leadership intend to use its conventional forces?

Although progress in weapons upgrading has been slow and small in absolute terms, it should hardly be dismissed as negligible. Even incremental improvement of old weapons can considerably increase their capabilities. Experience has shown that costly or complex weapons have not usually worked well on the battlefield, while weapons that were relatively simple for their day were by and large remarkably effective. What is critical is not how complex the weapons are, but how well they perform in combat.[105]

In this connection it should be noted that whereas some aviation experts take a dim view of the F-6, Pakistani pilots who have flown it in combat have a different opinion. They have praised the plane for its sturdiness and ease of handling, and have described it as highly effective in ground attacks and air battles.[106] Similarly, the renovation of old Chinese tanks must have substantially increased their fighting capacity. Relevant in this regard is the Israeli experience with outdated Soviet T-54 and T-55 tanks captured in the 1967 and 1973 wars. These tanks were refitted to accommodate a new 105 mm gun instead of the original 100 mm gun, and re-equipped with new fire-control systems, among other improvements. In combat the born-again

Soviet tanks were judged superior to the T-54 and T-55, and on a par with the T-62 models.[107]

Very similar improvements have apparently been carried out by the Chinese, with or without Israeli help, on their old tanks. The same presumably applies to a broad range of other weapons which the Chinese have renovated. It is these weapons that have been shipped to the Middle East. While both Iraq and Iran are in dire need of military equipment, neither they nor other countries, such as Pakistan, would pour money into weapons that did not prove effective on the battlefield.

While the PLA's conventional military equipment has become better in the past few years, it is still backward compared to the Soviet arsenal. What then are the PLA's chances against a conventional Soviet attack? These depend very much on the nature of the attack. If the Soviets launch an all-out massive invasion – aiming at China's heartland from several directions and forcing the Chinese to disperse their more modern divisions – obviously China's defences will be put in dire straits by Soviet superiority in the quantity and quality of military equipment. Despite this, the Chinese cannot equip the PLA for a conventional response to such an invasion. The astronomical costs of the required hardware and the problems of availability and absorption puts this course beyond their reach in the short term. Nor is it necessary. As already emphasized, the possibility of a full-scale Soviet invasion of China is virtually unimaginable. While it is the duty of military planners to imagine the unimaginable, it is also their duty to distinguish between the essential and the expendable. And a strategy of meeting a general invasion head-on is eminently expendable. Especially since the Chinese can confidently fall back on the notion that should such an invasion take place, they will counter it by resorting to the Maoist strategy of 'people's war'. The Chinese, in short, do not have to build the PLA for a mission that it will not conceivably be called upon to carry out. To judge their modernization strategy in these terms is to miss its essence.

The essence of this strategy, as pieced together from Chinese pronouncements and practice, is to rebuild the PLA for far narrower ends. Chief among these is to strengthen its ability to put up a conventional defence against a limited Soviet attack, which is apparently seen by the Chinese as the most serious threat they will face if hostilities break out. However, even in a limited confrontation, observers point out, the gap between Soviet and Chinese forces will be such as to give the Soviets overwhelming superiority. This is true, but superiority is not an absolute and fixed position. The purpose of the Chinese is clearly not to close the gap, which is unrealistic in the short run, but to reduce it gradually on the implicit assumption that incremental improvements in their force posture will make it more difficult for the Soviets to contemplate an attack. In other words, by increasing the price of an invasion, the Chinese will decrease the probability of its occurring. Viewed from this vantage point, even the modest progress made by the PLA in the post-Mao period is significant.

It is significant for other reasons as well. The upgrading of China's capacity to wage a limited conventional war against the Soviets also greatly enhances its ability to take on a smaller power like Vietnam. In fact, advances which are minute in relation to Soviet might, become much more important in the balance of power with countries like Vietnam. The implications of such advances for China's regional stature are self-evident. Particularly significant is the inordinate emphasis the Chinese have put on naval development, which is aimed in the long term not only at strengthening their power in the waters close to the mainland, but also at showing their presence on the high seas, primarily for purposes of prestige.

In short, the Chinese seem realistically to have tailored the ends of weapons modernization to their limited means. Although they have only begun to move towards the attainment of these ends, progress has been considerable. Given the commitment of China's leaders to improving military hardware, this movement can be expected to accelerate in the coming years.

6

Reforming the PLA: Professionalism First

If the modernization of military equipment is limited by economic and technological constraints, no such constraints exist in other areas – such as leadership, training and organization – which are no less vital than hardware to overall fighting capability. From the standpoint of the professional military, these were disaster areas when the Maoist period ended. As has been seen, prolonged domination of military affairs by Maoist dogma and the shattering effects of the Cultural Revolution had severely damaged professional competence throughout the armed forces. The post-Mao leaders are acutely aware that it is pointless to expend efforts on upgrading weapons and equipment without concomitant efforts to improve the professional quality of the entire infrastructure. They consider professional skills to be of primary importance and freely admit that such skills are lacking in the PLA. Unlike the Maoists, they are no longer prepared to put their faith primarily in the political attributes of the soldiers. As Yang Shangkun wrote in *Hongqi* in August 1982, echoing numerous similar statements by other leaders:

> Human factors still play a primary role in modern warfare. However, it is necessary to understand human factors in an all-round way. They include not only human courage, consciousness and the spirit of sacrifice but also human wisdom and talent as well as mastery and application of science, culture and technology . . . . It should be noted, however, that the scientific, cultural and technological level of our cadres still fails to keep abreast of the requirements of modern warfare. If we fail to change this state of affairs speedily, we shall not be able to master skilfully and operate proficiently more up-to-date equipment, let alone bring its efficiency into full play.[1]

The need for radical change is rooted in the recognition – axiomatic in other armies but not publicly articulated in China until the break with Maoist dogma – that modern war is complex and fighting it requires diverse and

119

special skills. The acquisition of such skills constitutes the central focus of military reforms. A 1982 article in *Hongqi* put it this way:

> New conditions which did not exist before, have appeared in contemporary warfare. The most salient feature is three-dimensional warfare. It means that warfare will be simultaneously carried out in the air, on land and at sea, and it will be difficult to differentiate between the frontline and the rear areas. To adapt to the demands of this kind of warfare, we must further build the PLA into a powerful composite army able to operate in concert with various branches of the services under modern conditions. The organizational system, weaponry, strategy and tactics as well as cadre training . . . must be oriented in this direction.[2]

To prepare the PLA for modern warfare, the Chinese leaders have carried out far-reaching reforms in all areas of its activities. Its structures have been simplified and streamlined. Its systems have been modernized. Its style has been made more professional. Although the full impact of China's military reforms will be felt only in the future, by the mid-1980s they have already changed the face and character of the Chinese armed forces. The following statement by Yang Shangkun gives what appears to be an eminently fair interim assessment:

> Since Comrade Deng Xiaoping took charge of the work of the Military Commission . . . our Army has carried out some reforms with notable success. For example, we have streamlined and reorganized the Army, carried out structural reform, attached strategic importance to education and training, restored the military academies and institutions, readjusted Army, divisional and regimental leading bodies, jointly built a socialist spiritual civilization with the people, acquired some scientific and cultural knowledge, trained people to be capable of doing both army and civilian work, revised various rules and regulations and so on. These reforms have brought about a new situation in all areas of the work of our Army. However, the reform of the entire Army, we should say, has just begun.[3]

The Officer Corps: A New Look

The most important task in the view of the Chinese high command is to improve the quality of leadership at all levels of the armed forces. It is an article of faith in the post-Mao PLA that on this task hinges the fate of military modernization in all other areas. Answering an army magazine reporter's question about training programmes for 1981, Han Huaizhi, then assistant to the chief of the General Staff, emphasized that 'with regard to training, cadres are a key point'. His explanation has been repeated numerous times by all senior military leaders: 'In peacetime, cadres are the ones who organize training; in wartime, they are the ones who command operations. The level of their modernization in military affairs and the strength of their command capability have a direct effect on the combat effectiveness of our armed forces'.[4]

All efforts, therefore, are directed at producing officers who, in the catchphrase of the 1980s, are 'younger in age, better educated and professionally more competent'. It is on this new breed of modern professional officers that the high command has pinned its hopes for the future. An article in the army paper put this forthrightly at the outset of military modernization in 1979: 'While we must have the industrious efforts of our veteran cadres who are still vigorous, we need the joint efforts of our youthful new cadres even more to solve the new problems which now confront our army building.'[5]

Producing such officers has not been easy due to the damage done by the Maoist legacy. Nowhere did this legacy hurt the PLA more than in its officer corps. Viewed by Maoist radicals as the citadel of antagonistic values and attitudes, the officer corps, it will be recalled, became the chief target of their crusade against military professionalism. This crusade left the officer corps in shambles. Military efficiency was sacrificed to political and factional calculations. Military involvement in politics drew officers away from professional duties and threw them into sectarian stuggles. Political rivalries and bureaucratic inertia froze the officer corps in a little-changing mould of programmes and personnel. The result was an officer corps that was oversized, over-aged, incompetent and incapable of adjusting to new times. As Deng Xiaoping complained in 1975, 'bloating, laxity, conceit, extravagance and inertia are to be found in certain degrees',[6] adding 'weakness and laziness'[7] to the list two years later.

In a single-minded effort to put the officer corps on an entirely new footing, the post-Mao leaders have introduced basic reforms in all phases of an officer's career, from recruitment to retirement. The common feature of these reforms is that they are governed by the requirements of military professionalism and the realities of modern war. Reforms of such scope profoundly affect the lives and interest of powerful personalities and are bound to generate some resistance and disquiet. Nevertheless, the Deng leadership has demonstrated its determination to rebuild the Chinese officer corps in line with the imperatives imposed by 'modern conditions'.

The starting point for this process has been the system of selecting officers. Dropping the past practice of promoting officers from the ranks, the leadership has stipulated that new officers should be graduates of military academies.[8] To enrol in these academies, candidates have to be graduates of senior middle schools and have to pass examinations set down by the Ministry of Education for entrance into institutes of higher learning. In addition, candidates have to meet specific conditions required by the PLA. After admission, candidates are subjected to further scrutiny of their qualifications, and only if they pass are they accepted by the military academies.[9] Candidates for pilot training have since 1983 been recruited from among college graduates.[10]

Just how strict the new enrolment conditions apparently are was illustrated by a circular issued in 1980 by the PLA's Discipline Inspection Commission, which cautioned against the practice of 'going through the back door' in seeking access to military academies. The circular noted that 'since the documents on the adoption of the system of enrolling local young students and soldiers into military academies and schools by means of a unified examination were distributed', high-ranking officers 'began to manoeuvre in the hope of getting their children and those of their friends and relatives into military academies and schools ... through irregular means'. The circular called upon officers to refrain from taking advantage of their position to seek special treatment, and directed staffs of military academies to accept only those who were qualified. Furthermore, candidates who had been improperly admitted were to be disqualified.[11]

The centrepiece of the campaign to raise the quality of officers is the military academies, which are viewed by the leadership as the foundation of the new army and the key to the success of military modernization. 'The quality of a commander', wrote Xiao Ke, commandant of the PLA Military Academy in 1983, 'determines to a great extent the quality of the troops, whereas the standard of colleges and academies determines the quality of commanders.' He then elaborated graphically:

> The relationship between the academies and troops is like that between the head and body of a dragon while performing a dragon dance. If the dragon head performs well, its long body will soar aloft and dance freely in the air. In the course of building a modern, regular and revolutionary army, the building of colleges and academies is the key link that determines the building of the army.[12]

As the prime breeding ground of military professionalism, the military academies bore the brunt of radical assaults during the Cultural Revolution. Of the 140 institutions that had been in operation before the upheaval, only forty were intact in 1977.[13] This, for example, was the fate of the principal institution, the PLA Military Academy: 'Its teaching staff was disbanded. Its teaching materials and files were bundled into sixteen trucks and were reduced to ashes. Books in its library and its teaching equipment were practically all demolished.'[14]

Since then, the Chinese high command has made an enormous effort to rebuild and refine the military academies in order to make them capable of producing the type of officer required by the modernizing army. In 1983, Xiao Ke said that the Military Commission had decided 'to step up further the building of the military colleges and made clear its intention truly to raise education and training in military colleges to a strategic level'. According to the decision, by or before 1985 over 70 per cent of officers of platoon rank and above would have had to go through training in military academies. The majority should have reached the level of middle schools or specialized schools, and a small portion should be of college level. Commanders of naval vessels and pilots should all be graduates of academies and should have reached the cultural level of colleges or middle and specialized schools.[15]

A 1983 meeting of PLA academies, convened to discuss measures for strengthening their work, called upon the entire armed forces to do several things. First, it urged that the best officers be assigned to run military academies. Although such officers are important in commanding combat units, they can, it was said, make an even greater contribution to army building by training qualified officers. Second, it was asked that outstanding officers be sent for training at military academies, even if their absence from units adversely affected current work. Third, priority, it was said, must be given to military academies in the allocation of advanced technical equipment. Finally, necessary funds must be given to academies, even if this meant reducing the number of soldiers.[16] The meeting also ventured into sensitive ground that affects the careers of numerous officers. It suggested that in future, decisions on promoting and assigning officers should be based mainly on their educational background and academic record. For this reason, academies should make recommendations on the assignment of graduating officers.[17] Since such a step involves the vested interests of various organs, it is not known to what extent it has been acted upon. However, the very fact that it was put forward by the academies is one indication of their new stature.

The continuous importance which the Chinese leadership attaches to military education was underlined by Li Peng, vice-premier of the State Council and chairman of the State Education Commission, in his speech to an all-army conference of military academies in February 1986. In advancing the modernization of the armed forces, Li said, military education should look to the future: it should 'effectively assimilate and apply the latest achievements in the world's military sciences and technology to improve our school system'; and it should concentrate on training capable personnel for the 1990s and the twenty-first century. Therefore, 'while concentrating mainly on the study of military affairs, military academies and schools should also train skilled personnel for both Army and local construction'.[18]

In 1984 there were over 100 academies divided into two broad categories of command and specialized technical schools. The command schools are in junior, intermediate and senior levels, and are designed for training commanding officers at the platoon, regimental and corps levels. The specialized technical schools are in intermediate and advanced levels. The junior-level command schools enrol outstanding squad leaders and soldiers of senior-middle-school graduate level, as well as the current year's crop of senior-middle-school graduates. They are trained to become platoon leaders in the ground forces and navy, pilots (although, as has been seen, the intention is to enlist college graduates for pilot training) and company quartermasters. The intermediate-level command schools take in battalion and deputy regimental commanding officers, as well as a small number of company-level commanders who graduated from junior-level command schools. They are trained to become regimental-level military, political and logistics commanding officers and staff officers for division and regimental level organs. These academies mainly teach division- and regimental-level tactics and organization, as well as command of joint operations. The senior-level command schools enrol division-level officers and a small number of outstanding regimental-level commanding officers who graduated from intermediate-level command schools. They are trained to become senior military, political and logistics commanders and senior staff officers. They study primarily strategy as well as command of military campaigns.

The intermediate-level specialized technical schools offer two-year courses to train technical and medical officers. The advanced schools offer three-year specialized college courses and four- to six-year regular college courses to train advanced technical officers. Under the overall supervision of the Military Commission, military academies are subordinate either to one of the PLA's General Departments or to one of the major units.[19]

At the highest 'seat of learning' of the Chinese armed forces, the PLA Military Academy, according to one report, there were in 1985 more than 700 cadets studying in five classes: advanced command, advanced rotational training, command, rotational training and military theory. The students in the first two classes were either officers from army-level units or from divisional-level units attached to combined arms outfits. The other two classes trained outstanding officers at divisional level and some regimental commanders. In line with the effort to make officers younger, it was emphasized that the average age in the first two classes was forty-six and thirty-five in the command class. Three tracks of study were offered: military affairs, politics and science and technology. The first consisted of the theory of people's war; strategic principles of active defence; strategy and campaigns; the theories, organization and deployment of various arms and services in joint operations under conditions of modern warfare; the theories of prominent military thinkers, ancient and modern, Chinese and foreign; the history of wars; and specific examples of battles. The politics track consisted of philosophy, political economy and political work in the army, as well as the international situation and China's foreign policy. No information was given in the report on the third track.[20]

The teaching staff was drawn from outstanding graduates of the academy, graduates of civilian institutions of higher learning, commanders with combat experience, and 'returned students from the Soviet Union in the 1950s'.[21] The mention of this last category illuminates how far the PLA has moved away from the Maoist period, when for almost twenty years anything that smacked of Soviet practices was derided as 'dogmatism'. It also illuminates how acutely the Chinese need exposure to the experience of a modern army, even though they had to settle for an experience absorbed by Chinese officers a very long time ago.

Another report on the same academy stressed that its main task was to train officers to command modern service arms in combined operations. One means was to study modern military campaigns, such as the Falklands campaign and the Middle Eastern wars.[22] An American military observer who visited the Academy in 1980 noted the fundamental reassessment of military doctrine and the realistic appreciation of China's strengths and weaknesses.[23] At the end of 1985 the PLA Military Academy was incorporated into the newly-established National Defence University.

A different kind of institution, whose importance has risen in recent years, is the National Defence Science and Technology University. Founded in 1953 as the PLA Military Engineering Academy, the institution has reportedly trained a total of 16,000 undergraduate students, 200 graduate students and 200 foreign students. Over 2,000 students have pursued advanced studies. The University carried out hundreds of research projects and won many PLA scientific and technical awards. At the beginning of 1985, the University established a graduate school, the first in the PLA, 'for educating high-standard and high-quality scientists and technical personnel' with doctoral and master qualifications for national defence purposes. By the end of the year, the school was expected to have 670 students.[24]

The need for integrated military studies at a high level led to the establishment of the National Defence University at the end of 1985. Scheduled to open in September 1986, the new University was formed by merging the PLA Military Academy, the PLA Political Acadamy and the PLA Logistics Academy. Its basic task is to train commanders at and above army level for the three services, and also to train staff officers at and above the military-region level, as well as senior researchers in military theory. Another task is to investigate strategic issues and to perform an advisory role in policy decisions of the Military Commission and the General Staff. The University is subordinate directly to the Central Military Commission. Its commandant is Zhang Zhen, formerly a deputy chief of the General Staff and its political commissar is Li Desheng, former commander of the Shenyang Military Region and, before that, director of the PLA's General Political Department.[25]

The National Defence University, it was said, 'will be run in the manner of opening up to the outside world. It will invite foreign military leaders, experts and scholars to give lectures in the university, carry out academic exchanges at home and abroad, and select and send in a planned manner officers, teaching and research workers, and students to conduct inspection tours and give lectures abroad.' Its focus will be on training senior commanders capable of meeting the requirements set by the modernization of the Chinese armed forces in the 1990s and the early twenty-first century.[26]

The rationale for the establishment of the National Defence University was summed up by its commandant, Zhang Zhen:

> The key to accelerating defence modernization is training a large number of personnel, especially senior leaders, well versed in modern military affairs. As a new technological revolution is occurring in the world, military science and technology are constantly being updated, and strategy and tactics have undergone and will continue to undergo a series of major changes. In a modern war, the Army's senior commanders will be required to have both 'advanced knowledge and diversified skills'. They must possess a strategic mind and the ability to command a combined battle; they must be able to direct military, political and logistics work in an all-round manner .... Hence, it is necessary to adapt the training system of senior Army cadres to the new situation and requirements.[27]

In order to make the academies more efficient, nine regional co-operation centres have been established since 1980 by more than eighty PLA academies. The purpose has been to pool resources, so as to make up for individual deficiencies, and to share strong points, so as to overcome the limitations of individual schools. The co-operation has reportedly resulted in extensive exchanges of experiences, in transfer of information and in the popularization of new technology. Large amounts of teaching materials have been reproduced and circulated.[28] Commenting on the result of this co-operation, the army paper called it 'a new achievement of the reform being carried out in various PLA institutes', a sure way of overcoming shortages by using limited resources more effectively.[29]

The pivotal role assigned by the high command to formal education in the making of the professional officer was reflected in a 1983 decision of the General Political Department, approved by the Military Affairs Commission, on strengthening education in science, culture and political theory for officers throughout the armed forces. Current levels, the decision noted, were far from able to meet the requirements of army building, and raising them was essential to speeding up modernization. The decision stipulated that all officers under forty years of age should strive to reach high-school level or equivalent professional-school level by 1990, while those over forty, or those who are high-school graduates, should take special courses connected with their work. To this end, it called on army units to use all available means to further the education of officers. These included the use of facilities of military academies for running special classes in army units; spare-time classes and correspondence courses; and other forms of self-tuition.[30]

To emphasize the practical significance of these regulations, the decision called for the creation of an examination and evaluation system for officers who had studied science, culture and political theory. An officer who took the appropriate courses and passed examinations would be issued with a graduation certificate. Study records which detailed the officer's performance and experience, would be put in the officer's file. Most important, the decision ordained that henceforth an officer's educational record would be as important as experience and performance in determining placement and promotion.[31]

The new importance of formal education reportedly galvanized units throughout the PLA into action. For example, the Shenyang PLA units invited professors from Liaoning University to aid them in establishing a university affiliated with the army to improve the cultural level of officers.[32] The Nanchang Infantry School set up full four-year college courses with instructors from universities in the province.[33] Similar courses were established by twenty other academies.[34] Instructors from the Missile Units Academy visited various air bases in order to impart the latest technological developments to officers unable to attend military academies.[35] The Lanzhou PLA units formed a spare-time educational network.[36] The Beijing PLA units ran basic courses for officers who were preparing to take examinations in higher education.[37]

The pride of place accorded to education has elevated the status of officers with an intellectual background. Shortly after his appointment as defence minister, Zhang Aiping made a case for the proper use of such officers. 'In modernizing our national defence and developing sophisticated military equipment,' he wrote in *Hongqi*, 'we must rely on scientific and cultural knowledge and on intellectuals who have mastered the most advanced science and technology.' Therefore, all officers should recognize the role of intellectuals in military modernization and create better working and living conditions for them. Most important, 'we should select and promote fine scientific and technical workers to leading technical posts and to leading posts at all levels and ensure that they have the power of and responsibility for their offices'.[38]

Judging by reports in the Chinese news media, placement of intellectuals in positions of responsibility has been fairly widespread in recent years. For example, since the 1978 Third Plenary Session of the Central Committee, Party Committees at all levels of the General Logistics Department reportedly implemented Party policies concerning intellectuals, with the result that by 1982 more than half of the officers in the Department had scientific or technological backgrounds.[39] In a surface-to-air missile regiment, the promotion of six college graduates to the commanding group was said to have wrought great improvements in the performance of the regiment.[40] An air force aviation engineering department made 'intellectual investments' by filling two-thirds of the positions in section-level command groups with officers who were college graduates.[41]

Perhaps nothing better illustrates the desire of the leadership to raise the professional quality of officers than its new promotion policies. The long-range aim is that all officers should be graduates of military academies, that only graduates of intermediate academies should be assigned to command battalions and regiments, and that only officers who received training in senior academies should become division and army commanders.[42] In the meantime, army units were told to drop past practices of promotion, and to give more weight to formal training in advancing officers. They were also told to stop drawing officers mainly from the ground forces, and to select more and better-educated officers from technical and non-combat units for command positions. Most significantly, they were told to discard the practice of promotion through seniority.[43] Defence Minister Zhang Aiping made a passionate plea for doing away with this practice:

> Some insist on the rule of seniority, believing that younger ones, who have worked under them, must not outrank and lead them. We communists, ever since the day we took an oath to join the party, are not destined to be officials all our lives, but to work for the motherland's prosperity .... For this objective, thousands upon thousands of martyrs have ... departed from us. We fortunate survivors will be condemned by history if we refuse to select and promote reliable successors .... Leading comrades ... in charge of cadre affairs should be the first to change their old notions and methods of work.[44]

This, however, is easier said than done, since the leadership's efforts to put new promotion policies into effect have run into considerable resistance. One source of resistance, according to the PLA leadership, is the lingering influence of 'leftist' ideology, which holds intellectuals in contempt. Officers who cling to this ideology are particularly hostile to military academies, where intellectuals are concentrated, and to their graduates.[45] They contend that officers who had never been to military academies had proved their worth in battle, that officers who began their careers in academies lacked the experience to command troops, and that, since the cultural level of the peasant-based PLA is not high, it should not be overly exacting for officers. They also contend that since the PLA is not highly modernized, there is no need for officers to acquire complex skills in military academies.[46] Some veteran commanders, moreover, regard knowledge as incompatible with ideals and integrity, and take the view that emphasizing knowledge weakens the role of ideology and erodes political consciousness.[47] Behind such arguments, of course, lurks the fear of veteran commanders that they will have to vacate their positions in favour of younger and more qualified officers, and lose the power and perquisites that come with high posts.

These attitudes are unacceptable to the Deng leadership, which is determined to promote only qualified officers over the long haul. This determination is reflected in the new 'Military Service Law', which was adopted in 1984. The Law stipulates that active-duty officers are to be drawn only from graduates of military academies, from enlisted men who received officer training in an institution approved by the Military Affairs Commission and who passed officer fitness tests, and from graduates of institutions of higher learning and special technical secondary schools who are suited to serve as officers.[48] The Military Service Law also restored the system of military ranks, which was abolished in 1965, although no date was set for its implementation. [49] This step was deemed essential for raising the prestige of officers, strengthening the army's sense of organization and discipline, and easing large-scale and complex joint-service operations.[50] Several years earlier the leadership had already promulgated regulations on the service of officers, which dealt with all aspects of a regular officer's career, and were designed to institutionalize the life-long service of the professional military.[51]

The preoccupation of the high command with infusing new blood into the officer corps has led to the introduction of an innovative measure, which is not customary in modern armies: demotion of officers for lack of achievement. In an interview with the army paper in 1985, Zhu Yungqian, deputy director of the General Political Department, said that the old system was harmful to army building in that it encouraged officers to be content with things as they were, and prevented talented officers from taking up important jobs. It also gave rise to favouritism and malpractices. The new system would enable getting rid of officers who had committed no serious mistakes, but who also had accomplished nothing. Such officers would be given a chance to do what they could, and their demotion would not be regarded as personal dishonour or disgrace.[52] This is hardly realistic, and it is unlikely that the far-reaching measure has been widely implemented, especially since nothing more has been heard of it. However, the very fact that it was suggested, and became the subject of discussion in the armed forces sponsored by the army paper,[53] is another illustration of the determination of the Chinese military leaders to improve the quality of the PLA.

The effort to advance younger officers to positions of high command has apparently borne fruit at all levels of the PLA. At any rate, reports to that effect, supported by statistics, are prominently played up in the media. For example, in 1983 it was reported that following the readjustment of corps-level combat units throughout the PLA, the average age of commanding officers has been lowered by 7.9 years. 'Many outstanding young cadres have been promoted to important leading positions regardless of personnel rules'.[54] In the Hunan Military District, the average age of army and divisional commanding officers after the reorganization was fifty and forty respectively.[55] In the air force, in the course of 1982 'a large number of cadres in the prime of life' had been promoted to commanding organs at or above divisional and regimental levels. Consequently, the number of officers at divisional level who were in their forties had increased by 22.6 per cent, and at the regimental level those in their thirties by 11.2 per cent. At the same time, young officers had been selected to continue their studies in academies 'to lower further the average of the contingent of cadres and raise their level of education and professional competence'.[56] In line with the leadership's policy, a submarine unit selected young officers to become submarine commanders and deputy commanders. Their ages ranged from twenty-seven to thirty-one.[57]

The trend towards promoting younger and more professionally fit officers extended to the higher echelons of the military hierarchy. In September 1985 it was reported that the readjustment of the leading bodies of the PLA General Staff and all the major military regions, services and arms had been completed. Following the readjustment, the average age of the leading members of these bodies had been lowered from 64.9 to 56.7. Each leading body, it was said, consisted of officers who were in their forties, fifties and sixties.[58] Major changes in this direction took place at the top of the structure – in the General Departments of the General Staff. Although the directors had not been changed, by mid-1985 their deputies were new faces. In the General Staff Department, the permanent deputy chief of staff was forty-nine years old and the two deputy chiefs of staff were forty-four. In the General Political Department, the permanent deputy director was about fifty and the two deputy directors about forty. In the General Logistics Department, the deputy director was about fifty, as were the two deputy directors.[59] All these officers were about twenty years younger than the veterans they had replaced. Speaking about the changes in the age structure of the officers, Yu Qiuli, director of the General Political Department, said that 'the key to a lower average age for army officers lies in a break with the rules. Without making a break, we cannot become bold. In terms of reform, this is the biggest task for the Army and also the most complicated and difficult one.'[60]

Retirement of Veteran Officers

The fate of the efforts to place younger professional officers in positions of responsibility throughout the armed forces hinges largely on such positions becoming available through the retirement of veterans. Deng Xiaoping highlighted the problem succinctly in 1980: 'The reason lower-level cadres could not be promoted is that older ones have stood in their way'.[61] This has been a major obstacle to military modernization because 'older' officers are incapable of adjusting to new circumstances, but are 'content with their old way of doing things'. They persist in 'solving new problems by old standards' and do not attach 'due importance to the creation of new military theories and operational tactics'.[62] It is also primarily the veteran officers, mainly from the ground forces, who are presumably most afflicted with 'leftist' tendencies, and who have opposed not only the military policies of the Deng leadership, but also its social and economic reforms. Replacing these veterans with younger and more competent commanders, who can also be expected to support Deng's national policies, is thus beneficial to the leadership in several respects.

However, the problem has been getting the old soldiers to fade away. Understandably reluctant to part with the benefits of high office which they had enjoyed for years, if not decades, ranking officers have been less than enthusiastic in responding to the leadership's prodding to retire gracefully. But mass retirement there has to be, if plans for military modernization are to proceed smoothly.

The Deng leadership has treated the problem gingerly. Since there is no formal requirement for retirement in the PLA, the leadership has chosen to coax rather than coerce ageing officers to leave the armed forces. This approach probably stems in part from the leadership's reluctance to antagonize veteran commanders who have vast networks of personal ties, and whose support it needs. The dispatch of large numbers of disgruntled veteran commanders into civilian life is clearly something the leadership wants strongly to avoid. Another reason probably derives from a recognition of the long and loyal service rendered by veterans, and a genuine desire to end their careers in a dignified and comfortable manner, which will ensure their co-operation.

The approach of the leadership was well illustrated by Wu Kehua, commander of the Guangzhou PLA units, in his speech at the the 12th Congress of the Party in 1982.[63] 'We veteran comrades', he said, should take the lead in 'setting an example ... and promote young and middle-aged cadres ... to leading posts'. To do this, Wu went on, several questions had to be settled. First, it was necessary to put to rest the 'feeling of worry' of 'some comrades' who 'do not trust the young and middle-aged cadres,

[and] are worried that they "may not be able to shoulder important responsibilities" ... '. Such worries, Wu said, were groundless. 'Weren't we in our twenties and thirties when we became division and army commanders? Of course, we had been tested and tempered in actual combat. ...' Nevertheless, today's officers have also 'come through a great deal of tempering and tests' and were fully capable of assuming the 'important responsibilities of building a modern ... army'.

Second, 'veteran comrades should accept the fact that they are getting old .... The law of nature is irresistible. Neither vigour nor physical strength permit us to continue to shoulder arduous leading tasks.' Therefore, Wu said, they should relinquish their posts, which will enable talented officers to be promoted and will enable the veterans to pass on their experience to their successors.

Finally, Wu came to what is probably the most sensitive aspect of retirement: the treatment of retiring veterans. Two things had to be done. One was to 'create a fine social atmosphere of respect for the old and virtuous'. The other was to 'make proper arrangements for and take good care of the veteran cadres'.

The importance which the leadership attaches to the welfare of retiring officers was underlined by Deng's personal concern with the details of the problem. Training courses, he said in 1980, should be set up for officers whose posts are eliminated to prepare them for the professions and trades they will enter. 'If the localities have no buildings to house classes, army barracks can be used and the localities can provide the teachers.' After training, these officers can be placed in various ministries or employed in the localities in public security and legal organs, 'where the skills required are pretty close to those of army cadres'. In particular, he said, there was a shortage of policemen, as well as judges, lawyers and procurators. Another possibility was for retired officers to become primary or secondary school teachers. Former officers were also especially qualified to become administrators because 'commanding troops is a kind of administration'.[64]

The effort to take good care of former officers was said to be widespread throughout local army units. For example, from the Guangxi Military District it was reported that the new leadership group 'respects and cares for comrades who have withdrawn from the leadership group and the retired old cadres. It has taken steps to solve practical problems in housing, transportation, cultural entertainment and so on.' The new commanders 'used their spare time ... to visit the homes of these comrades to seek their advice and views and also promptly did a number of good things for the old cadres'. These included designating housing areas located in a good environment close to the district headquarters for the retired officers as well as establishing a study and entertainment centre. These officers were also given priority in the use of military cars.[65] Commenting on such measures, the army paper pointed out that 'respecting retired veteran cadres and showing concern for them to make them glad they retired ... ' would speed up the turnover of officers in the armed forces and 'create a new situation in army building'.[66]

With the rapid rise of demobilized officers in the mid-1980s, cushioning their departure from the armed forces required a national effort. In 1985 and 1986, according to one account, some 47,000 officers were to retire from the army. These officers had joined the army during the war against Japan and the civil war and had reached junior rank up to regimental level. An additional 70,000 to 80,000 officers in this category were expected to retire in the next few years.[67] This is on top of the normal demobilization process.[68] In January 1986, it was reported that demobilization was running ahead of schedule and that more than 100,000 officers had already been discharged.[69]

A national meeting on the placement of retired officers and servicemen in early 1985 called on local authorities to make arrangements for the transfer of the first group of 33,000 retired officers and another group of 14,000, who would be transferred to the localities after the first one. Yang Chen, vice-minister of civil affairs, particularly urged the local authorities to speed up the construction of housing, which was vital to the transfer of retired officers.[70] Interviewed by the Chinese news agency in mid-1985, Cui Naifu, the civil affairs minister, said that localities throughout the country were making preparations to receive demobilized officers in the second half of the year. The state had already allocated one billion yuan for this purpose. Thirty thousand residential quarters had been completed and arrangements had been made for the livelihood, political study and medical care of retired officers, as well as for work and schooling for their families.[71]

The pace of the demobilization process apparently outran the estimates. At the end of June 1985, the vice-minister of civil affairs told a reporter that the resettling of the first batch of over 100,000 retired officers would start the following month. These officers would be assigned work mainly in their native place or in the localities where they had joined the army.[72] To cope with the tide, another national meeting, sponsored by the State Council and the Central Military Commission, was held in mid-1985. Participants from various local authorities were assigned quotas of demobilized officers for the year. They pledged to take appropriate steps for resettling the veterans, such as opening training classes for officers transferred to civilian jobs, providing housing for them and their families, as well as employment for family members and education for children.[73]

Commenting on officer demobilization, the *Renmin Ribao* again reflected the sympathetic attitude of the leadership. These officers, it said, had made important contributions in fighting, construction and army building. 'Now they are old and weak, or have either been injured or disabled in war or work.' Therefore, ministering to their needs in retirement is an 'unshirkable duty' of all organizations. Although they had left their posts, demobilized officers have not retired from active life and should be given every opportunity to make further contributions.[74]

A Smaller Army

The mass retirement of officers has been only the most conspicuous aspect of a deeper and daring reform: a radical reduction in the size of the PLA. The vast size of the armed forces has been a vexing problem for the leadership for at least a decade. By 1982, they had more than 4.2 million men, a figure that was probably higher by at least 20 per cent than before the Cultural Revolution.

The reasons for this rise can only be surmised. One was probably the wide range of new non-military tasks that the PLA had taken on during the Cultural Revolution. At the height of the turmoil, no less than two million men were reportedly involved in political and administrative activities, from restoring order to running factories.[75] Another was the apparent disruption of demobilization procedures, which was evidently not paralleled by a freeze on recruitment. This was presumably due in part to 'empire building' tendencies of increasingly autonomous local commanders, primarily in the ground forces. Such tendencies were doubtless intensified by the upheaval, since in the uncertain situation high-level commanders were probably reluctant to let loyal officers leave the army. Finally, in the absence of a strong leadership for most of the decade following the outbreak of the Cultural Revolution, aged and incompetent officers could not be compelled to retire.

Due to a combination of these reasons, by 1975 the PLA had become 'bloated', as Deng Xiaoping said at a meeting of the Military Affairs Commission. 'We can't say that every division is bloated,'Deng went on, 'but it is definitely true to some extent of the army as a whole.'[76] The meeting of the Commission was 'aimed at solving precisely this problem'.[77]

Five years later, however, the problem was still acute. Speaking to the Standing Committee of the Military Commission in 1980, Deng noted that since 1975 'some work' had been done but 'ran into complications and was halted'. Consequently, 'in the last few years, army organizations at various levels have again been expanded ... '. The adverse effect was twofold. One was that 'if a war really breaks out, we will find it difficult even to disperse our forces, let alone direct operations', due to 'organizational overlapping and overstaffing'. Another was 'the fact that the armed forces are over-manned also makes it harder to modernize their equipment'. Therefore, Deng said, it was necessary to decrease the number of personnel, mainly officers, 'if we want to carry out the four modernizations or to streamline the army and raise its combat effectiveness'.[78] Since operating costs have been estimated to absorb about 35 per cent of the military budget, the link between the reduction of men and the renewal of weapons is plain.

There are, in the view of the Chinese leadership, other important links between the cutback of manpower and combat effectiveness. Talking to a reporter after the decision to slash the size of the PLA, Yang Shangkun pointed to a few such links. First, cutting manpower, and the consequent improvement of hardware, will enable the PLA to develop further as a composite force. Second, the command structure at all levels will be more flexible and suited to the requirements of modern war. Third, the quality of officers will be raised. Fourth, the proportion of officers to soldiers will be more rational. Fifth, the work style of commanding groups will be improved and efficiency will be enhanced. Sixth, the structure of military schools will be better suited to the needs of a modern army. Seventh, the reserve system will be strengthened, enabling the PLA to respond effectively if war suddenly breaks out.[79]

Paring personnel has additional advantages. For one thing, a smaller army, better armed and trained, conforms to China's new military doctrine. This doctrine, it will be recalled, postulates that a limited attack on China will not be met by a Maoist strategy of 'people's war', but by a positional defence and swift counter-attacks. Such a strategy requires fewer troops than in the Maoist scheme. But it also requires troops equipped with modern weapons and capable of waging a modern war. A reduction in the size of the army also provides the Deng leadership with an appropriate opportunity for dismissing officers who have ideological qualms regarding its policies inside and outside the PLA. Such dismissals can be effected for organizational rather than political reasons simply by reorganizing units and cutting the ground from under unwanted officers.

A major milestone on the road to troop reduction was the adoption of the new Military Service Law in May 1984.[80] Until then, China had no formal reserve system, although the militia had provided a reserve pool of military manpower. In the 1950s, Peng Dehuai began to organize reserve divisions in line with the Soviet model, which he allegedly intended to use for reducing the size of the army and, ultimately, for replacing the militia. His aim was to decrease defence spending by relying on a trained reserve and not only on large forces-in-being.[81] By establishing a formal reserve system and merging it with the militia, the Military Service Law in effect adopted Peng's policy, and laid the groundwork for an extensive reduction of the standing army.

Just how extensive was revealed by Hu Yaobang, secretary-general of the Chinese Communist Party, during a visit to New Zealand in April 1985. Responding to a question about China's military role in the South Pacific, Hu said that China would cut one million troops from the army in the course of 1985 and 1986.[82] Whether the revelation was planned in advance or came spontaneously when an opportunity arose, it turned the spotlight on changes that were obviously in the throes of intensive implementation.

These changes were given the highest seal of approval at an unusual meeting of the Central Military Commission, held between 23 May and 6 June 1985. The importance of the meeting was reflected in its extraordinary length and in the exceptional turnout of almost the entire Politburo. The meeting reportedly 'discussed the Chinese Government's strategic policy decision to reduce the Armed Forces by one million . . . during the next two years'.[83] In his speech, Hu Yaobang again affirmed that national defence must be subordinate to economic development and praised veteran officers 'for putting the general interest first' and 'submitting themselves to the needs of the overall situation'. Deng Xiaoping highlighted the 'identical views and unanimity' that had been reached on the reorganization plans, and said this showed officers were 'able to view an issue by taking the interests of the whole into account', a phrase that was repeated by Yang Shangkun.[84] Such protestations usually suggest the existence of sentiments diametrically different from those being praised. This is hardly remarkable, since the meeting of the Central Military Commission finally dashed whatever hopes many senior commanders may still have had about retaining their positions – especially because it was reiterated that following strength reduction a large number of officers would be retired, and because the leadership organs of several military regions were readjusted at the meeting.[85] What is remarkable is the firm resolve of the Deng leadership to push through radical reforms despite the difficulties.

This resolve was underlined by an army paper editorial on the meeting. Terming it 'epoch-making' the paper said that the meeting was convened 'amid the floodtide of reform', without which it would be impossible to improve combat capability. The achievements of the meeting, the editorial concluded, 'will have a broad and far-reaching impact' on building a modern army, an impact which will become stronger over the years.[86] The principle guiding the reforms associated with troop reduction, said Yang Shangkun in another commentary, was to substitute quality for quantity.[87]

One striking example of the Chinese leadership's determination to implement this principle is the plan to reduce the size of the Air Force by about 30 per cent. The plan, as announced in July 1985, is to dismiss 120,000 out of the more than 400,000 personnel.[88] This awesome undertaking was assigned to the newly appointed commander, Wang Hai, who replaced Zhang Tingfa. The first commander with a combat record, Wang had served for three years as deputy commander before taking over the top post.[89]

The aim of the massive reduction, Wang said, was to build the air force into 'a more competent and efficient military power'. The reduction would facilitate saving limited finances for the development of modern technology. It would also improve training conditions for pilots by making available more facilities and flying time. In modern warfare, Wang emphasized, 'combat capability hinged on the quality rather than quantity of the rank-and-file'.[90]

Streamlining Structures and Styles

Raising quality and reducing quantity is also the essence of other organizational reforms in the PLA. As the size of the army grew, its organizational structure became cumbersome, top-heavy, inefficient and wasteful. The efforts to eliminate these defects went hand in hand with the attempts to reduce the size of the armed forces. At the 1975 enlarged session of the Military Affairs Commission Deng Xiaoping said that 'our present meeting will decide on a new size and organizational structure for the army, with a view to making them less unwieldy . . . . If we can do away with bloating, streamline the army establishment and restructure it as a whole, we will pave the way for the proper solution of other problems.'[91] Two years later, Deng returned to the problem, complaining that a new structure for the army had not yet been created. 'We have failed', he said, 'to make it sufficiently clear that there must be streamlining and no overstaffing'. Some units were not adequately manned while others were overstaffed. 'It has become the fashion to set up new offices and sign up more personnel whenever there is a problem to be solved.' The reform, Deng warned, will not be short-term: 'If we now cut back in accordance with the newly determined size and structure of the army, will we still have more streamlining to do in the future? Yes, we will.' The target of this streamlining will be mainly high-level leading organs, from the General Staff to the provinces.[92]

Deng's pep talks did not produce progress. Speaking to the Standing Committee of the Military Affairs Commission in 1980, Deng said that 'in the last few years, army organizations at various levels have again been expanded, leading to a revival of bureaucracy'.[93] He again called for measures 'to solve such problems as organizational overlapping and overstaffing with the consequent inefficiency of command at various levels'.[94] The main purpose of these measures, he said, was to 'reduce the number of unnecessary non-combatants and of personnel in leading and commanding organs – mainly cadres'.[95] He then gave an example. Some officers suggested, Deng said, that in a regiment, in addition to the commander and political commissar, two deputy commanders and one deputy political commissar were enough, which meant that in practice the number of deputy commanders and deputy political commissars was higher. 'This is a good idea,' Deng agreed. 'It should be applied to the divisions as well. The present leading bodies are really too big.'[96] To make them smaller, the leadership coined the slogan 'reducing the swelling, paring the fat, and simplifying the administrative structure', which was supposed to inspire an ongoing campaign to streamline structures. One result was the abolition of the PLA Engineering Corps, the incorporation of the Railway Corps into the Railway Ministry, the merging of some local troops with the Ministry of Public Security, and the trimming of head-quarters staff.[97] But the campaign really got under way in the spring of 1985 in conjunction with the accelerated drive to reduce troop numbers.

Addressing a forum of the National Defence, Science, Technology and Industry Commission in April 1985, Defence Minister Zhang Aiping said that 'streamlining and reorganization is, currently, the biggest reform in the army and involves both local and large areas'.[98] A few days later the army paper reported that a number of leading PLA organs had dispatched work groups to grass-roots PLA units 'to ensure smooth progress of the work of structural reform and the streamlining of army organizations and simpli-fication of the administration'.[99] In the air force, for example, the campaign cut a wide swathe, involving personnel arrangements, stocktaking and transfer of equipment, installations and expenditure.[100] That the movement was making an impact, painful to many officers as it turned out, was illustrated by the fact that the Air Force Party Committee found it necessary to issue a list of 'eight prohibitions' which had to be observed at all levels. According to the list, it was prohibited to do the following: to pursue the private interests of cliques and individuals; to make illegal transfers and arrange posts for relatives or to interfere with their employment by an organization; to launch sudden drives to promote people, to recruit Party members or to make arrangements for family dependents to accompany the units; to use surplus funds and income not covered by the budget to give dinners, present gifts, indulge in lavish eating and drinking, and squander money; to launch sudden drives to parcel out public funds and property; arbitrarily to dispose of equipment at low prices;

forcibly to take possession of barracks and furniture; privately to remove or pass on documents, files and data.[101]

Structural reform was also a subject of discussion and decisions at the important mid-1985 meeting of the Central Military Commission, which approved the reduction of troops. The meeting altered the structure of military regions – the highest level of command and organization below the PLA's central organs – and made changes in their commanding personnel.[102] The reshuffle, as subsequently reported, was extensive. The number of military regions was cut from eleven to seven by merging the Wuhan Military Region with Jinan, Lanzhou with Urumchi, Chengdu with Kunming, and Fuzhou with Nanjing. Four of the seven commanders were new appointees, a ratio that was presumably retained, if not increased, in the commanding organs of the regions.[103] One casualty was the veteran leader Li Desheng, who had served as commander of the Shenyang Military Region for twelve years. A powerful military figure, Li had close ties with Maoist radicals, but despite this was widely considered to be untouchable because of his seniority and political connections. As it turned out, the Deng leadership thought otherwise, although it took its time before removing Li, presumably for the same reasons. Later in the year, as noted, Li was appointed political commissar of the National Defence University.

More extensive reforms were promised by Yang Shangkun in July 1985. These, he said, would range from readjustments involving military regions and regrouping of units to the incorporation of the people's armed police into local establishments and the transfer of frontier units to public security departments. The readjustment would focus in particular on organs directly under the General Departments of the PLA; the Commission of Science, Technology and Industry for National Defence; the military regions; and various arms and services. The number of levels would be reduced, organizations would be eliminated or merged, and the positions of some units would be downgraded. Outdated equipment would be phased out and some military installations would be closed down. The make-up of units would be adjusted to strengthen combined arms units. Leading organs, Yang said, had already reduced the number of deputy positions, appointed no advisers and provided officers strictly according to needs of units.[104] In short, structural reform involved 'the amalgamation, disbanding, downgrading and transformation of military units, the changing of leading cadres and the transfer of personnel'.[105]

The changes did not bypass the organs at the top of the PLA's command hierarchy – the General Staff Department, the General Political Department and the General Logistics Department – which were likewise streamlined and trimmed. As a result, it was reported, the work of the Departments became more practical, efficient and smooth. At the same time, the authority of the General Staff was centralized, because the headquarters of the specialized forces – such as artillery, armour and engineers – which had been separate arms, were transformed into administrative units of the General Staff Department.[106] Another change was the transformation of the essentially infantry field armies into group armies, which consist of various arms and services, and which are more suitable to the needs of modern warfare.[107]

A central object of structural reform and streamlining has been the logistics system. First, because the Chinese belatedly discovered, at least in public statements, that a modern support system is an integral part of a modern army. Speaking to an all-army logistics conference in 1982, Defence Minister Zhang Aiping noted that 'food and fodder have gone before troops and horses since ancient times. This always applies to the army no matter how developed its equipment is'.[108] The conference concluded that 'logistic work is a science. Modern warfare has presented increasingly higher demands for logistic work .... Under certain circumstances in a war it can even determine victory or defeat.'[109] Another reason is that 'since logistics work involves army building and every aspect of army life, as well as the country's economic construction',[110] it is by its very nature prone to waste and inefficiency. It is against these tendencies that reforms in the support services have been directed. In the words of Hong Xuezhi, director of the General Logistics Department, speaking in 1982:

> In the past two years, while allotting the budget, we have carefully and rationally planned our projects ... and eliminated ... non-essential projects .... Regarding management, we have mobilized the entire armed forces to make careful calculations and strict budgeting, practise economy, check warehouses and storage rooms to tap potential ... cut non-productive expenses, strictly follow the standardization system and strive to do more jobs properly and economically.[111]

By 1984, 'after many years' efforts', the PLA had 'preliminarily established a comprehensive logistics support system' consisting of networks which covered supply of materials, equipment repair, communications and transport, medicine and health, and military goods production. Logistics-support equipment and techniques had also been improved.[112] Further progress was noted by Hong Xuezhi, director of the PLA's General Logistics Department, in February 1986. Speaking to a reporter, Hong said that a three-level – general headquarters, military regions and group armies – logistics and administrative system had been set up which met all the requirements of the armed forces and was suitable for joint operations. Advanced technology, such as computers, was widely applied to logistics work. In future, 'our main efforts will be placed on establishing a more efficient and rational ... organizational system, building systematized logistics bases, and providing facilities so that we can readily deal with all possible emergencies'. The purpose is to ensure 'systematic, rapid and uninterrupted supplies'.[113] In 1985 it was reported that the entire logistics system, from the headquarters to units such as factories, research institutions, colleges and hospitals, was slated to be cut by half, in line with the leadership's decision to streamline the armed forces.[114]

The efforts to effect savings were not limited to the logistics services. At the beginning of 1982, the Military Affairs Commission issued a directive calling on the entire army to 'cut down military spending, strengthen economic management, simplify administration and practise economy'. It said that 'particular attention should be paid to conserving oil, electricity, coal . . . water and . . . energy . . . '. It also said that troop training should be carried out thriftily and that financial discipline should be upheld.[115] Consequently, several steps were taken. PLA units diversified agricultural and sideline undertakings to broaden sources of income.[116] Training methods were reformed and simulation used extensively to reduce expenses.[117] Expenditure on banquets, gifts and excessive consumption was cut down.[118] All PLA units were subjected to a 'thorough and general financial audit' in order 'to improve financial management' and to ensure that 'defence expenditures fully produce economic results . . . '.[119]

A new efficiency measure is the introduction of enterprise-type management into the production and service units of the PLA. A directive issued by the General Political Department in 1984 ordered that 'all units that can be managed as enterprises be changed into enterprises'. The Department, it was reported, had established a 'general service company' consisting of companies dealing with construction, coal, medical equipment, farming, animal husbandry and fishery production. A service company responsible for catering and boarding was slated to be set up. These companies, it was emphasized, would not receive money from the defence budget but would be run on a profit-and-loss basis.[120]

Making the PLA function better also requires fundamental reforms in the 'work style' of officers – their leadership practices and personal conduct. A well-justified source of pride to the Red Army leadership during the long struggle for power, the 'work style' of commanding personnel began to deteriorate with the emergence of military professionalism and the consequent erosion of revolutionary values and dynamism. In the late 1950s and early 1960s, the Maoist leadership reacted with extreme measures which damaged professional competence but held these tendencies in check.[121] During the Cultural Revolution, the dam burst. Catapulted to positions of authority, exposed to factional struggles and unrestrained because norms had collapsed, many officers were quickly corrupted by their new power and privileges.

A frank description of this deterioration was provided by Deng Xiaoping in his 1975 speech to the Military Affairs Commission. Deng's personal and detailed concern with the problem [122] – to which he devoted the first half of his speech – is a clear indication of its seriousness. This is hardly surprising, since the faults listed by Deng obviously cannot be tolerated if the PLA is to become an effective armed force.

Topping the list was factionalism. Always a problem in an army formed by the blending of disparate units, this problem, Deng said, had been overcome previously by rectification campaigns. 'Why, then, should we raise it now? Because this problem has reappeared' in the course of the Cultural Revolution. 'Many persons became involved in factional activities, some siding with one faction, some with another. Since the army people had great authority, they became the real power behind the different factions . . . . Later they brought the same attitudes into the army . . . and this damaged unity within the army.' The effects were deleterious. Officers practised favouritism, did not co-operate with those who differed with them, and engineered transfers of colleagues who held different views.

No less serious was lax organizational discipline. 'The army used to have a very strong sense of organizational discipline, and orders were carried out without hesitation. But things are different now. Sometimes, not only individuals but even whole units act in defiance of orders.' Deng related this phenomenon to factionalism. 'Those who disobey orders have the interests of their own factions in mind . . . . They seek fame, gain and position, and when they fail to secure them, they take offence and even refuse to obey orders of transfer.'

Arrogance was another by-product of the Cultural Revolution. Wielding great power, some officers became conceited and overbearing, inclined to throwing their weight around. 'At present there is not sufficient unity inside the army itself, between the army and the government and between the army and the people.'

Furthermore, 'a bourgeois way of life' had replaced the tradition of hard work and plain living. 'Examples of this abound . . . . Some seek ease and comfort, higher salaries, more housing space and indeed top conditions in every respect. Some even treat public property as their own . . . entertain guests with lavish dinners and give them generous gifts, or erect buildings, halls and guesthouses that are not needed.' In their pursuit of luxuries, some army units confiscate things from civilians or buy them at reduced prices. Some army farms and enterprises spend their profits carelessly.

Finally, there was bureaucratism. 'Some high-ranking cadres, their revolutionary will failing in their later years, seek their own self-interest instead of maintaining their revolutionary integrity.' Officers with minor ailments request benefits as if they were seriously ill 'or they moan and groan

142

without being ill at all'. They are not conscientious in their work and do not put in any effort. They do nothing themselves and do not use their minds. 'They rely on their secretaries to do everything and even ask others to write a five-minute speech for them – and then they sometimes read it wrong.'

The elimination of these flaws has been high on the leadership's agenda. 'It is imperative', wrote Yang Shangkun in *Hongqi* in 1982, 'to improve work style in order to achieve the goal of improving work efficiency and command capability.'[123] This meant breaking with past patterns of administration, such as minute definition of duties, unclear division of labour, multiple command levels, shifting of responsibility, long delays in making decisions and passing the buck to higher levels.[124] It has also meant breaking with widely prevalent practices of conspicuous consumption and financial corruption.[125] To achieve this, the leadership has launched various campaigns, and the media have frequently exhorted officers to change their ways and highlighted their supposed successes. For example, an article in the army paper discovered the virtues for high-ranking officers of hard work and plain living, which it described with the enthusiasm of a convert.[126] The Party committee of a PLA division in Nanking was commended for displaying discipline, honesty and modesty.[127] Discipline inspection committees have been established in all major units of the PLA and periodic all-army conferences have been convened to review their work. At the 1985 conference, these committees were told to strengthen supervision in matters such as implementation of orders, personnel assignments, handling of finances and material resources, and the activities of commanding officers.[128]

It is clear that the leadership has strenuously tried to correct the 'work style' of officers. Less clear is the extent of its success. While progress has doubtless been made, many reports have a propagandistic rather than realistic ring. An uncertain point is how far it is possible to change veteran officers, used to power and privileges and set in their ways. Given this, the Deng leadership seems to be banking not so much on altering the habits of these officers as on getting rid of them. This makes structural reforms and streamlining all the more significant.

Training for Modern War

The most concentrated expression of the leadership's resolve to modernize the army is surely to be found in the new training programmes. 'The key to the modernization of our Army', declared Yang Shangkun, 'lies in training able troops as without them there will be no modernization'.[129] If the PLA's overriding mission in peacetime is to increase its capacity to make war – a principle which the post-Mao leadership accepts without reservation –

training is the main means to this end. The Chinese media constantly reiterate the truism that 'only through much training and much sweating in peacetime will it be possible to suffer less and spill less blood in wartime'.[130] It follows naturally that 'combat readiness is the most fundamental guiding thought in military training'.[131]

This had not been the case for many years. In the Maoist period 'Lin Biao and the "gang of four" equated military training with the purely military view . . . and slapped on political labels and wielded a big stick' against those who wanted to engage in military training.[132] The results were disastrous: 'military training was not strict, or at times . . . no training at all was given. Some soldiers had been in the armed forces for several years without ever touching a rifle, and some cadres could not lead troops. The combat capabilities of the whole armed forces declined markedly.'[133] The post-Mao leadership, therefore, had to adopt an entirely new approach to training which, in the words of a senior officer, includes 'a reform of everything that is not suitable for warfare under modern conditions and a restoration . . . of those ways . . . that practice has proven to be good'.[134]

The chief change has been from training infantry units to training armoured formations, and from single-service exercises to combined-arms manoeuvres.[135] In 1978, for example, the PLA Lanzhou units held their first large-scale exercise in ten years. Since then, such exercises have become the order of the day.[136] In the autumn of 1981 the PLA held a huge combined-services exercise, the largest in its history. A variety of units took part: tanks, motorized infantry, paratroops, artillery, as well as surface-to-air, anti-tank, engineer, logistic and electronic warfare units, aircraft and helicopters.[137] Speaking to the participating troops, Deng Xiaoping said that 'these exercises have given us an opportunity to assess our achievements in building modern, regularized armed forces, and have simulated modern warfare fairly well. They represent part of our effort to explore combined operations by the various services and arms under modern conditions . . . . This will give a great impetus to our efforts to build up the armed forces.'[138] Less than a year later, another large-scale exercise took place in Ningxia, which deployed various arms and included the simulated use of tactical nuclear weapons.[139] In 1982, the number of combined arms manoeuvres reportedly set a record in the PLA's history.[140] The air force and the navy, including marines, held exercises of their own.[141]

In line with the strategy of 'active defence', joint-services exercises were conducted against invading tanks, aircraft and paratroops, and were designed to improve the abilities of Chinese officers to command and co-ordinate complex operations under modern combat conditions.[142] Battlefield training has not been the only means to this end. In 1983, it was reported, for example, that for the past four years the general staff had been bringing together middle- and high-ranking officers for lectures on military science and modern war to speed up the emergence of a new generation of combat commanders. The PLA's proudest product among this generation is Li Lianghui, commander of the PLA Airborne Force, who at age forty-three in 1983 commanded a massive airborne tactical exercise involving hundreds of planes, several thousand soldiers and numerous types of weapon.[143]

High technology has been incorporated into the command systems of combined forces to ease control and co-ordination. For example, an anti-airborne command exercise conducted by a corps under the Jinan Military Region in 1984 used computers and television to monitor and manage the operation.[144] In the Fuzhou Military Region, advanced computers in the command post aided in the direction of manoeuvres.[145]

High technology has also been used to develop training programmes, particularly in producing laser and electronic simulators.[146] The Military Training Equipment Institute of the Shenyang Military Region developed a laser simulator for tactical exercises. The simulator, it was reported, replaces live ammunition with lasers, emits smoke and sounds, and immobilizes weapons which are hit. This not only creates more realistic combat conditions, but also saves ammunition and reduces wear and tear on weapons. In the opinion of experts, this equipment has opened new vistas for the training of the armed forces.[147] Advanced electronic technology has likewise been used by the navy in simulated warship control, in the flight simulator produced by the air force, and in the command simulator for ground artillery made by artillery troops.[148] In October 1985, the Chinese organized a military exercise which was attended by foreign military attachés and in which laser and electronic simulation devices were used.[149]

While introducing technology, the leadership has at the same time re-emphasized the traditional virtues of discipline and decorum. Every army has to tighten discipline periodically, but in the PLA elementary concepts of conduct had to be reinculcated and institutionalized because of the disruptions caused by radical Maoists. In an attempt to drive a wedge between upper and lower ranks, the Maoists had propagated notions such as that 'to observe discipline was to practice slavishness', that 'rules and regulations were restrictions', and that 'only attacking the leadership was allowed'. The credo of the 'gang of four', according to the post-Mao leaders, was that 'going against the tide' was justified and that 'those at a lower level can oppose those at the next higher level . . . '.[150] Allowing for the exaggerations inherent in such formulations, they nevertheless provide a general picture of the situation that had prevailed at the height of radical influence.

To eliminate this influence and upgrade standards of behaviour, the Deng leadership issued 'regulations concerning discipline'.[151] In its comment, the army paper stressed that 'army discipline, appearance and bearing are symbols of the army's fighting capacity'. It rejected the views of 'some people' who maintain that these features are of 'little significance' and do not affect fighting capacity. 'This attitude', said the paper, 'is wrong' because 'an army that is sloppy, undisciplined and unorganized in peacetime can hardly pass the stiffest test when fighting'.[152] To strengthen the execution of orders, in 1981 the Standing Committee of the National People's Congress adopted provisional regulations on punishing servicemen who commit offences in the line of duty.[153] The day-to-day enforcement of discipline in army units at all levels is the task of discipline inspection committees. These committees, said Yang Shangkun in 1983,'have done a great deal of work' but 'their continuous efforts are still needed'.[154]

These efforts have also been aimed at making the army look better. For example, one morning in 1983 the commander, political commissar and leading officers of the Xizang Military District descended on the main streets of Lhasa to inspect the behaviour of military drivers and off-duty soldiers.[155] In Shaanxi, high-ranking officers spread out through the streets of Xi'an to check on military personnel after citizens had complained to the commander about the conduct and appearance of soldiers who, it was alleged, bared their chests, wore their hats at an angle, dangled cigarettes from their mouths and grew beards and long hair, while female soldiers wore jewellery.[156] In the navy, the appearance of ports, ships and soldiers was improved after high-ranking officers made inspections.[157] Air force units in Shanghai, Tientsin and Canton took similar steps.[158]

The leadership has also sought to strengthen discipline and decorum by making the soldiers proud of serving in the PLA and tightening their commitment to it. One means has been the institution of parades.[159] Another has been the introduction of oath-taking ceremonies upon enlistment.[160] A third has been the issuance of new uniforms as of May 1985. Smarter and more attractive than the simple ill-fitting uniforms worn by officers and men for years, the new uniforms, according to the army paper, are 'beneficial for strengthening the tight-knit organization, unified command and tidy military appearance' of the armed forces and will boost the soldiers' 'sense of honour and pride'.[161]

The most important measure for regularizing all aspects of troop activity in the period of modernization has been the promulgation in 1984 by the Central Military Commission of internal service regulations. An order signed by Deng Xiaoping said that the new regulations would 'provide the basis for the whole Army to establish and maintain sound internal and external relations and a regular interior service system, perform its duties well, conduct management effectively and foster a fine work style'. The regulations spell out the duties and rights of servicemen pertaining to discipline, training, study, rest and physical appearance as well as procedures for daily routine and combat readiness.[162]

An additional aspect of troop training, peculiar to the PLA, has been the fostering of 'dual-purpose personnel'. This aspect of training follows Deng Xiaoping's instruction that 'after receiving training, our cadres and soldiers should not only be able to fight in a war, but should also be able to conduct socialist construction'.[163] Its aim is to provide soldiers with skills in the course of their military training which can be used in civilian life after their release. A unit of the Nanjing PLA units, for example, ran vocational courses from the end of 1980 in subjects such as photography, arts and crafts, radio operations, gardening, sewing and cooking. Some 90 per cent of the soldiers attended these classes.[164] A regiment in Chengdu provided courses in writing techniques, medicine, farm machinery, veterinary medicine, accounting and plant cultivation.[165] Many officers were initially worried that dual-purpose training would adversely affect military training, but eventually they reportedly realized that this type of training, if properly carried out, could actually promote military training. This was because the new knowledge acquired by the soldiers was useful in solving some military problems, and because the enthusiasm of the troops for training increased.[166]

An Assessment

That Deng Xiaoping and his colleagues are determined radically to reshape the institutional structures and operational procedures of the PLA is hardly in doubt. That they have initiated wide-ranging reforms to achieve this objective is hardly in doubt either. This still leaves open the question of how effective the reforms have been.

The difficulties in attempting an answer are obvious, particularly since it is impossible to observe the Chinese military establishment at first hand. To be sure, foreign military delegations and reporters occasionally visit Chinese military units and installations. However, their reports have to be treated with some scepticism, because such visits are obviously stage-managed, and there is no way of knowing to what extent their observations of select outfits are representative of the entire army. In the end, an assessment of the reforms has to rely on reports made public by the Chinese.

These reports seem to be realistic and fairly balanced. While the Chinese have been expansive in playing up achievements, they have also been frank in pointing out difficulties. While they have described these achievements in glowing terms, they have not made unrealistic or absurd claims. And while they have highlighted the progress made by the reforms, they caution that this is only a beginning. There is no reason to dispute this balance sheet.

An assessment of the reforms also has to take into account the time lag between initiation and impact. Some reforms – such as the replacement of senior veterans with younger and more professionally oriented officers – have doubtless already changed the modes of command and management in the PLA. Other reforms – such as the training of a new generation of officers and their integration into operational units – will clearly take considerably longer. The same holds true of the whole reform process.

A curious characteristic of this process is that the Chinese hail as progress the introduction of basic features which are commonplace in modern armies. This, however, is hardly a reason for derision. After years of stagnation and ossification, the modernization of the PLA has to start virtually from scratch. Rudimentary and seemingly banal reforms are the essential first step.

7

Civil–Military Relations: Deng in Command

The post-Mao modernization of the PLA has been paralleled by a transformation of its political role and relations with the Party. The two processes have been inseparable. Without the political transformation, the military reforms initiated by the Deng leadership could not have been carried out effectively. The reason is plain: prolonged involvement in politics had made the PLA utterly unfit for the imperatives of modernization.

Military intervention in the struggles of the Cultural Revolution had turned the PLA into a pivotal political force at the expense of professional competence. Its leaders acquired a powerful voice in policy-making councils, and its officers and men assumed wide-ranging political and administrative responsibilities throughout the country. As a result, the PLA became far removed from military concerns. It also became, in practice if not in theory, largely autonomous from civilian control.

After the storm of the Cultural Revolution subsided, China's civilian leaders tried to retrieve the political power that they had unwittingly given the PLA. However, the military resisted, and the ensuing civil–military conflict reached a climax in the bizarre Lin Biao affair – the alleged attempt by an increasingly beleaguered defence minister and his colleagues to assassinate Mao and seize power. Following the downfall of the Lin Biao group, the PLA disengaged from the political arena, but only to a limited extent. When the Maoist era ended, the military was still a key factor in Chinese politics. This was demonstrated by its central role in the succession struggle and in propping up the new regime. After Deng Xiaoping became China's paramount power-holder, one of his prime aims was to complete the withdrawal of the PLA from politics and to reassert political control over it.

The attainment of this aim has been essential not only for military modernization, but for carrying out Deng's reform programme in all other

149

areas as well. The political involvement which had made the PLA unfit for modernization had also made it singularly fit for intervening in national affairs. And in an era of radical reforms and coalition politics, such intervention can be crucial. This is because assertive military leaders, deeply involved in politics and dissatisfied with the policies of the Party leadership, can, in co-operation with dissident groups in the Party, try to impede the implementation of these policies. This is what happened in China in the early 1980s, and this is a situation that Deng has sought to avert.

Both military and political considerations have, therefore, impelled Deng to redress the balance in civil–military relations that had been completely upset by the far-reaching effects of military intervention in politics. To this end, he has carried out major changes in the functions, personnel and political work of the PLA. An examination of these changes and the consequent state of civil–military relations is the subject of this chapter.

Back to the Barracks

Although the withdrawal of the PLA from politics had made substantial headway by the late 1970s, when Deng came to power the military still played a prominent role at all levels of the Chinese power structure. This was because the processes essential for the completion of the withdrawal – the consolidation of a strong political leadership, the reconstruction of civil organizations and the return of the PLA to professional pursuits – had not yet made adequate progress. The completion of these parallel processes occurred only after Deng's ascent to the dominant leadership position.

Although Deng needed the support of the military for his policies, his personal prestige, political experience and power bases throughout the ruling structure did not make him critically dependent on this support. These assets were reinforced by Deng's retention of the top posts in the military hierarchy, even though he refrained from assuming similar posts in the Party or government. Until 1980 Deng served as the PLA's chief of staff and, more importantly, he has remained chairman of the Party's Military Affairs Committee and, concurrently since 1982, chairman of the state Central Military Council. Deng has thus been in a position to exert close control over the military establishment. After Deng's return to rule, moreover, the reconstruction of Party and administrative organs, which had proceeded at a slow pace for a decade, was stepped up in conjunction with the introduction of reforms in all sectors of society and the reversal to bureaucratic modes of operation. As a result, these organs regained the capacity to assume the civil functions still performed by the PLA. Finally, under Deng's leadership, the concentration on modernization in the PLA has returned it to an exclusive preoccupation with professional tasks, which by their nature are incompatible with activities outside the military sphere.

The convergence of these processes laid the groundwork for the disengagement of the PLA from politics. The disengagement, however, has not been uniform in speed and scope at all levels of the PLA's involvement. At the basic and provincial levels, the relinquishment of the PLA's political functions proceeded at a faster pace than the reduction of its power in the central policy-making organs. In any event, by the end of 1985 the role of the PLA at all levels had been changed radically.

The extent of the change at the grass-roots level is the most difficult to ascertain, since there is no way of determining how far the PLA was still involved in non-military affairs in the late 1970s. Judging by the Chinese media, such involvement was minimal, since it was hardly mentioned in press and radio reports. However, both the civilian and military leaders were interested in downplaying the presence of the PLA outside the military sector: the civilians in order to underline the reassertion of Party control over the PLA; and the military in order to underpin its demands for resources to bolster military preparedness.

In this connection, it is relevant to note that in the early 1970s the Chinese media also downplayed the preoccupation of the PLA with non-military functions, but the actual situation turned out to be quite different. Just how different was described by Doak Barnett, a seasoned and astute observer of the Chinese political scene:

> In eight major cities – and nearby rural areas – that I visited in late 1972 and early 1973, it was apparent that despite the recent reduction in the PLA's political roles military men still permeated much of civilian society in China (at least in key urban areas) and continued to occupy very influential positions. In every factory and university, as well as every province and municipality that I visited active military men still made up a significant portion of the membership of both the Party Committees and Revolutionary Committees.[1]

Barnett goes on to note that although for some time the Chinese media had not mentioned the Military Control Committees set up during the Cultural Revolution as a vehicle for direct military rule, he found that in Shanghai the Military Control Commission still operated. Presumably, similar commissions operated in other places as well.[2] Thus, the widely prevalent assumption that the Military Control Commissions had been disbanded after the turmoil of the Cultural Revolution had subsided turned out to be false. The extent of the military's pull-out from civilian sectors had also been underestimated. According to Barnett:

> In all but one city that I visited, the military still exercised direct control over the police, and in Shanghai the army was still directly involved in some economic fields as well.

In every city and suburban area that I visited, moreover, ordinary rank-and-file soldiers, sailors, and airmen were ubiquitous. We were rarely, in fact, out of sight of military personnel. They were in uniform, but most were unarmed and remarkably few seemed to be engaged in military activity.[3]

There is no doubt that by the late 1970s the PLA's intervention in society had been substantially reduced in comparison with the situation described by Barnett. However, as already noted, the processes that were essential for the full-scale return of the army to the barracks were just beginning to materialize. Therefore, although the profile of the PLA in society had been greatly lowered, its presence was presumably still substantial.

One telling indication of this presence was the resentment it aroused among the population. As Yu Qiuli, director of the PLA's General Political Department, said in 1983: 'In the past, the relations between the Army and the government and between the Army and the people were always good. During the ten years of civil disorder, these relations were undermined.'[4] This happened because military men abused the political power which they had acquired. And abuses were apparently acute and widespread. They ranged from high-handed treatment of civilians and their property, through conspicuous consumption and the flaunting of special privileges, to outright corruption.[5] One channel for the expression of popular resentment against the military elite was the publication of poems which gave vent to rage and bitterness the likes of which had not been seen in China since the establishment of the Communist regime. One poem contained these lines: 'The magnificent medals are studded with decorative patterns, which are the bloodstains of the soldiers . . . . Generals wear medals . . . . The bloodstained bones of soldiers rot in the soil and have long since been forgotten.'[6] Another poem assailed a general who had been a revolutionary hero, but had become a member of a selfish and privileged ruling class that flourished while the masses suffered.[7] Such poems could hardly have been published without the tacit support of Party officials. Although they were widely discussed and criticized,[8] as far as is known no action was taken against the poets or the journals that published them. These poems were doubtless only one extreme manifestation of sentiments that were widespread throughout society,[9] and were a direct offshoot of military intervention in civilian affairs. The existence of such sentiments pointed to the continued presence of the PLA in society and the consequent frictions it aroused, especially due to the arrogant behaviour of high-ranking officers. From the vantage point of the Deng leadership, this situation added urgency to its effort to return the army to the barracks.

This effort was carried out in several ways. One was to relieve the PLA of the non-military functions that it was still performing in society. The most visible and extensive function apparently related to public security. Because of its pivotal importance, this function both turned the public spotlight on the military and provided it with the capacity to meddle in the daily life of the population. One indication of this capacity was a report that between the beginning of 1979 and mid-1981, the PLA had dispatched more than 160,000 officers and men to help localities in maintaining social order.[10]

In 1983 the regime began to transfer public security functions from the PLA to the public security organs. In January it was reported that following a joint decision by the Party's Central Committee, the State Council and the Military Affairs Committee, the Beijing Garrison Command handed over the maintenance of internal security in the capital to the Public Security Bureau, which operates under the civilian Ministry of Public Security.[11] Similar transfers presumably took place in other cities. A very significant step was taken in April with the formal establishment of the People's Armed Police as an arm of the Ministry of Public Security.[12] This organization had dis-integrated during the Cultural Revolution as a result of Red Guard onslaughts on the Party and its affiliated organs. The functions of the People's Armed Police devolved to the PLA, which became the chief guardian of social order and public security. After the Cultural Revolution, efforts were made to rebuild the Armed Police, but it was not revived until the late 1970s.[13]

According to its political commissar, the Armed police and the PLA are 'both armed forces of the state but they have a division of labour. The PLA is responsible for the exterior. The Armed Police is responsible for internal security.'[14] To carry out this responsibility, by 1985 the Armed Police had established 29 divisions, 564 regiments and 1,029 battalions. It had also set up three academies for basic-level officers, as well as a naval academy and medical school.[15] The formidable size of this organization provides a striking illustration of the extent to which the PLA must have been absorbed in civil affairs after it had taken on internal security duties. The transfer of these duties to the Armed Police was, therefore, a major move towards the withdrawal of the PLA from non-military matters at the basic levels of society.

The Deng leadership also moved to relieve the PLA of functions which, though devoid of direct political significance, greatly enhanced the presence of the military in the civilian sector and added to its power. A conspicuous function of this type was the general-purpose construction work carried out by the PLA's railway engineers. Active since the establishment of the regime, the PLA's Railway Engineer Corps had played a major role in building the nation's transportation system. In July 1981 it was reported that since the Third Plenum of December 1978 alone, the Corps had constructed more than 1,000 kilometres of railways along with 7,900 metres of tunnels and 8,300 metres of bridges. The railways built by the military accounted for about 43 per cent of China's new lines.[16] In January 1984 the PLA Railway Corps was abolished as a military unit and was transferred to the Ministry of Railways.[17]

The withdrawal of the PLA from non-military functions has gone hand in hand with a redefinition of its role in society. The aim has been to restore the PLA to its traditional role of assisting the population in times of need rather than ruling over it. The Chinese media have assiduously cultivated this image by publishing numerous reports about troops enthusiastically performing old-fashioned good deeds, such as relief work, agricultural production, aiding industry and promoting public health.[18] In a marked reversal of roles, the PLA was urged by Deng himself to release resources for civilian use to advance national construction.[19] Responding to this call, the PLA reportedly vacated land and barracks to facilitate the construction of civilian facilities and opened military installations for civilian use.[20] According to a March 1985 report by Yang Dezhi, chief of the General Staff, the PLA had made available fifty-nine airfields and several ports and piers for civilian or joint military–civilian use. It also turned over thirty-nine military installations, many army camps and large amounts of land for purposes of civilian construction.[21]

The main manifestation of the PLA's new role in society has been its contribution to the construction of so-called 'civilized villages', 'civilized towns' and 'civilized units'. Initiated in 1981, these activities have been described as a 'great undertaking' in which large numbers of soldiers were 'mobilized to help masses of people, under the leadership of local party committees and governments, build the countryside and cities where they are stationed into a stronghold of socialist spiritual civilization'.[22] What this undertaking meant in practice is not clear at all. Its aim has been vague – 'an effective measure for achieving a radical turn for the better in the general mood of our society'.[23] And its achievements have been no less vague – 'through the activities of developing "civilized villages", the appearance of our villages has become clean and tidy and the hygienic conditions have greatly improved . . . . People pay greater attention to the new morality and customs . . . .'[24] At bottom, the campaign appears to have provided little more than new packaging for the traditional activities of the PLA among the population. It was presumably meant primarily to placate conservative leaders who were dismayed by the erosion of revolutionary values as a result of Deng's reforms. For them the message was that the Deng leadership was determined to preserve these values by promoting 'spiritual civilization', and that the military was in the forefront of this effort both inside and outside the armed forces. But whatever the purpose, the campaign does not appear to have developed much steam and it fizzled out by the middle of the decade.

Although the Chinese media frequently portray the PLA as busily engaged in rendering various kinds of assistance to the population on a very large scale, such a picture can hardly be realistic, for two reasons. First, whatever they may occasionally say, military leaders themselves do not attach much importance to the non-military activities of the PLA. This is most strikingly demonstrated by the fact that these activities are almost never mentioned in major statements on military affairs by PLA commanders or in the press. They are dealt with only in reports specifically devoted to relations between the PLA and the population, and appear to be more ritualistic than realistic. The explanation obviously lies in the total preoccupation of military leaders with improving the professional standards of the PLA, an endeavour which can only be hindered by extensive outside activities. And this leads to the second reason. An army completely absorbed in the full range of military tasks – as the PLA clearly has been from the early 1980s – can simply have very little time and energy for other activities. This does not mean that the PLA has stopped participating in such activities, for it still devotes some effort to this sphere. But the effort can only be sporadic and circumscribed by its main responsibilities. Thus, the role of the PLA at the basic levels of society has been not only redefined but also restricted.

This development has been supported by an assault on the ideological underpinnings of the intervention. The aim has been to destroy the rationale for the initial entry of the PLA into politics and, by extension, for the lingering effects of its intervention. The method has been to discredit the Cultural Revolution, which had spawned the circumstances for the PLA's intervention, and, in particular, the PLA's participation in it. The result has been the reinterpretation of recent history which has completed stripped the Cultural Revolution of any positive aspects, and has stressed only its deleterious impact on the PLA.

It took the Deng leadership some time to come up with this reinterpretation publicly. The reason is obvious. Several high-ranking military leaders, most prominently Ye Jianying, not only survived the storm but were identified with the Maoist leadership to one degree or another. Vast numbers of field officers took an active part in implementing the policy of intervention under the slogan of 'three supports and two militaries' (supporting the Left, industry and agriculture, exercising military control and conducting military and political training). And the PLA as an institution was extensively and almost exclusively engaged in such activities for several years. An unequivocal condemnation of this policy could not but reflect on the personal stature of these leaders and officers, and damage the prestige of the PLA.

Until 1984 the Deng leadership trod delicately with regard to this sensitive issue. Speaking to officers of the PLA's General Political Department in March 1981, Deng steered a middle course:

> We must say two things. First, that at the time it was correct for the army to go to the civilian units and deal with the situation there, which otherwise would have been uncontrollable. So the 'three supports and two militaries' did prove useful. But second, they also did great harm to the army, for in their wake they brought many

155

bad things that greatly detracted from the army's prestige. Among other things they were responsible for much of the factionalism and some 'Left' notions and practices.[25]

The landmark resolution on the history of the Party, adopted at the Sixth Plenary Session of the 11th Central Committee in June 1981, was even more restrained and fuzzy on the issue of intervention:

> The chaos was such that it was necessary to send in the People's Liberation Army to support the Left, the workers and the peasants and to institute military control and military training. It played a positive role in stabilizing the situation, but it also produced some negative consequences.[26]

In subsequent years the issue was not mentioned prominently, but in the spring of 1984 the leadership decided to take it on frontally and forcefully. The immediate reason derived from the realization that, as a deputy commandant of the PLA Political Academy put it, the Cultural Revolution's 'pernicious influence has not been totally eradicated and its legacy still remains'.[27] This was brought home to the leadership after it decided, at the Second Session of the 12th Central Committee in September 1983, to conduct a three-year rectification drive of Party organizations. When the drive began in the PLA, 'the problem of how to deal with issues left over from the "Cultural Revolution" was encountered everywhere . . . the "leftist" influence exposed in many units was . . . relatively deep. . . '. Consequently, in April the Central Military Commission concluded that 'it was essential totally to negate the "Cultural Revolution" . . . '.[28]

For the PLA this meant that first of all it was necessary to 'totally negate' its intervention in politics under the 'three supports and two militaries' policy. The new verdict was unequivocal: intervention had been wrong. The reason was provided succinctly by the *Renmin Ribao*: 'All factions in the "Great Cultural Revolution" were wrong. Hence, "supporting the Left" in carrying out "three-support and two military" work always meant supporting particular factions, and no matter which faction was supported it was wrong.'[29] The verdict was plainly prompted by the pressing need to put an end to continued infighting between factions whose origins lay in the intervention and its aftermath. As the army paper explained it: 'The reason for the existence of factionalism at present is that some comrades still think there were a "correct line" and "correct aspects" in the Cultural Revolution, and that their faction represented the "correct line". . . . Hence they compete with the other faction whenever there is a chance.'[30] This greatly hindered the proper functioning of the PLA because behaviour of officers was conditioned not by professional standards but by factional considerations.[31] 'Therefore, in order to thoroughly eliminate factionalism, it is necessary thoroughly to negate the "Cultural Revolution", just like "removing firewood from under a cauldron".'[32]

The verdict on intervention had additional significance. If it had been wrong for the PLA to intervene from the start, then the political power that it had acquired in the process was acquired in a wrongful manner. The implication was that whatever power the PLA still retained should be given up. Furthermore, if it had been wrong for the PLA to become involved in factional fights, it should not have intervened, even though ordered to do so by the Maoist leadership, because intervention inevitably compelled it to support one faction against another. The message is clear: the PLA should refrain from intervening in political conflicts in the future.

The renewed assault on the Cultural Revolution and the PLA's role in it was thus used by the Deng leadership to rationalize and reinforce the removal of the PLA from the political arena. Such an assault, as already observed, could not but reflect on the personal stature of senior military leaders and many field officers, as well as on the PLA as an institution. That the Deng leadership nonetheless launched it suggests that several developments had preceded the campaign. The first is that the power of senior leaders, primarily Ye Jianying, had dwindled to such an extent, due mainly to old age and infirmity, that they were unable to block the attack even if they had tried. Another is that the turnover of officers in the PLA, during which officers with a background of political involvement were replaced by more professional commanders, had by the mid-1980s proceeded enough so that an attack on the PLA's political intervention was not apt to send shock waves throughout the officer corps. Finally, the prestige of the modernizing PLA is determined by its military achievements in the present rather than by its political past, so that an attack on the past is not considered an intolerable affront.

The final push for the army's withdrawal from politics was provided indirectly by the 1985 decision to reduce the size of the armed forces by 25 per cent over two years. A smaller and leaner army will have even less time and taste for non-military pursuits. In such an army, moreover, there will be a stronger stress on military competence, because of the need to offset the reduced size by higher professional standards. More significantly, the reduction will result in the dismissal of officers who had exercised political functions, and the rise of a new generation whose sole preoccupation is professional.

The PLA in the Regions and at the Centre

At the provincial level, the withdrawal of the military from politics under Deng was more distinct than at the grass-roots. It was at this level that the transformation of the PLA into the dominant political and administrative authority in the provinces had been most cogent. Regional commanders and political commissars became first Party secretaries of most provinces, while military men took the majority of seats in provincial Party secretariats. Thus, when the reconstruction of provincial Party committees that had disintegrated during the violent phases of the Cultural Revolution was completed in August 1971, the PLA emerged as the paramount force. Of the twenty-nine first secretaries, twenty-two were military men. Of the 158 members of provincial level Party committee secretariats, ninety-eight or 62 per cent were military men.[33]

From these powerful posts, military commanders were able to project their influence throughout the vast reaches of the Chinese mainland. From these posts, they could also undergird the political power of military leaders in central policy-making organs. It is hardly surprising, therefore, that these posts became a source of bitter conflict between civilian and military leaders. After the defeat of Lin Biao, the Party leadership made a concerted effort to remove military men from these posts, but results came slowly. This was due chiefly to the reluctance of officers to relinquish their power if they could not ensure that they would be replaced by veteran cadres, capable of keeping disruptive revolutionary elements under control.[34] By the time of Mao's death, eight military men had given up their concurrent positions as provincial Party first secretaries, bringing the number down to fourteen. When Deng Xiaoping rose to the pinnacle of power in late 1978, ten military men still held the top political positions in the provinces.

Since then, all officers have been removed from the posts of provincial first secretaries. Military men have apparently also been removed almost entirely from provincial Party secretariats. For example, when Sichuan province held a Party congress in 1983, only four of the 100 members of the provincial Party committee were identified with the military – a situation that was presumably repeated in other provinces. Moreover, while military men have given up political posts, senior provincial Party functionaries have been given political posts in the PLA as a way of ensuring closer control of the military by the Party. Thus, beginning in 1979, Party committee secretaries at provincial and lower levels have been appointed concurrently as political commissars of parallel military units.[36]

Deng not only relieved military men of all formal political posts, he also acted to break up the informal power that they had accumulated through long tenure in the same area. As early as 1975, in a speech to the Military Affairs Committee, Deng pointed to the dangers inherent in this situation:

> it is not good for cadres to function in one place for too long. Since some cadres have become involved in factionalism in civilian units to the detriment of the work there, it would be best to transfer them elsewhere. Wherever a 'mountain stronghold' exists, we must get rid of it – demolish it by transferring the cadres involved so that they don't gather in one place . . . .To sum up, it is not good to have a cadre work in one place for too long.[37]

Action, however had to be put off until Deng consolidated his power. Then, in a series of shifts unprecedented in scope since the early years of the regime, Deng reshuffled and replaced regional commanders, and reorganized the structure of the military regions. These moves elevated new commanders, with more professional records than their predecessors, into top positions of regions that had been adapted to the requirements of a modern command structure.

The first reshuffle took place in 1980, affecting eight of the thirteen military region commanders and five political commissars. Seven of the commanders, about whom information is available, had served as division and corps commanders in the Korean War.[38] Another change, much more significant in the long term, was the restructuring of the Military Regions in 1985. As a result, the eleven Military Regions, as already noted, were reduced to seven by merging the Jinan Military Region with Wuhan, Nanjing with Fuzhou, Lanzhou with Urumqi, and Chendu with Kunming. The Beijing, Guangzhou and Shenyang Military Regions remained intact.

At the same time, vast changes were made in the make-up of the leadership organs. By 1985, only one commander appointed in 1980 – Qin Qiwei of the Beijing Military Region – remained in his post. Xiang Shouzhi of Nanjing and Yu Taizhong of Guangzhou had been appointed in 1982, while Zhao Xianshun of Lanzhou, Fu Quanyou of Chengdu, Li Jiulong of Jinan and Liu Jingsong of Shenyang had all been appointed in 1985. What little information is available indicates that all these commanders have strong professional backgrounds. Liu Jingsong of Shenyang, for example, was fifty-two when appointed, had risen from platoon to army commander, had attended the PLA's Infantry Academy, and had commanded mechanized units. Many officers in the regional commands were also apparently replaced. According to a report on the mid-1985 meeting of the Central Military Commission, which decided on the structural reform, 'the meeting successfully selected and appointed members of the leading groups of military regions'.[39] These officers were described as being 'in the prime of their lives', with 'practical experience in the service', 'well educated and knowledgeable'.[40]

Although the motive for reforming the structure of the regions was military – to increase the combat capability of the PLA by streamlining its command system – the reform also had important political ramifications. Whereas previously, operational control over service arms was exercised by the headquarters of the respective arms, in the new regions control over units of service arms stationed in the regions has been transferred to the regional commands. For example, tank units attached to a certain region were placed under the control of the regional command, whereas previously they had been under the control of the Armoured Forces Command.[41] As a result, the new regional commanders control a much greater area and a far larger number of troops than their predecessors, in addition to exercising the newly transferred control over service arms.

The initial impression is that these shifts have greatly increased the authority of the regional commanders. However, a distinction has to be drawn between their military and political authority. From a military standpoint, there is no doubt that their authority has been greatly increased, which is exactly what the Deng leadership wanted, because this increase conforms to the needs of the modernizing army and its new operational doctrine. From a political standpoint, however, the most likely effect of the shifts has been to decrease the authority of the regional commanders and their associates, for several reasons. First, if the experience of the 1980s is anything to go by, the Party leadership will most probably not allow regional commanders to remain in one place for long periods. Second, even if they do remain, it will be much more difficult for them to build up particularistic political connections – the main source of their political power – in a large area than in a smaller one. Third, the more extensive and complex responsibilities of the regional commanders will leave them little time and energy for other activities. Most importantly, these responsibilities require regional commanders to be thorough professionals, which is the best barrier against their becoming deeply involved in political affairs, particularly if such involvement is detrimental to the effectiveness of the armed forces. In short, the changes in the regional structure and commands not only decrease the political power of regional commanders in the present, they will also presumably militate against the growth of such power in the future.

The removal of the military from executive political posts has had an intimate connection with the decline of its influence in central policy-making organs – the Central Committee and the Politburo. The connection has been intimate because it was the massive intervention of the PLA during the Cultural Revolution, and its ensuing emergence as the foremost ruling authority in the localities, that had vastly extended the political power base of the military and greatly magnified its influence in the Central Committee and the Politburo. This was strikingly illustrated by the PLA's representation in these organs.

In the Central Committee set up by the 9th Party Congress in 1969, when the political power of the PLA was at its zenith, military representation amounted to slightly more than 50 per cent. The 11th Party Congress which was held in 1977 – the first congress in the post-Mao period – reduced military representation to about 30 per cent. In the 12th Central Committee, which was elected in 1982 – the military received approximately 22 per cent of the seats. At plenary sessions of the 12th Central Committee, which were held in September 1985, the share of the military was further reduced – to about 13 per cent. This was the lowest military representation in the Central

Committee since the 8th Party Congress – the first congress to have elected a central committee after the establishment of the regime. The representation of the military in the 8th Central Committee had amounted to about 24 per cent.

Assessing the influence of the military in the Politburo – China's top policy-making organ – is more difficult than in lower-echelon organs. At this level of seniority, it is not always possible to determine whether a leader, whose primary affiliation is with the PLA, is acting as a representative of the military, or as a national figure whose concerns transcend military matters. This difficulty derives from the historical characteristics of the Chinese Communist leadership.

During the revolutionary struggle, there was little to distinguish civilian from military leaders, since their activities were inextricably intertwined. Top military commanders were in almost every case important leaders of the Party, while Party leaders who held no direct command played key roles in the direction of military affairs. Consequently, when the Chinese Communists came to power, PLA leaders were 'not co-opted into the top circles of the Chinese Communist Party – they were there from the outset'.[42] And from the outset they were there not merely as military leaders, but also as national leaders who were deeply involved in affairs of state.

This dual role was retained by the old marshals until the last of their number retired in 1985. This role, however distinguished them from most professional officers, who stayed out of politics when possible, and who did not necessarily share the views of the marshals on national issues. Therefore, in their role as national leaders, the marshals cannot be said to have always represented 'the military' on national issues. On these issues, they first of all represented themselves in their capacity as national figures. At the same time, however, the chief concern and main power base of the marshals was the PLA, and on military issues they doubtless sought to advance its institutional interests in the Politburo.

Their ability to do this was determined first of all by the number of military men in the Politburo. In the Politburo of the 9th Central Committee elected in 1969, after the Cultural Revolution had catapulted the PLA to the peak of its political influence, about 50 per cent of the seats were given to the military: ten out of the twenty-one full members and two of the four alternates had a primary affiliation with the PLA. In the Politburo of the 11th Central Committee, which was elected after Mao's death, military leaders retained their proportionate share of power (about 50 per cent): twelve of the twenty-three members and two of the three alternate members were military men. In the 12th Central Committee's Politburo, which was elected in 1982, military representation dropped sharply to about 30 per cent: eight out of the twenty-five full members and one out of the three alternates.

However, the drop was apparently not as sharp as Deng had desired. Although the 12th Congress set up a Central Advisory Commission to accommodate ageing leaders who retired from active service, most senior general refused to transfer themselves to this powerless body despite Deng's prodding. Deng's inability to dislodge them was more a mark of their personal stature than of the PLA's political power, although the continued presence of senior military leaders in the Politburo undoubtedly enhanced the PLA's influence. However, by the autumn of 1985 Deng's increased power, and the infirmity of some leaders, combined to produce a major shake-up of the Politburo: ten of its members retired en masse, among them seven military men.[43] Of the six new members, not one was identified with the PLA. Hence, in the new Politburo of the 12th Central Committee, only three out of the twenty full members were military men (about 15 per cent), as was one of the two alternate members.

Thus, by the end of 1985, Deng had completed the process of removing the PLA from politics. After returning the troops to the barracks and dislodging military commanders from regional political posts, he greatly reduced the influence of the military in the central policy-making organs. The remarkable feature about this process is not that it took time and encountered resistance, but that it was completed without serious and disruptive struggles, or even visible tensions, between the civilian and military leaderships. Given that 'military disengagement from politics appears to be rare . . .'[44] this was a major feat.

This feat should be attributed to Deng's personal prestige, national stature and political acumen. At the same time, it should be attributed to the professional ethic of the Chinese officers, which made them receptive to Deng's directives. Formed during the great modernization drive of the mid-1950s, the ethic remained in force despite the assaults of Maoist radicals. Its strength stems from several sources.

The first has been the modernization of the PLA, which has required increasingly higher levels of expertise on the part of officers, and which has tended to mould their outlook above all other considerations. Another has been the special status of officers – the product of professional requirements and of the post-revolutionary stratification of society – which has made officers inward-looking and caste-conscious. Greatly reinforcing the professionalism of Chinese officers has been the immense integrative power of modern Chinese nationalism, which is fuelled by the searing memory of China's past impotence, and by the overriding desire to see it strong and unified. Another factor has been the commitment of China's military leaders to the principle of civilian supremacy over the military, a commitment born out of their indoctrination, training and experience. Finally, organizational strength has been added to these factors by the network of controls instituted by the Party in the armed forces which, despite its weakness during certain periods, has been a powerful check on military officers.

The professional ethic of the Chinese officers has kept the PLA out of politics when possible, although it did not prevent its commanders from clashing with the Party leadership when their professional interests were jeopardized. When the PLA could no longer stay out of politics due to the convulsions caused by the Cultural Revolution, the professional ethic suffered partial breakdowns. Some local commanders flouted central directives and some military leaders defied the civilian leadership.[45] However, such breakdowns occurred primarily because the civilian authority ceased to function effectively, and not because the military had set out deliberately to defy this authority. Once this authority was restored, the military co-operated with the Party leadership in transferring power back to civilian institutions. To be sure, this process was slow and difficult: in the beginning, military leaders were reluctant to relinquish power for fear that radicals would be its recipients; in general, power, once acquired whatever the initial circumstances, is not easily given up. What matters, however, is that in the end the PLA withdrew from politics and returned to professional pursuits.

Restoring Political Control

The removal of the army from political involvement in the localities and the reduction of its power in policy-making organs went a long way towards restoring political control over the military. The two processes have been parallel and complementary. The decrease of the PLA's influence in ruling organs naturally increased Deng's ability to formulate policies without interference from its representatives, or from senior leaders whose power base was the PLA. The political quiescence [46] of the military has thus been the essential condition for the maintenance of civilian control over it.

However, it has not been enough. Quiescence alone does not guarantee that within its own establishment the military will pursue programmes in line with Party policies. Despite its formal subordination to civilian authority, the military can deviate from Party policy in the course of implementation, refrain from implementing it by bureaucratic stalling, or implement it listlessly. The decline of the political-control apparatus in the PLA during the mid-1950s, despite the Party's insistence on its maintenance, is only one example of such behaviour[47] on the part of the military. To prevent such occurrences, Deng has supplemented the army's retreat from power with the reassertion of internal control over it. This he has done in two ways: personnel changes and institutional controls.

For Deng, as for any leader, the most effective means of ensuring organizational compliance is to appoint 'his men' to key posts in the organization. This, in fact, is what Deng has done, but the process has been difficult and drawn out. It could hardly have been otherwise. Placement requires displacement, and this affects office-holders where it hurts most: their power and perquisites. Dislodging high-ranking officers, who have held their positions for long periods and are well connected, has obviously been no easy matter.

Despite this, Deng has steadily placed officers of his choice in key positions. This conclusion is not based on a knowledge of special connections between Deng and newly appointed officers; in fact, at levels below the very top of the hierarchy, the new officers are much younger than Deng, and in most cases surely have no personal relationship with him. However, given Deng's concern with the army and his own political standing, it is safe to assume that no important positions in the military command structure can be filled without his approval.

At the top level of the hierarchy, Deng made four key appointments.[48] The first was that of Yang Dezhi as chief of staff in 1980. Yang replaced Deng himself, who had held the post in 1975–76 and again after his return from political exile in 1977. As already observed, Deng was a political rather than military chief of staff, and he most probably took the post in order to enforce Party control over the military, as well as to placate the military by acting as their spokesman at the highest levels of the Party hierarchy. However, given his other responsibilities, Deng could hardly have devoted himself to daily involvement in military activities, and as soon as circumstances permitted, he relinquished the post in favour of a professional commander. And, indeed, Yang has been highly visible in directing the effort to introduce the sweeping reforms initiated by Deng in the armed forces.

Another appointment was that of Zhang Aiping as defence minister in 1982. Zhang replaced Geng Biao, also a Deng appointee, and the first civilian to hold that post in China. However, Geng, it will be recalled, was an anaemic minister at a time of rapid change, and he must have been a disappointment to both Deng and the military. Zhang is cast in an entirely different mould. Coming from the high-technology sector of the military establishment, he is intimately acquainted with the complex problems of weapons procurement and absorption, and is clearly a highly qualified choice to oversee the transition of the PLA to a new stage dominated by much more advanced hardware.

The third appointment was that of Yu Qiuli as head of the PLA's General Political Department. Yu took over from Wei Guoqing, who was ousted in 1982 because, as will be seen in detail later in the chapter, of the crude attempt by senior officers in the General Political Department to intervene in politics on the eve of the 12th Party Congress by publishing an article in the army paper that was highly critical of Deng's policies and leadership. The paper is controlled by the General Political Department and Wei paid the price. Until his appointment, Yu had worked in the heavy-industry sector, and it is not at all clear why he was chosen for this post. What is clear is that he is not a Party ideologue, and his tenure has been characterized by a low-key approach to the role of politics in the armed forces, and by a conscious effort to prevent political considerations from interfering with military modernization. Perhaps this is precisely why Deng chose Yu to head the General Political Department.

The final important appointment was that of Yang Shangkun as secretary-general of the Military Affairs Committee – China's highest military decision-making organ. In this capacity, Yang has been able to control the daily work of the Committee and to supervise the implementation of its directives in the armed forces. Lacking a military background, Yang's main qualifications were presumably his organizational skills and his commitment to Deng's programme. As it turned out, he has become a faithful and forceful spokesman for the military policy of the Deng leadership.

Through these appointments Deng tightened his grip over the key levers of power in the military establishment. Yang Shangkun controls the formulation of directives for the military, Zhang Aiping the development of weapons and equipment, while Yang Dezhi and Yu Qiuli head two of the three departments that comprise the general staff – the General Staff Department and the General Political Department. The third – the General Logistics Department – remained under its veteran director, Hong Xuezhi. A staff officer of long standing, Hong was dismissed along with Peng Dehuai in 1959, presumably for advocating the professional viewpoint. His approach and activities clearly conform to Deng's policy.

These were only the most significant appointments at the highest echelon of the military hierarchy. As already detailed, numerous personnel changes were also made at lower echelons – from the deputy directors of the three General Departments and their staffs, the managers of the military industry, the regional commanders and their subordinates, and down to commanders of combat units. The common qualities of these officers is that they are generally much younger and better educated than their predecessors, they have worked for long periods in their speciality, and they have climbed the rungs of the military command ladder.[49] They are, in short, professional officers. And from Deng's standpoint, this is the best guarantee for the maintenance of civilian control over the military. Officers of this type can be expected to devote themselves to military duties and to shun involvement in politics. More important, because of shared concepts on the development of the armed forces, they can also be confidently expected to support Deng's reforms and to ensure their implementation in the PLA.

In the Maoist period, control of the army through the choice of politically reliable personnel went hand in hand with institutional controls, which were designed to ensure the organizational subordination of the PLA to the Party. These controls were exercised through a political hierarchy, which consisted of Party committees, political commissars and political departments, and which ran parallel to the military chain of command. Ideally, leadership in the armed forces was based on the principle that, except in emergencies, decisions in military units were made by Party committees and implemented by military commanders and political commissars according to their respective functions. This ideal was never fully realized. Once Chinese officers developed professional attitudes, they resented and resisted this system on the grounds that it was detrimental to combat effectiveness in modern warfare. After Peng Dehuai's dismissal, it turned out that the political system in the PLA had been allowed to fall into disarray. Lin Biao revived the system in a limited fashion, but it broke down during the Cultural Revolution due to radical attacks on Party organizations in the armed forces, and the General Political Department ceased operations for some two years. Although it resumed operations in 1969, the General Political Department never regained its past prominence, and neither did the political organs subordinate to it. Despite this deterioration, the Maoist leadership remained committed to the political control system as the mainstay of Party predominance over the armed forces.

In the post-Mao period, the system in its Maoist mould has been watered down beyond recognition. Most significantly, the basic principle of this system – the supreme decision-making power of Party committees in military units, and the equal status of military commanders and political commissars as executors of its decisions – has in effect been jettisoned by the Chinese leadership. This has been unequivocally demonstrated by the total absence of reference to this principle in statements on the role of political work in the PLA, and in descriptions of political activities throughout the armed forces.

The explanation for this dramatic departure is not hard to find. The interference of Party committees and political commissars had been one of the main sources of conflict between professional officers and Party leaders since the late 1950s. The officers opposed such interference on the grounds that it was completely incompatible with the needs of a complex army in modern warfare. Instead, they favoured the institution of the 'single commander' system, which put full operational control over units in the hands of the military commanders. However, Maoist leaders turned down this demand on two counts. First, because they feared that it would lead to the growth of an officer class that enjoyed a special status and was impervious to political control. And second, because under the 'people's war' doctrine the political conditioning of troops was viewed as no less important than their military preparedness, and this conditioning was to be ensured by Party intitutions in the armed forces.

The rationale for limiting the professional authority of officers no longer exists in the Deng era. Whereas in the Maoist period it was the professionalism of the officer corps that moved the leadership to curb its autonomy in military matters, under Deng it is this very professionism that has moved the leadership to lift these curbs. The commitment of the Deng leadership to the supremacy of 'experts' over 'reds' in management, and the abandonment of 'people's war' as a force-building doctrine, have elevated the military commander to the dominant position in military units. Consequently, the Deng leadership has not infringed on the professional prerogatives of the military. It sets policy for the PLA but also gives military leaders and commanders broad autonomy to carry it out.

The essence of the new approach is that political work in the armed forces must serve military objectives. As an article in *Hongqi* put it: 'Our political work must become a forceful guarantee for our troops to have a good fighting will, and acquire superb military skills and military measures, so that the tasks of war can be successfully accomplished.'[50] The novelty of this approach, and the difficulty of implementing it, were explained by Zhang Tingfa, when he was commander of the air force:

> In the past political work was carried out under the erroneous principle of 'taking class struggle as the key link', and was greatly affected by 'putting politics in command'. Political work was elevated to a position 'higher than everything'.... Since the Third Plenary Session of the 11th CPC Central Committee, such absurdities as 'putting politics in command' have been negated, and the situation has undergone a great change. However, the influences in this respect have not been completely eliminated. Some political cadres do not like and are not used to the role of 'service' and 'guaranteeing', believing that by doing so, political work will become unnecessary and aimless. They worry that if 'putting politics in command' is not mentioned and the 'leading role' of political work not emphasized, the position and role of political work will be lowered and the prestige of political organs and cadres will be affected.[51]

Such misgivings are understandable, given the much more modest role accorded to political functionaries in the armed forces. This role was described in an army paper report on the operations of a division political department under the Wuhan Military Region during military training in 1984.[52] The operational principle, according to the report, was that political work should not interfere with the command structure and that it should play a supporting role during military training. When the division went on manoeuvres, 'the comrades from the propaganda, organization, cadre and training sections of the division and various regiments ... conducted propaganda to cheer the troops during various phases.... The political department also had liaison officers at headquarters, keeping the troops informed of combat results to heighten their morale.' Another task of the department was to support and promote the whole range of military reforms carried out by the leadership. Commenting on the activities of the political department, the army paper called them 'a good step' because they advanced the completion of military tasks and negated Lin Biao's theory of putting politics first, which had damaged military training.[53]

The removal of political organs from intervention in military affairs does not mean that they have been reduced to the role of cheerleaders. These organs still exercise important functions. The most prominent is the conduct of political education and indoctrination, which takes several forms. The first is an ongoing effort, not linked to specific events, to explain and disseminate Party policies. Yang Shangkun described this effort in the following way in 1983:

> While the whole Party was effecting a historic change, party committees at various levels throughout the army ... made considerable efforts to educate commanders and fighters in the principle of practice being the sole criteria for the test of truth, party lines, principles and policies laid down since the Third Plenary Session of the IIth CPC Central Committee, the four fundamental principles, and the 'Resolution on Certain Questions in the History of our Party since the Founding of the People's Republic of China'. Now education on the guidelines laid down by the 12th Party Congress and on the new Constitution is being carried out in the army.[54]

Education is also carried out in order to prepare for or explain important measures undertaken by the army. For example, when the reduction of the army's size was being put into effect, a comment in the army paper said that 'the mood of personnel in the units that are being reorganized may become unstable, and unhealthy trends may occur in personnel readjustment and the handling of property and materials'. In view of this, said the paper, 'it is necessary first to do ideological work among such personnel and then to step up the work of discipline inspection.'[55]

Party organs in the armed forces are also responsible for carrying out campaigns of ideological rectification. For example, when the nationwide movement against 'spiritual pollution' was launched in late 1983, these organs were instructed to implement the campaign in the army: 'party committees and political institutions at all levels in our army must pay close attention to resisting spiritual pollution and have a very strong sense of urgency and responsibility in this regard. They must try to discover weak links and step up ideological and political work; measures must be taken to clear away and prevent spiritual pollution.'[56]

Another function of Party organs is to enforce political discipline throughout the armed forces. For example, secretaries of discipline inspection committees of the Kunming PLA units were told by their political commissar that 'discipline inspection committees of party committees at all levels must regard unconditional maintenance of political unanimity with the Central Committee as the focus of current party discipline inspection work'. It was, he added, essential 'to have the party organizations at all levels and the whole body of party members obeying the decisions of the upper-level party organizations . . . '. The commissar then instructed the discipline inspection committees to 'deal severely with and resolutely investigate anyone who runs counter to and opposes the party's line . . . no matter how high his position or how great his merits'.[57] In political matters, in short, Party organs in the PLA still wield considerable clout.

In sum, Deng's success in reasserting political control over the PLA, as in removing it from politics, should be attributed largely to the co-operation of the military, for which there are two reasons, First, the Chinese military, as emphasized previously, have always been committed to the principle of civilian supremacy, and have not resisted its implementation when the civilians demonstrated a capacity to rule effectively. Second, they have not resisted political control provided it was exercised in a moderate fashion and did not interfere with their professional duties. These conditions have been fully met by the Deng leadership.

Political Dissent and Civil–Military Relations

The co-operation between the Deng leadership and the military in transforming the role of the PLA has not prevented conflict between them on other issues. The conflict was most evident in the early 1980s, but subsided by the middle of the decade because most of its causes were removed. However, other causes are inherent in the civil–military relationship. How then has the conflict affected this relationship and Deng's position vis-à-vis the military?

The basic premise in assessing civil–military conflict is that the Party and the PLA have not always faced each other as separate entities, because in some instances groups within the Party and the PLA formed coalitions that cut across institutional boundaries. As a rule, the strength of the dividing line between the Party and the PLA has depended on the issues at stake. When the issues concerned the corporate interests of the PLA, the military have tended to coalesce around these interests and to present a common 'military view' to the Party leadership. However, when the military became involved in political issues that departed from their professional interests, they were no longer united by an overriding 'military view'. Instead, the military split along professional and political lines, each of which was supported by different segments of the armed forces.

At the inevitable risk of oversimplification, these segments can be classified in two broad and amorphous groups. One group consists of professional officers whose main interest has been the modernization of the PLA, and who have limited their activities to advancing this interest. The second group consists of senior military leaders who, while sharing the institutional interests of the professional military, have not limited their concerns to these interests. Whereas the professional military tended to stay out of politics, these leaders intruded into political affairs and spoke out against the policies of the Deng leadership. Although they were supported by certain groups in the PLA, these leaders acted primarily in their capacity as national figures and as members of the Party's highest policy-making organs – a capacity which, as noted earlier, derived from their special status in the Chinese leadership. Owing to conflicting interests, these groups have not coalesced against Deng on political issues. On the contrary, the differences between Deng and the professional officers have been reduced sufficiently to give Deng strong support against his critics in the PLA, as well as in the Party.

The accommodation achieved by Deng and the professional military may seem implausible at first glance. After all, as seen in earlier chapters, they differed on the central issue of resource allocation for weapons acquisition, and the military did not get what it wanted. From this pivotal perspective, civil–military relations may seem doomed to perennial conflict. This, however, is clearly not the case. For one thing, professional officers surely realize that rapid and all-round hardware renewal is simply not possible due to astronomical costs. They surely also realize that such renewal is not urgent, because China is not faced with an imminent military threat. It is, moreover, plain to the officers that to attain massive re-equipment China has to turn to imports, but this is hazardous due to the difficulty of finding reliable suppliers, and the danger of becoming dependent on them. These officers also know full well that the Chinese armed forces are not capable of absorbing and maintaining large quantities of sophisticated weapons over the short haul.

In the light of these considerations, the leadership's argument for a policy of slow and selective weapons modernization until China builds an appropriate economic and technological base is surely persuasive even to officers who strongly desire the newest weapons – especially since, despite budgetary constraints, substantial progress has, as already shown, been made in weapons modernization. More important, in all other areas of military modernization, professional officers have been fully satisfied. Therefore, they have little grounds for serious disaffection, and many reasons to co-operate with the Deng leadership. And this is what they have done. Although there has been opposition to Deng's military policies in the armed forces, the main motives have been bureaucratic, not political.

If Deng and the professional military reached an accord, the same could not be said, at least until the mid-1980s, for another group in the military which opposed and criticized Deng's national reforms. Centred in the PLA's General Political Department and its subordinate organs, this group apparently gathered around Ye Jianying. Until his retirement in 1985, Ye was the archetype of the soldier–politician whose concerns embraced both military and national affairs. He obviously viewed himself – and was viewed by others in China – not solely as a representative of the military, but as a national leader whose activities were not restricted by institutional boundaries. Although in the past Ye had been a leader of the professional military, and for that reason was a prime target of the 'gang of four',[58] he apparently, for personal and political reasons, became the focus of opposition to the policies of Deng Xiaoping.

The personal reasons presumably stemmed from the fact that, despite radical attacks against him during the Cultural Revolution, Ye's stature was linked to the Maoist legacy. Furthermore, Ye's role as the central pillar in the coalition led by Hua Guofeng during the transition period after Mao's death reinforced this link, as Hua's tenure symbolized continuity with the Maoist era. Thus, an unrestrained repudiation of the Chairman's legacy could not but have had an adverse effect on Ye's position within the Party. Ye's political motives presumably derived from his abiding belief in the central facets of the Maoist ideology, and his concern for the future of the Chinese revolution, which he saw as stagnating because of Deng's policies.

It is not surprising, therefore, that a key issue in dispute between this group of officers and the Deng leadership was the evaluation of Mao's role in the history of the Chinese revolution. The Party's pronouncement on this important issue – the 'Resolution on Certain Questions in the History of Our Party since the Founding of the People's Republic of China', adopted after debates and delays at the Sixth Plenum of the 11th Central Committee in June 1981 – is generally considered by observers to have been watered down when compared with statements reportedly made by Deng,[59] and this modification is attributed to pressure from the military. Even if so, the resolution's verdict is still much harsher than that given by Ye Jianying in his highly significant statement marking the thirtieth anniversary of the regime in October 1979. The difference is particularly glaring with regard to the most sensitive and divisive question – Mao's responsibility for the Cultural Revolution. Whereas Ye simply glosses over this period and attributes its calamitous consequences to Lin Biao and the 'gang of four',[60] the resolution deals with the Cultural Revolution in detail and lays the blame for its excesses squarely on Mao.[61]

Related to the treatment of Mao's legacy has been the discontent of this group with the consequences of what it has perceived as the drift away from

Maoist values in Chinese society. Many articles and reports reflecting such discontent were published by the army paper, primarily in the early 1980s. One article, for example, praised the revolutionary Yan'an spirit and lamented its passing: 'What kind of fine social values and attitudes we had at that time, and how much we yearn for such fine social values and attitudes'.[62] It then implicitly criticized Party policies for abandoning such values:

> To turn China into a powerful, modern socialist country, we should demonstrate high material civilization as well as high spiritual civilization. This kind of spiritual civilization should not be represented by high developments in the fields of science and culture alone. First of all and most important, this spiritual civilization must manifest itself in communist ideals and beliefs, communist ethics and values, fine social practices, comradely relations among the people and so on.[63]

A more specific indication of the phenomena that irritated the critics of Party policies was given by Li Desheng, then commander of the Shenyang Military Region, when he refuted their criticism:

> For example, in early 1979 after the emergence of Xidan democratic wall, some comrades doubted whether the discussion on the criterion of truth and the slogan of emancipating the mind were correct; in early 1980 when the phenomena of indulging in social dancing, wearing flared trousers and singing hit songs appeared, some comrades favoured the slogan 'promoting what is proletarian and liquidating what is bourgeois'; in 1981 when *Unrequited Love* was criticized, some comrades held that it was necessary to exercise dictatorship in the ideological and cultural spheres; in 1982 when serious crimes in the economic spheres were cracked down on, some comrades held that this was a result of the policy of opening to the outside world and adopting flexible economic policies at home and that the policy of taking class struggle as the key link should not be done away with.[64]

The dissidents in the military blamed the Party's policies for the appearance of such phenomena. For example, a report outlining PLA efforts in Guangzhou Province to combat leftist attitudes said that 'some comrades . . . regarded certain erroneous trends of thought and unhealthy tendencies in society as the results of carrying out the policies [laid down by the Third Plenum of the 11th Party Congress]. They wondered whether the Party's principles and policies had deviated and become rightist.'[65] One political commissar, for example, did not wonder at all, but minced no words in linking Party policies with the emergence of pernicious trends in society: 'At present, under the new historical conditions in which our country is implementing an open-door policy and the policy of enlivening the economy, and owing to the corrosive influence of decadent bourgeois ideas abroad and the adverse influence of the remnant force of the exploiting classes in the country, anarchism, extreme individualism and bourgeois liberalization trends of thought have appeared in society.'[66]

A particularly galling manifestation of this trend, from the military dissidents' viewpoint, was the film script *Unrequited Love* by Bai Hua, an intellectual in a PLA unit in the Wuhan Military Region. The script was a bitter portrayal of a patriotic artist who was hounded to death by radical leftists. Although published in 1979, the script was not attacked in the army paper until the spring of 1981, when the debates over the evaluation of Mao's role were approaching a climax. In denouncing *Unrequited Love* for 'negating patriotism', and in depicting it as 'not an isolated phenomenon' but as a reflection of 'anarchism, ultra-individualism [and] bourgeois liberalism',[67] the dissidents in the military may have used the script to highlight the potential consequences of extreme de-Maoization, and thereby to influence the outcome of the debate over Mao's role in the history of the Party. Whether or not for this reason, the Party press did not take up the attack on Bai Hua, but joined in only after the verdict on Mao had been reached and after the army paper continued to press its campaign.

A much more blatant instance of military meddling in high politics occurred on the eve of the landmark 12th Party Congress, which was held 1–11 September 1982. This incident brought the simmering strains between the Deng leadership and dissident elements in the military to a head. The cause of the flare-up was an article by Zhao Yiya, an army propagandist, which was published in the Shanghai *Jiefang Ribao* of 28 August 1982 and which, as it later turned out, was reprinted from the previous day's army paper.[68] Taking up the time-old theme of 'redness' versus 'expertise' under the new slogan of 'socialist spiritual civilization' versus 'capitalist civilization', Zhao strongly criticized the overemphasis on material progress at the expense of the Communist ideology. 'We want to learn the advanced scientific and technological achievements of the capitalist world,' Zhao said, but 'we must also adopt an analytical attitude, and cannot copy them blindly and mechanically, still less praise them in extravagant terms'.[69] This, however, was exactly what 'some comrades' did. They 'one-sidedly emphasized "civilization" while neglecting "spirit" and, worse still, socialism. As a result, the difference between the two types of civilization was easily confused.'[70]

Had Zhao left matters there, the publication of his article would probably not have become a *cause célèbre*. After all, the army paper had published many articles warning about the effects of neglecting ideology. However, two features made Zhao's piece stand out. First, Zhao did not confine himself to criticizing Party policies, but in no uncertain terms also accused the Party leadership of dereliction of duty:

In the past few years, unhealthy ideas have really emerged inside and outside our party. However, what is more important is our lax and weak leadership on the ideological front. It was some of our comrades on the theoretical, literary and art, and journalistic circles who first took the lead in supporting and publicizing the erroneous viewpoint of bourgeois liberalism.... Moreover, this erroneous viewpoint was not promptly checked and corrected. As a result, it inevitably spread and grew.[71]

A second distinguishing feature of Zhao's article was the timing of its publication. As the army paper itself later emphasized, the article, which was 'in conflict with certain important points in the report to the 12th Party Congress', appeared after the report had been 'basically finalized'.[72] Its publication may have represented a last-ditch effort by Deng's opponents to pressure the leadership into altering the report in line with their views. More likely, the article may have been intended to provide the dissidents with ammunition against Deng so as to strengthen their hand in the tough bargaining over personnel appointments that apparently went on behind the scenes before and during the Congress. In any case, publication of the article at that time, the army paper admitted, was 'not only a case of serious carelessness, but ... a grave political and organizational mistake on our part.'[73]

This mistake did not pass without retribution from the Party leadership. On 27 September, the army paper published a long and abject self-criticism for printing the piece in the first place and refuted its arguments point by point. It concluded:

> The fact that Comrade Zhao Yiya's article was published in this paper (and also simultaneously in the Shanghai *Jiefang Ribao*) shows that among a very small number of comrades in the party and the army there indeed remains the pernicious influence of 'Left' ideas, which constitutes an obstruction to the party's line, principles and policies.... Organizationally and as a disciplinary matter, it is impermissible to propagate these erroneous viewpoints. It is precisely on this point that this paper has for a period of time in the past lacked understanding and must strive to correct from now on.[74]

As part of this effort, on the same day as the publication of the army paper's self-criticism, Wei Guoqing, the director of the PLA's General Political Department, which is responsible for the paper, was dismissed.

Supporting criticism of Deng's policies was not the only transgression committed by Wei Guoqing. The director of the General Political Department also turned out to be an adamant advocate of 'putting politics in command' in the armed forces – a principle that was forcefully rejected by Deng in the post-Mao period and that had always been anathema to the professional military. Wei, however, continued to cling to the concept that political considerations should reign supreme over military activities. In his speech at the all-army political work conference in 1980, Wei said: 'Experience shows that units that relax political–ideological work at any time are eventually penalized. Political work is the lifeline of our army. Putting politics in command and political ideology above everything else is an important principle. It still has to be adhered to after the emphasis of work has been shifted.'[75] Wei then called for upholding the system of Party committee leadership in the armed forces, according to which Party committees hold ultimate authority in military units and military commanders are subordinate to them.[76] This system, as we have seen, has been completely abandoned by the Deng leadership.

Speaking to the all-army political work conference in early 1982, Wei continued to propagate his view:

> In the new situation, political work is still the lifeblood of our army. . . . It cannot be weakened. The fine tradition and fundamental principles of our army in carrying out political work must be upheld. They cannot be violated. It is completely correct that they should be employed and developed in line with new conditions. The principle of putting politics in command and placing ideology at the fore is applicable to any task at any time.[77]

Wei's dismissal thus not only deprived the dissidents in the military of easy access to the army press, it also removed an obstacle to establishing the primacy of professionalism and to strengthening the co-operation between Deng and the professional military.

PLA dissidents also criticized the Party's economic policies, which they viewed as yet another manifestation of the Deng leadership's departure from socialist values. One target of attack was the Party's pragmatic policy of decentralizing agricultural production down to the family level: 'When some comrades saw that some places were permitted to fix production quotas for each household, they wondered how on earth that could happen and opined that this was taking the old road again.'[78] Others objected on more practical grounds, expressing their fears that the new reponsibility system would disrupt PLA recruitment and troop morale.[79] According to some accounts, a career in the military was becoming less attractive to peasant youths, as the 'income of army men's families was less than before, as a result of implementing the system of production responsibility'.[80] More generally, the Party's economic policies came under fire because they were seen as leading to moral laxity and corruption:

> For example, we have given enterprises greater decision-making power, have instituted the bonus system and have opened up a number of channels for the circulation of commodities in order to . . . accelerate the development of the national economy. However, due to the influence of various non-proletarian ideas, some persons have abused their decision-making power, have wantonly issued bonuses or have benefited themselves at the expense of the public interest. . . . Others have engaged in speculation and profiteering, have put profits first and have considered everything in terms of money.[81]

175

What then has been the significance of this dissent? How has it affected civil–military relations in general and Deng's position in particular? An attempt to answer these questions has to consider several factors.

The first factor is the extent of dissent. Because of the lack of data, it is difficult to identify with certainty the dissidents at the highest level of the military hierarchy. What is known generally is that the main source of opposition to Deng's policies at this level, as already pointed out, has been the General Political Department, and its former director, Wei Guoqing, who was dismissed from his post. Other high-level supporters of the dissident group may have included Xu Shiyou, former commander of the Nanjing and Guangzhou Military Regions, who lost his Politburo post at the 12th Party Congress;[82] Ye Fei, former commander of the navy;[83] and lesser figures such as Xiao Hua, until the mid-1960s director of the General Political Department and later political commissar of the Lanzhou Military Region.[84]

How strong has been the support of the officer corps for dissident military leaders? This question is extremely difficult to answer. Judging by the efforts of the leadership to refute criticism and to indoctrinate officers, dissatisfaction with Party policies had been extremely widespread in the early 1980s. For example, in April 1981 it was reported that 'over the past two years, some 70 per cent of cadres at and above the regimental level have attended various forms of study classes' in which the correctness of Party policies was explained.[85] And in January 1982 it was reported that in the previous year, 70 per cent of all army officers had attended political study classes lasting one month.[86]

This does not mean, however, that all the officers participating in such classes had disagreed with the policies of the Party. When criticism of Party policies began to well up in the PLA, the Party leadership launched a major educational drive to counter it, and it hardly distinguished between officers who had voiced criticism and those who had not. More important, it is unlikely that many professional commanders were among the critics, given their preoccupation with improving the combat capabilities of the PLA and their desire for material development, even at the expense of revolutionary values, as the basis for military modernization. At any rate, no high-ranking officer associated with the professional military, perhaps with the exception of the dismissed Ye Fei, has publicly spoken out against the leadership's economic or ideological policies.

The significance of the dissent also depends on the form of its manifestation. At the national level, the most obvious voice of the dissident leaders was the army paper, but they doubtless made their views known in inner Party circles as well. At the middle and lower levels of the armed forces, dissent from Party policies was presumably expressed in discussion sessions and speeches. Whatever the form of dissent, there is not the slightest indication that the military made any move to press their views by direct action of some kind. With regard to military policies which they have to implement, officers have the risky option, to which they have resorted in the past, of sidestepping or sabotaging distasteful directives in the course of implementation. However, with regard to national policies, such an option is hardly open to officers, since they generally have no control over the implementation of these policies. Short of direct action, therefore, military leaders can try to influence national policies by public statements, which they have done, and by working behind the scenes in whatever ways are customary in China's mysterious policy-making process, which they have also presumably done.

Another factor that has to be taken into account in assessing the significance of dissent in the military is the reaction of the Party leadership. One has obviously been personnel changes, but information linking such changes directly with criticism of Party policies is unavailable, and only the dismissal of Wei Guoqing, and perhaps Ye Fei, fall into this category. However, as has been seen, sweeping changes have occurred at all levels of the military hierarchy under Deng's aegis. While there is no information to connect these changes directly to disaffection with Deng's policies, such a connection is probable in at least some cases. At any rate, the new appointees, especially to sensitive posts, have doubtless been screened by the Deng leadership, and their support for its policies must have been taken into consideration.

The Deng leadership also reacted by cracking down on the critics of its policies. Party committees in various PLA units and institutes convened criticism and self-criticism meetings at which the influence of 'leftist' ideology was analysed and condemned.[87] At the same time, study classes for officers were held throughout the PLA in order to convince them of the correctness of Party policies.[88] In the air force, for example, it was reported in 1981 that 'study classes have been run in various ways. In view of the fact that air force cadres are large in number and that they are spread all over the country, study classes are held at the four levels from the divisional level to the leading organ of the air force in order to ensure that they are assembled to engage in study for one month each year.' For units scattered in far-away places, teams of instructors were sent to hold mobile study classes. And for pilots who could not interrupt their flight training for long periods, one-week classes were held. The results, according to the report, were satisfactory: 'In the past some leading cadres lacked a correct understanding of the Party's line and policies . . . and . . . some even had doubts and misgivings . . . . After engaging in theoretical study, they have not only gained a clear under-standing of the line and policies but have also been able convincingly to answer and explain . . . questions . . . raised by troops.'[89] At the beginning of

1983, the Military Affairs Committee looked back on its efforts with satisfaction.

> The all-army party organizations at various levels and the vast number of party members have shown further improvement in supporting the political views of the central authorities. Through education and a series of measures to set things right . . . marked . . . results have been achieved . . . . The overwhelming majority of cadres and party members believe that the leadership of the Central Committee is absolutely correct.[90]

Nonetheless, some officers apparently find it difficult to share the belief of the 'overwhelming majority' of their colleagues in the wisdom of Party policies. This attitude is attributed by Party spokesmen to the lingering effects of 'leftism'. For example, writing in *Renmin Ribao* the deputy political commissar of the Beijing PLA units explained the sources of this attitude:

> First, we must see that 'leftist' influence lasted a long time and had a profound effect. Beginning in the latter part of the 1950s, for over twenty years, our party made 'leftist' mistakes . . . . The young comrades grew up during this period and accepted many 'leftist' things. Comrades who had taken part in revolution . . . were similarly subject to many 'leftist' influences. In these historical conditions, many comrades formed certain 'leftist' concepts.[91]

He then described the effects of these 'concepts' in the armed forces:

> For example, some comrades have not completely eliminated the influence of 'giving prominence to politics'. When engaging in political work, they do not sufficiently stress its role as a guarantee, and when engaging in military training, they still 'have a lingering fear . . . of deviating to one side and demonstrating a purely military viewpoint'. There are also questions of belittling specialization and technical work . . . . We do not attach sufficient importance to science, culture and education . . . . In the utilization of cadres, we also have the problems of paying great importance to qualifications and records of service but looking down upon educational level.[92]

'Leftist' views also shaped the attitude of some officers to Deng's reforms:

> For example, when we talk about the production responsibility system in agriculture, they will think that this is tantamount to the division of the fields and to going it alone; when we talk about allowing some people to get rich before others, they are afraid that this will lead to polarization; when we talk about transporting goods from a long distance away for sale, they will relate this with speculation and profiteering; when we talk about implementing the bonus system, they will relate this with material incentive; and when we talk about attaching importance to knowledge and intellectuals, they are afraid that this will lead to belittling the workers, peasants and soldiers.[93]

Several years of political study, according to the deputy political commissar, have generally put such apprehensions to rest, but 'some comrades still take a sceptical attitude in their heart of hearts, being afraid that these policies do not conform to the socialist orientation and principles . . . '.[94]

In a major effort to eliminate 'leftist' views, the leadership decided in early 1984, as noted earlier, to make condemnation of the Cultural Revolution the central object of rectification in the armed forces. The reason was explained by the army paper:

> 'Leftist' thinking, though having already influenced our party before the 'Cultural Revolution', did not dominate the entire party at the time. However, during the 'Cultural Revolution', erroneous 'leftist' thinking . . . influenced every corner and every front throughout the country for fully ten years . . . . Our party has launched an all-round drive to set things right . . . . However, erroneous thinking, as soon as it takes shape . . . cannot be eliminated in a short time . . . . the influence of 'leftist' thinking is still alive to a different extent in the minds of many people.[95]

The conclusion is clear: 'Without thoroughly negating the "Great Cultural Revolution", we will fail to repudiate completely . . . "leftist" ideology . . . .'[96]

Such statements should not create an exaggerated impression of the strength of 'leftist' ideology. Even at the peak of its strength in the early 1980s, this ideology had no more than a marginal impact on Party policies and Deng's position. Although Deng may have made minor concessions and tactical retreats as a result of pressure from military dissidents, he was not swayed from the course he set himself. Disaffection in the military did not weaken Deng's position to a significant degree. If it had, he would have been compelled to make more than minor compromises with his critics. In fact, Deng did not give in to criticism, but mounted counter-attacks against the critics. By 1985, the combined effect of rectification campaigns and personnel changes greatly reduced the strength of 'leftist' ideology. At the same time, the retirement of Ye Jianying both removed the main focus for dissent in the military and deprived the dissidents of a voice in the Politburo.

In sum, Deng has been able to overcome dissent in the military primarily because this dissent has been limited to a segment of the PLA that has not included the professional officers. These officers support Deng because they have reached an understanding with him on vital military matters. And this understanding forms the basis for civil–military co-operation in the Deng era that provides the political force for China's march to military modernization.

Conclusion

This study has tried to survey and assess the changes that have taken place in the PLA in the post-Mao period. In conclusion, it may be useful to restate briefly the principal points made in the study and their main implications.

The starting point for the changes in the PLA has been the defence policy of Mao's successors, which differs dramatically from the Maoist approach. Driven by a desire to achieve quick material progress in all sectors of society, at the expense of revolutionary values if necessary, the new leaders have designated the modernization of the armed forces as one of their main objectives. However, they have ruled out the rapid renovation of the PLA's weapons, because such an endeavour would require massive arms imports, which are incredibly expensive and which would expose China to the dangers of dependence and the difficulties of absorbing sophisticated technology.

The leaders decided, therefore, that weapons renewal, while allowing for selected purchases from abroad, will be a slow process that relies primarily on indigenous efforts and has to be preceded by economic and technological development. Underlying this decision is the conviction of the leaders that China is not faced with an imminent security threat that calls for urgent measures to bolster defences. At the same time, they decided that reforms which do not require vast outlays but are essential to improving combat capability should be carried out quickly and across the board.

The doctrinal underpinning for the reforms has been provided by the revision of Mao's military concepts. Referred to by the Chinese as 'people's war under modern conditions', the revised doctrine attaches supreme importance to 'modern conditious' rather than 'people's war'. Elements of Maoist doctrine have been retained only as China's last resort against an all-out conventional invasion of the mainland. Only in this eventuality will the Chinese abandon population centres, lure the invader deep into China's hinterland and mobilize the population to wear the enemy down in a protracted guerrilla war of attrition. Short of such an invasion, which is virtually unimaginable, the Chinese will hold on to territory by waging positional warfare and mobile counter-attacks, conducted by mechanized forces in combined-arms operations.

The departure from 'people's war' also produced modifications in China's nuclear doctrine. For one thing the Chinese have discarded the simplistic scenario that a nuclear attack on China must inevitably be followed by a ground invasion, which the Chinese will successfully counter by relying on 'people's war'. Since they no longer consider this kind of war as a catch-all response to all contingencies, the Chinese have in effect severed the connection, integral in the Maoist scheme, between a war's nuclear and conventional phases. War, in short, is no longer viewed as unavoidably total.

Consequently, the Chinese have also implicitly altered their concept of deterrence. In Maoist days, they sought to deter a nuclear strike by playing up the notion that it could not subjugate China, while a ground invasion, which would have to follow such a strike to achieve victory, would be defeated by a 'people's war'. In the mid-1980s, the growing confidence of the Chinese in their nuclear second-strike capability, and the abandonment of their commitment to total 'people's war' as the only possible response to an invasion, produced a shift of emphasis – from deterring a nuclear attack through denial of ultimate victory to preventing one through the threat of retaliation.

Nowhere has the departure from Maoist doctrine been more cogently manifested than in the building, arming and training of the armed forces. The Maoist premise that the 'human factor' is more important than weapons and military expertise has been completely abandoned in favour of professional objectives. To attain these objectives, far-reaching reforms have been introduced in all the activities of the PLA. The selection, education and promotion of officers have been directed towards raising their professional competence, with special stress on staffing key positions with competent officers. The training of troops has been oriented towards preparations for a modern war, with particular emphasis on combined-arms operations. The structure of the PLA has been streamlined and made leaner, more centralized and more suitable to the needs of modern warfare. Weapons and equipment have, within the limits set by economic and technological constraints, been improved and increased.

The revival of professionalism in the PLA has been accompanied by a transformation of the PLA's political role and relations with the Party. Due to the Cultural Revolution and its aftermath, the army still held prominent political posts at all levels of the Chinese power structure when the Maoist period ended. This state of affairs has been changed completely. Under Deng Xiaoping's aegis, the PLA has been removed from involvement in political affairs in the localities, and its influence in central policy-making organs has been greatly reduced. At the same time, the Deng leadership has reasserted Party control over the defence establishment through personnel changes and institutional controls. Essential to the smooth completion of this process has been the co-operation between the Deng leadership and the professional military. This co-operation has extended to key issues of military modernization. Despite disagreements, Deng and the military have reached a consensus which is vital to the effective implementation of the radical reforms that are designed to transform the PLA into a modern and professional army.

The difficulties are obvious. Some of the reforms have run into resistance, some will require years to bear fruit, and some may prove to be unfeasible. Nevertheless, many of the reforms have already been put into effect, and have doubtless raised the efficiency and effectiveness of the PLA as a fighting force. The Deng leadership, moreover, seems to be fully aware of the difficulties, but is determined to pursue its policy of military modernization.

The essence of this policy is a sustained effort to raise the combat capability of the PLA through a slow improvement of technology and a sweeping improvement of the non-technological components of military power. How effective, then, has this effort been and what are its prospects? A major difficulty in attempting to answer this question derives from the backward state of the PLA's conventional forces at the end of the Maoist period. Because of this backwardness, even modest progress, which has undoubtedly been achieved, seems considerable when viewed against the starting line. However, because the PLA was so backward in comparison with modern armies, modest progress is not sufficient to bring it much closer to the level of these armies.

Nevertheless, even modest progress in improving China's conventional forces has already had important implications in the short term. It has made the prospect of invading China more daunting and, therefore, more remote. It has enabled the Chinese to contemplate a defence without resorting to the humiliating requirement of withdrawing into the interior and surrendering population centres to the invader. It has increased the confidence of the Chinese in their overall military capability and, presumably, has contributed to their more relaxed stance towards the Soviet Union. It has given China a much greater capability to act as a regional power. It has served notice that China is beginning to extend its naval presence beyond coastal waters. It has turned China into a significant arms trader. And, perhaps most importantly, it has laid the foundation for the long-term growth of China's military power.

The guidelines for this growth have been set by the Deng leadership. If they are followed, China's military strength will increase slowly but steadily. To what extent they will be followed depends, first of all, on what happens on the political scene after Deng departs. If his successors remain committed to China's 'second revolution', the PLA can be expected to continue its march to modernization.

Notes

Chapter 1: The Maoist Legacy

1   Melvin Gurtov and Byong-Moo Hwang, *China under Threat: The Politics of Strategy and Diplomacy* (Baltimore: The Johns Hopkins University Press, 1980); and Gerald Segal, *Defending China* (Oxford University Press, 1985).

2   See, for example, Robert F. Dernberger, 'The Economic Consequences of Defense Expenditure Choices in China', in *China: A Reassessment of the Economy*, A Compendium of Papers Submitted to the Joint Economic Committee, Congress of the United States (Washington, DC: US Government Printing Office, 1975), pp. 467–98.

3   On the modernizationof the PLA in the 1950s see Ellis Joffe, *Party and Army: Professionalism and Political Control in the Chinese Officer Corps, 1949–1964* (Harvard University: East Asian Research Center, 1965); and John Gittings, *The Role of the Chinese Army* (Oxford University Press, 1967).

4   Joffe, *Party and Army*, pp. 2–3.

5   *Ibid.*, pp. 10–11.

6   On China's intervention in the Korean War see Alexander L. George, *The Chinese Communist Army in Action: The Korean War and its Aftermath* (New York: Columbia University Press, 1967); and Allen S. Whiting, *China Crosses the Yalu: The Decision to Enter the Korean War* (New York: Macmillan, 1960).

7   XINHUA, 1 August, 1979; in Foreign Broadcast Information Service: People's Republic of China (National Technical Information Service, US Department of Commerce, Washington DC) (hereafter cited as FBIS), 3 August, 1979, p. L/2.

8   George, *The Chinese Communist Army in Action*, pp. 199–200.

9   On the growth of professionalism in the PLA and its effects see also Harlan W. Jencks, *From Muskets to Missiles: Politics and Professionalism in the Chinese Army* (Boulder, Colorado: Westview Press, 1982).

10   *Zhongguo Xinwen She*, 22 January, 1982; in FBIS, 25 January, 1982, p.K/16.

11   Donald S. Zagoria, *The Sino-Soviet Conflict, 1956–1961* (Princeton University Press, 1962), chs. 5–7.

12   Mao Zedong, 'On the Ten Great Relationships', in Stuart Schram, ed., *Chairman Mao Talks to the People* (New York: Pantheon Books, 1974), p. 68.

13   Information on this agreement, the existence of which was apparently unknown in the West, was provided several years later in the course of acrimonious exchanges between China and the Soviet Union. The Chinese statement on this agreement reads as follows: 'As far back as 20 June, 1959. . . the Soviet government unilaterally tore up the agreement on new technology for national defence concluded between China and the Soviet Union on 15 October, 1957, and refused to provide China with a sample of an atomic bomb and technical data concerning its manufacture.' From 'Statement by the Spokesman of the Chinese Government', 15 August, 1963; *Beijing Review*, 16 August, 1963.

14   Joffe, *Party and Army*, p. 96.

15   Jonathan D. Pollack, 'China as a Nuclear Power', in William H. Overholt, ed., *Asia's Nuclear Future* (Boulder, Colorado: Westview Press, 1977), pp. 36–41.

16   Zagoria, *The Sino-Soviet Conflict*, ch. 7.

17   *Hongqi*, no. 5, 1 March, 1983; in FBIS, 17 March, 1983, pp. K/4–5.

18   Roderick MacFarquhar, *The Origins of the Cultural Revolution 2: The Great Leap Forward 1959–1960* (Oxford University Press, 1983), ch. 10.

19   Ellis Joffe, *Between Two Plenums: China's Intraleadership Conflict, 1959–1962* (Ann Arbor: Center for Chinese Studies, University of Michigan, 1975), pp. 8–22.

20   Jürgen Domes, *Peng Te-Huai: The Man and the Image* (London: C. Hurst, 1985).

21   On Lin Biao's stewardship as defence minister until the Cultural Revolution see Ellis Joffe, 'The Chinese Army Under Lin Piao: Prelude to Intervention', in John M.H. Lindbeck, ed., *China: Management of a Revolutionary Society* (University of Washington Press, 1971), pp. 343–74.

22   Jencks, *From Muskets to Missiles*, p. 196.

23   On the role of the PLA in the Cultural Revolution and its aftermath see Ellis Joffe, 'The Chinese Army in the Cultural Revolution: The Politics of Intervention', *Current Scene* (Hong Kong), vol. VIII, no. 18, 7 December, 1970, pp. 1–25; and Ellis Joffe, 'The Chinese Army After the Cultural Revolution: The Effects of Intervention', *China Quarterly*, no. 55, July–September 1973, pp. 450–77; see also Harvey W. Nelsen, *The Chinese Military System: An Organizational Study of the Chinese People's Liberation Army* (Boulder, Colorado: Westview Press, 1977), chs. 2 and 4; and Jencks, *From Muskets to Missiles*, ch. 4.

24   Ellis Joffe and Gerald Segal, 'The Chinese Army and Professionalism', *Problems of Communism*, November–December 1978, pp. 1–5.

25   Harry Harding, 'The Domestic Politics of China's Global Posture, 1973–1978', in Thomas Fingar, ed., *China's Quest for Independence: Policy Evolution in the 1970s* (Boulder, Colorado: Westview Press, 1980), pp. 110–21.

26   *Hongqi*, no. 2, 2 February, 1978: in FBIS, 22 February, 1978, P. E/4.

27   XINHUA, 30 January, 1978: in British Broadcasting Corporation (BBC) (Summary of World Broadcasts), FE/ 5729/B11/9, 2 February, 1978.

28   *Beijing Review*, no. 32, 5 August, 1977, p. 16.

Chapter 2: Leadership Politics and Perceptions

1   The section on the politics of the post-Mao period draws from the following:

Richard D. Nethercut, 'Leadership in China: Rivalry, Reform and Renewal', *Problems of Communism*, March–April 1983, pp. 30–46; Michel Oksenberg and Richard Bush, 'China's Political Evolution: 1972–1982', *Problems of Communism*, September–October 1982, pp. 1–19; Dorothy Grouse Fontana, 'Background to the Fall of Hua Guofeng', *Asian Survey*, vol. XXII, no. 3, March 1982, pp. 237–60; Dorothy J. Solinger, 'The Fifth National People's Congress and the Process of Policymaking: Reform, Readjustment and the Opposition', *Asian Survey*, vol. XXII, no. 12, December 1982, pp. 1,239–75; William B. Mills, 'Generational Change in China', *Problems of Communism*, November–December 1983, pp. 16–35; Thomas P. Bernstein, 'Domestic Politics', in Steven M. Goldstein, ed., *China Briefing*, 1984 (Boulder, Colorado: Westview Press, 1985), pp. 17.

2 The section on bureaucracy draws from the following: John P. Burns, 'Reforming China's Bureaucracy, 1979–1982', *Asian Survey*, June 1983, vol. XXIII, no. 6, pp. 692–722; Hong Yung Lee, 'China's Twelfth Central Committee: Rehabilitated Cadres and Technocrats', *Asian Survey*, *ibid.*, pp. 673–91; H. Lyman Miller 'China's Administrative Revolution', *Current History*, September 1983, pp. 270–4; Tony Saich, 'Party and State Reforms in the People's Republic of China', *Third World Quarterly*, July 1983, pp. 627–39; Bernstein, 'Domestic Politics'.

3 Christine Wong, 'Economic Performance', in Goldstein, *China Briefing*, p. 110.

4 *Ibid.*

5 *Deng Xiaoping Wenxuan* (Selected Works of Deng Xiaoping) (Beijing), 1 July, 1983; in JPRS, 84651, *China Report*, no. 468, p. 50.

6 On Chinese threat perceptions see Gerald Segal, 'The Soviet "Threat" at China's Gates', *Conflict Studies*, no. 143, 1983; and David Armstrong, 'The Soviet Union', in Gerald Segal and William T. Tow, eds., *Chinese Defence Policy* (London: Macmillan, 1984), pp. 180–95.

7 Paul H. B. Godwin, *Doctrine, Stategy, and Ethic: The Modernization of the Chinese People's Liberation Army* (Air University, Alabama, Maxwell Air Force Base, 1977), p. 67.

8 Quoted in Harold Hinton, ed., *The People's Republic of China: A Documentary Survey*, vol. 5, 1971–1979 (Wilmington, Delaware, Scholarly Resources, Inc., 1980), p. 2,466.

9 Cf. Harry Harding, 'The Domestic Politics of China's Global Posture, 1973–1978', in Thomas Fingar, ed., *China's Quest for Independence: Policy Evolution in the 1970s* (Boulder, Colorado: Westview Press, 1980), pp. 102–9.

10 *Beijing Review*, no. 25, 22 June, 1981, pp. 22–5.

11 *Renmin Ribao*, 30 September, 1978; in FBIS, 10 October, 1978, p. A/9.

12 Beijing Domestic Service, 18 February 1981; in FBIS, 19 February 1981, pp. C/2–5.

13 The section on China's foreign policy draws from the following: Carol Lee Hamrin, 'China Reassesses the Superpowers', *Pacific Affairs*, Summer 1983, pp. 209–31; Banning Garrett, 'China Policy and the Constraints of Triangular Logic', in Kenneth A. Oye, Robert J. Lieber and Donald Rothchild, eds., *Eagle Defiant: United States Foreign Policy in the 1980s* (Boston, Little, Brown, 1983), pp. 237–71; Jonathan D. Pollack, *The Lessons of Coalition Politics: Sino-American Security*

Problems (Santa Monica, The RAND Corporation, 1984); Robert Sutter, 'The United States', in Segal and Tow, Chinese Defence Policy, pp. 196–206; Harry Harding, 'China's Changing Role in the Contemporary World', in Harry Harding, ed., China's Foreign Relations in the 1980s (New Haven: Yale University Press, 1984), pp. 177–223; Gerald Segal, 'Sino-Soviet Relations: The Road to Detente', The World Today, May 1984, pp. 205–12; and Gerald Segal, Sino-Soviet Relations After Mao, The International Institute for Strategic Studies, Adelphi Paper, no. 202, Autumn 1985.
14   Ta Kung Pao (Hong Kong), 16 February, 1986; in FBIS, 18 February, 1986, p. W/12.

Chapter 3: A New Military Policy

1   Beijing Domestic Service, 10 April 1977; in FBIS, 13 April 1977, p. E/4–5.
2   Beijing Domestic Service, 10 April 1977; in FBIS, 15 April 1977, p. E–22.
3   Beijing Domestic Service, 20 January 1978; in BBC, FE/5721/B11/3–4.
4   Hongqi, no. 2, 2 February 1978; in FBIS, 22 February 1978, p. E/17.
5   XINHUA, 30 July 1978; in FBIS, 1 August 1978, pp. E/4–15.
6   New York Times, 4 January 1980.
7   Chinese Defense Spending, 1965–1979 (Central Intelligence Agency, National Foreign Assessment Center, July 1980), pp. 1, 3.
8   Beijing Domestic Service, 5 February 1977; in FBIS, 7 February 1977, pp. E/5–9.
9   See, for example, Ye Jianying's speech to the Conference on Learning from Daqing in Industry, 9 May 1977; Beijing Review, no. 21, 20 May 1977, pp. 15–19.
10   Quoted in Chu-yuan Cheng, China's Economic Development: Growth and Structural Change (Boulder, Colorado: Westview Press, 1982), p. 276.
11   Ibid.
12   A. Doak Barnett, China's Economy in Global Perspective (Washington, DC: The Brookings Institution, 1981), p. 39.
13   Ibid, pp. 45–63.
14   Beijing Review, no. 10, 10 March 1978, p. 22.
15   Cited in David L. Shambaugh, 'China's Defense Industries: Indigenous and Foreign Procurement', in Paul H.B. Godwin, ed., The Chinese Defense Establishment: Continuity and Change in the 1980s (Boulder, Colorado: Westview Press, 1983), p. 85, note 82. See also Francis J Romance, 'Modernization of China's Armed Forces', Asian Survey, vol. XX, no. 3, March 1980, pp. 298–310.
16   BBC, FE/5951/i, 25 October 1978.
17   Strategic Survey 1979, p. 82
18   Chu-yuan Cheng, China's Economic Development, pp. 278–9.
19   Barnett, China's Economy in Global Perspective, pp. 83–98.
20   New York Times, 6 March 1979; Harlan W. Jencks, 'China's "Punitive" War on Vietnam: A Military Assessment', Asian Survey, vol. VIII, no. 4, August 1979, pp. 811–14.
21   XINHUA, 1 August 1979; in FBIS, 2 August 1979, p. L/2.
22   Hongqi, no. 10, 2 October 1979; in FBIS, 18 October 1979, pp. L12–19.

23 *Renmin Ribao*, 8 September 1980; in FBIS, 12 September 1980, p. L/14.

24 *Hongqi*, no. 21, 1 November 1982; in FBIS, 19 November 1982, pp. K/20–6.

25 *Hongqi*, no 5, 1 March 1983; in FBIS, 17 March 1983, pp. K/2–7.

26 *Hongqi*, no. 15, 1 August 1984; in FBIS, 21 August 1984, pp. K/8–18.

27 *Hongqi*, no. 15, 1 August 1985; in FBIS, 8 August 1985, pp. K/1–7.

28 See note 22, p. L/14.

29 David Crane, 'The Harrier Jump-Jet and Sino-British Relations', *Asian Affairs*, vol. 8, no. 4, March–April 1981, pp. 227–49.

30 Cited in Douglas T. Stuart and William T. Tow, 'Chinese Military Modernization: The Western Arms Connection', *China Quarterly*, no. 90, June 1982, p. 264

31 *Ibid.*, p. 265.

32 Edward N. Luttwak, 'Problems of Military Modernization for Mainland China', *Issues and Studies*, vol XIV, no. 7, July 1978, pp. 53–65.

33 *Financial Times*, 23 June 1981, cited in note 31.

34 *Guofang Xiandaihua* (National Defence Modernization), July 1983; in Joint Publications Research Service (Washington, DC) (hereafter cited as JPRS), CPS-85-011, p. 26.

35 Jonathan D. Pollack, *The Lessons of Coalition Politics: Sino-American Security Relations* (Santa Monica: The RAND Corporation, 1984). The following paragraphs are drawn from this study.

36 Lawrence Freedman, 'The Triangle in Western Europe', in Gerald Segal, ed., *The China Factor: Peking and the Superpowers* (London, Croom Helm, 1982), pp. 121–3.

37 Ellis Joffe, *Party and Army: Professionalism and Political Control in the Chinese Officer Corps, 1949–1964* (Harvard University: East Asian Research Center, 1965), pp. 157–8.

38 Note 25, p. K/3.

39 *Ibid.*

40 *Ibid.*

41 The following account is drawn from Jonathan Pollack, 'The Modernization of National Defense', in Richard Baum, ed., *China's Four Modernizations* (Boulder, Colorado: Westview Press, 1980), pp. 249–50; and Denis Fred Simon, 'China's Capacity to Assimilate Foreign Technology: An Assessment', in *China Under the Four Modernizations*, Part I, Selected Papers Submitted to the Joint Economic Committee, Congress of the United States (Washington, DC: US Government Printing Office, 1982), pp. 534–5.

42 Note 38.

43 *Ibid.*

44 Note 34.

45 Note 22, p. L/16.

46 Article by Li Desheng, reprinted from *Lilun Yu Shijian* (Liaoning), no. 4, in *Renmin Ribao*, 13 April 1983; in FBIS, 14 April 1983, p. K/4. On China's policy of military modernization in the 1980s see Thomas W. Robinson, 'Chinese Military Modernization in the 1980s', *China Quarterly*, no. 90, June 1982, pp. 231–52; and Paul Godwin, 'Towards a New Strategy?', in Gerald Segal and

William T. Tow, eds., *Chinese Defence Policy* (London: Macmillan, 1984), pp. 36–49.

Chapter 4: 'People's War Under Modern Conditions'

1   On Maoist military doctrine see Ralph L. Powell, 'Maoist Military Doctrines', *Asian Survey*, vol. VIII, no. 4, April 1968, pp. 239–62; Jack H. Harris, 'Enduring Chinese Dimensions in Peking's Military Policy and Doctrine', *Issues and Studies*, July 1979, pp. 77–88; Paul H. B. Godwin, *Doctrine, Strategy and Ethic: The Modernization of the Chinese People's Liberation Army* (Air University, Alabama: Maxwell Air Force Base, 1977); Georges Tan Eng Bok, 'Strategic Doctrine', in Gerald Segal and William T. Tow, eds., *Chinese Defence Policy* (London: Macmillan, 1984), pp. 3–17.
2   See Jonathan D. Pollack, 'The Logic of Chinese Military Strategy', *Bulletin of Atomic Scientists*, January 1979, pp. 22–33.
3   Sining Tsinghai Provincial Service, 2 August 1977; in FBIS, 7 August 1978, pp. E/11–13.
4   Beijing Domestic Service, 10 July 1977; in FBIS, 12 July 1977, pp. E/6–11.
5   Beijing Domestic Service, 28 June 1977; in FBIS 1 July 1977, pp. E/1–6.
6   Beijing Domestic Service, 3 July 1977; in FBIS, 6 July 1977, pp. E6–10.
7   Beijing Domestic Service, 27 June 1977; in FBIS, 29 June 1977, pp. E/12–18.
8   Beijing Domestic Service, 5 July 1977; in FBIS, 11 July 1977, pp. E/1–5.
9   XINHUA, 19 January 1979; in BBC, FE/6023/B11, 23 January 1979, p. 6.
10 XINHUA, 9 September 1979; in FBIS, 10 September 1979, p. L/13.
11 Beijing Domestic Service, 10 April 1977; in FBIS, 15 April 1977, p. E/10.
12 Beijing Domestic Service, 5 February 1977; in FBIS, 7 February 1977, p. E/6.
13 XINHUA, 5 August 1977; in FBIS, 8 August 1977, pp. E/10–21.
14 *Ibid.*, p. E/21.
15 *Selected Works of Deng Xiaoping* (Beijing: Foreign Languages Press, 1984), pp. 127–140.
16 Note 9.
17 *Ibid.*, p. 5.
18 Note 10, p. L/14.
19 XINHUA, 17 September 1979; in FBIS, 19 September 1979, p. P/4.
20 *Hongqi*, 2 October 1979; in FBIS, 18 October 1979, pp. L/12–19.
21 *Ibid.*, p. L/15.
22 *Ibid.*, p. L/16.
23 XINHUA, 1 August 1979; in FBIS, 2 August 1979, pp. L/1–4.
24 XINHUA, 14 March 1980; in FBIS, 20 March 1980, pp. L/14–17.
25 Nanjing Jiangsu Provincial Service, 19 September 1979; in FBIS, 21 September 1979, p. O/1.
26 XINHUA, 19 November 1979; in FBIS, 23 November 1979, p. L/2.
27 *Hongqi*, no. 16, 16 August 1981; in FBIS, 17 September 1981, pp. K/10–23. See also Paul H. B. Godwin, 'Mao Zedong Revised: Deterrence and Defense in the 1980s', in Paul H. B. Godwin, ed., *The Chinese Defense Establishment: Continuity and Change in the 1980s* (Boulder, Colorado: Westview Press, 1983), pp. 21–40.

28 For a different interpretation see Harlan W. Jencks, ' "People's War Under Modern Conditions": Wishful Thinking, National Suicide, or Effective Deterrent?', *China Quarterly*, no. 98, June 1984, pp. 305–19.

29 *Shijie Zhishi*, no. 15, 1 August 1983; in JPRS, 84508, no. 461, 11 October 1983, pp. 78–83.

30 *Zhongguo Qingnian Bao*, 30 December 1982; in JPRS, 82806, no. 387, 4 February 1983, p. 4.

31 *Ibid.*, pp. 4–5.

32 Note 20, p. L/14.

33 *Jiefangjun Huabao*, no. 181; in JPRS, 77978, no. 188, 1 May 1981, p.1.

34 *Hongqi*, no. 1, 1 August 1984; in FBIS, 21 August 1984, p. K/12.

35 Quoted in Jonathan D. Pollack, 'China as a Nuclear Power', in William H. Overholt, ed., *Asia's Nuclear Future* (Boulder, Colorado: Westview Press, 1977), p. 52. See also Gerald Segal, 'China's Nuclear Posture for the 1980s', *Survival*, January–February 1981, pp. 11–18; and Gerald Segal, 'Nuclear Forces', in Segal and Tow, *Chinese Defence Policy*, pp. 98–113.

36 *Hongqi*, no. 21, 1 November 1982; in FBIS, 19 November 1982, p. K/22.

37 XINHUA, 18 October 1982; in FBIS, 19 October 1982, p. K/1.

38 *Renmin Ribao*, 29 October 1984; in FBIS, 30 October 1984, p. K/1.

39 *Renmin Ribao*, 3 October 1984; in FBIS, 3 October 1984, p. K/1.

40 The article appeared in the army paper on 16 September 1979. Its author, Xu Baoshan, was not identified. It was reproduced in JPRS, 75825, no. 88, 4 June 1980, pp. 97–9.

41 *Ibid.*, p. 99.

42 *Ibid.*

43 See, for example, report in *Jiefang Huabao*, no. 11, 1980; in JPRS, 76928, no. 144, 4 December 1980, p. 20.

44 *Ningxia Ribao*, 29 June 1982; in FBIS, 3 August 1982, p. K/8.

45 XINHUA in English, 12 June 1984; in FBIS, 12 June 1984, p. K/10.

46 See, for example, Shanghai City Service, 28 November 1976; in FBIS, 29 November 1976, pp. E/4–10.

47 Thomas C. Roberts, *The Chinese People's Militia and the Doctrine of People's War* (Washington, DC: National Defense University Press, 1983), pp. 51–77.

48 XINHUA, 30 July 1978; in FBIS, 1 August 1978, pp. E/4–15.

49 *Hongqi*, no. 10, 2 October 1979; in FBIS, 18 October 1979, pp. L/12–19.

50 *Shansi Ribao* (Taiyuan), 24 November 1982; in FBIS, 16 December 1982, pp. R/4–6.

51 Military Service Law, chapter 6.

52 *Renmin Ribao*, 5 June 1984; in FBIS, 6 June 1984, p. K/11.

53 XINHUA, 4 June 1984; in FBIS, 6 June 1984, p. K/17.

54 This section is drawn from Cd. L. Bruce Swanson, 'The Navy of the People's Republic of China', in Barry M. Blackman and Robert P. Berman, eds., *Guide to Far Eastern Navies* (Annapolis, Maryland: Naval Institute Press, 1978), pp. 65–167; David G. Muller, Jnr, *China as a Maritime Power* (Boulder, Colorado: Westview Press, 1983); and Bruce Swanson, 'Naval Forces', in Segal and Tow, *Chinese Defence Policy*, pp. 85–97.

55 Muller, *China as a Maritime Power*, p. 168.
56 Gerald Segal, 'China and Arms Control', *The World Today*, vol. 41, nos. 8–9, August–September 1985, pp. 162–6, esp. p. 164.
57 Interview with British newspaper publisher Robert Maxwell, *International Herald Tribune*, 7 August 1985.

Chapter 5: Weapons and Equipment: Backward but Better

1 Drew Middleton, *The Duel of the Giants: China and Russia in Asia* (New York, Charles Scribner's Sons, 1978). 'Unarmed Giant' is the title of Chapter 9 which gives a succinct summary of the state of the PLA at the end of the Maoist period. See also Ellis Joffe, 'The Chinese Army: A Balance Sheet', *Quadrant* (Sydney, Australia), vol. XXII, no. 11, November 1978; The Hebrew University of Jerusalem, Truman Institute Reprints, 11 pp.; *Newsweek*, 21 January 1980; *Washington Post*, 31 October 1983; and yearly surveys of the International Institute for Strategic Studies, *Military Balance*.

2 *New York Times*, 6 March 1979; Harlan W. Jencks, 'China's "Punitive" War on Vietnam: A Military Assessment', *Asian Survey*, vol. XIX, no. 8, August 1979, pp. 801–15; Jonathan Mirsky, 'China's 1979 Invasion of Vietnam: A View from the Infantry', *Royal United Services Institution Journal*, June 1981, pp. 48–52; King C. Chen, *China's War Against Vietnam, 1979: A Military Analysis*, University of Maryland, Occasional Papers/Reprint Series in Contemporary Asian Studies, no. 5, 1983 (58), reprinted from *Journal of East Asian Affairs*, vol. III, no. 1, Spring–Summer 1983, 31 pp. The figures for Chinese casualties – estimated by Chen (p. 25) on the basis of several sources – seem incredibly high. However, even if exaggerated, they are an indication of the price paid by the PLA for its technological and logistic deficiencies.

3 The section on the air force is drawn from Paul H. B. Godwin, *The Chinese Tactical Air Forces and Strategic Weapons Program: Development, Doctrine and Strategy*, Documentary Research Division, Air University Library (Air University, Alabama: Maxwell Air Force Base, 1978); Rear Admiral James B. Londer, USN (Retd) and A. James Gregor, 'The Chinese Communist Air Force in the "Punitive" War Against Vietnam', *Air University Review*, vol. XXXII, no. 6, September–October, 1981, pp. 67–77; Bill Sweetman, 'Air Forces', in Gerald Segal and William T. Tow, eds., *Chinese Defence Policy* (London, Macmillan, 1984), pp. 71–84; Madelyn C. Ross, 'China's Air Defense', *China Business Review*, vol. II, no. 4, July–August 1984, pp. 31–3; *Jane's Defence Weekly*, 14 December 1985; *Hangkong Zhishi* (Aerospace Knowledge Magazine), no. 7, July 1985 (citing an unnamed Japanese report); in JPRS-CST-85-035, 17 October 1985, pp. 70–2.

4 The section on the navy is drawn from Cd. L. Bruce Swanson, Jr., 'The Navy of the People's Republic of China', in Barry M. Bleckman and Robert P. Berman, eds., *Guide to Far Eastern Navies*, esp. pp. 94–109; and David G. Muller, Jr., *China as a Maritime Power*, esp. chs 6 and 11.

5 Swanson, 'The Navy of the People's Republic of China', p. 109.

Notes

6   Edward N. Luttwak, 'Military Modernization in the People's Republic of China', *Journal of Strategic Studies*, vol. 2, no. 1, May 1979, pp. 3–16.
7   XINHUA, 11 June 1983; in FBIS, 30 June 1983, p. K/11.
8   XINHUA, 12 March 1983; in FBIS, 14 March 1983, p. K/22.
9   Harlan W. Jencks, 'The Chinese "Military–Industrial Complex" and Defense Modernization', *Asian Survey*, vol. XX, no. 10, October 1980, pp. 965–89; David L. Shambaugh, 'China's Defense Industries: Indigenous and Foreign Procurement', in Paul H. B. Godwin, ed., *The Chinese Defense Establishment: Continuity and Change in the 1980s* (Boulder, Colorado: Westview Press, 1983), pp. 43–69; *Chinese Defense Spending 1965–1979* (Central Intelligence Agency, National Foreign Assessment Center, July 1980); Sidney Jammes, 'Military Industry', in Segal and Tow, *Chinese Defence Policy*, pp. 117–32.
10   *Kwangming Daily*, 20 January 1977; in FBIS, 31 January 1977, p. E/2.
11   *Jingji Ribao*, 7 May 1983; in FBIS, 16 May 1983, pp. K/5–6.
12   *Ibid.*, p. K/6–7.
13   *Ibid.*, p. K/7.
14   See note 8.
15   Jencks, 'The Chinese "Military–Industrial Complex" ', p. 987.
16   Shambaugh, 'China's Defense Industries', pp. 66–7.
17   *Ibid.*, p. 54.
18   Jammes, 'Military Industry', p. 125.
19   XINHUA, 12 March 1983; in FBIS, 14 March 1983, p. K/23.
20   *Jingji Guanli*, no. 4, 5 April 1985; in FBIS, 14 June 1985, p. K/16.
21   *Jingji Guanli*, no. 8, 5 August 1984; in FBIS, 25 September 1984, p. K/12.
22   *Ibid.*, p. K/13.
23   Note 20.
24   Note 21, p. K/13.
25   Richard E. Gillespie, 'Marketing to the PLA', *China Business Review*, vol. II, no. 4, July–August 1984, pp. 38–9.
26   Ross, 'China's Air Defense', p. 33.
27   *International Herald Tribune*, 25 August 1982; *Aviation Week and Space Technology*, 4 November 1983; *Wirtschaftswoche* (Düsseldorf), 15 February 1985; in JPRS-CPS-85-032, 2 April 1985, p. 108.
28   *Jane's Defence Weekly*, 11 August 1984, p. 179.
29   *Jane's Defence Weekly*, 1 March 1986, p. 351.
30   ANSA (Rome) in English, 5 April 1985; in JPRS-CPS-85-040, 29 April 1985, p. 98.
31   *Jane's Defence Weekly*, 21 December 1985, p. 1,343.
32   *Jane's Defence Weekly*, 29 June 1985, p. 1,290.
33   *Financial Times*, 11 April 1986.
34   *Aviation Week and Space Technology*, 18 June 1984, p. 31; note 28.
35   *The Economist*, 10 May 1966, p. 34
36   *Aviation Week and Space Technology*, 16 January 1984, p. 29.
37   Note 35 and Beijing UPI, 30 December 1985.
38   Note 35 and *Jane's Defence Weekly*, 19 October 1985, p. 852.
39   *Far Eastern Economic Review*, 2 January 1986, pp. 11–12; *Jane's Defence Weekly*, 19 April 1986, p. 694; note 35.

40 See, for example, *Jane's Defence Weekly*, 24 November 1984, p. 915; *Guardian*, 23 November 1984; *Die Welt* (Bonn), 17 October 1984, in JPRS-CPS-85-003, 9 January 1985, pp. 100–1.
41 *Jingji Ribao*, 15 October 1984; in FBIS 7 November 1984, p. K/10.
42 *Ibid.*, p. K/11.
43 *Jane's Defence Weekly*, 9 March 1985, p. 401.
44 Note 42.
45 Karen Berney, 'Dual-Use Technology Sales', *China Business Review*, vol. 11, no. 4, July–August 1980, p. 25.
46 Note 41, p. K/13.
47 *Ibid.*, p. K/12.
48 *Ibid.*
49 See, for example, *Renmin Ribao*, 24 March 1981; in FBIS, 31 March 1981, pp. A/1–3; *Bingqi Zhishi* (Ordnance Knowledge), no. 3, 1982; in JPRS 81700, 3 September 1982, no. 334, pp. 65–8.
50 *Zhongguo Xinwen She*, 10 December 1984; in FBIS, 11 December 1984, pp. K/7–8.
51 *Ibid.*, p. K/8.
52 *Die Welt*, note 40; and *Jane's Defence Weekly*, 27 July 1985, pp. 171–4, and 1 February 1986, pp. 159–61.
53 *Far Eastern Economic Review*, 9 July 1982; *Asiaweek*, 26 October 1984.
54 Note 41, p. K/14.
55 *Renmin Ribao*, 21 September 1984; in FBIS, 24 September 1984, p. K/5.
56 *International Defense Review*, December 1984, p. 1,789.
57 *Jane's Defence Weekly*, 21 December 1985, p. 1,367.
58 *Ibid.*, pp. 1,367–8.
59 *Aviation Week and Space Technology*, 27 January 1986, p. 29.
60 *Asian Defense Journal*, March 1986, p. 67.
61 *Ningxia Ribao*, 23 April 1984; in JPRS-CST-84-016, 6 June 1984, p. 32.
62 Ross, 'China's Air Defense', p. 32. See also a collation of reports from *Aviation Week and Space Technology* and *Aerospace News* which was reprinted in *Hangkong Zhishi*, no. 10, October 1984, (in JPRS-CST-84-042, 17 December 1984) and which gives a similar picture of the state of the air force. Although the editors noted that the publishing of these reports does not represent an endorsement, they obviously would not have published these reports had they been considered grossly incorrect.
63 Ross, 'China's Air Defense', p. 32.
64 *Aviation Week and Space Technology*, 3 February 1986, p. 31.
65 *Jane's Defence Weekly*, 13 September 1986.
66 Sweetman, 'Air Forces', p. 77.
67 *Hangkong Zhishi*, no. 9, September 1984; in JPRS-CST-84-037, 8 November 1984, pp. 31–4. The Chinese article reprints an article from *Jane's Defence Weekly* of 26 May 1984 which, in turn, uses information provided by the Chinese.
68 Sweetman 'Air Forces', p. 78.
69 Ross, 'China's Air Defense', p. 33.
70 *Aviation Week and Space Technology*, 13 August 1984, p. 28.
71 *Guangming Ribao*, 1 August 1984; in JPRS-CPS-84-069, 18 October 1984, p. 85.

72   XINHUA, 23 November 1984; in FBIS, 27 November 1984, p. K/7.
73   *Ibid.*
74   XINHUA, 24 July 1984; in FBIS, 27 July 1984, p. K/2.
75   Note 71.
76   *Ibid.* See also Beijing Domestic Service, 20 September 1984; in FBIS, 26 September 1984, p. K/13; and esp. *Zhongguo Xinwen She*, 13 November 1984; in FBIS, 14 November 1984, pp. K/18–19.
77   Note 74.
78   Beijing Domestic Service, 20 September 1984, in FBIS, 26 September 1984, p. K/13.
79   *Yangcheng Wanbao* (Guangzhou), 29 September 1983; in FBIS, 4 October 1983, p. K/15.
80   XINHUA, 2 November 1982; in FBIS, 2 November 1982, pp. K/1–2.
81   See, for example, *Renmin Ribao*, 3 August 1981; in FBIS, 7 August 1981, p. K/10; and XINHUA, 25 October 1982; in FBIS, 28 October 1982, pp. K/19–20.
82   Bruce Swanson, 'China's Emerging Navy', *China Business Review*, vol. 11, no. 4, July–August 1984, p. 26. See also Bradley Hahn, 'Hai Fang', *Proceedings of the* U.S. *Naval Institute*, March 1986, pp. 114–20.
83   Swanson, 'China's Emerging Navy', p. 27.
84   *Zhongguo Xinwen She*, 26 September 1985; in FBIS, 1 October 1985, pp. K/10–11.
85   Note 72.
86   *International Herald Tribune*, 12 November 1982; *Daily Telegraph*, 22 March 1983.
87   *The Economist*, 9 February 1985; *International Herald Tribune*, 14 and 15 January 1985.
88   Swanson, 'China's Emerging Navy', p. 28.
89   Robert G. Sutter, *Chinese Nuclear Weapons and American Interests: Conflicting Policy Choices* (Congressional Research Service, The Library of Congress, 1983), pp. 13–21.
90   *Far Eastern Economic Review*, 24 April 1986, p. 14.
91   Sutter, *Chinese Nuclear Weapons*, p. 21.
92   Swanson, 'China's Emerging Navy', p. 27.
93   See, for example, *Beijing Review*, no. 27, 30 July 1984, p. 21.
94   Bradley Hahn, 'China in Space', *China Business Review*, vol. II, no. 4, July–August 1984, pp. 12–24; *Hangkong Zhishi* (Beijing), no. 11, 6 November 1984; in JPRS-CST-85-004, 5 February 1985, pp. 64–8.
95   See, for example, *Newsweek*, 17 October 1983, and Gillespie, 'Marketing to the PLA', pp. 34–9.
96   *Jane's Defence Weekly*, 13 April 1985, p. 620.
97   *Aviation Week and Space Technology*, 20 February 1984, p. 29.
98   Anne Gilks and Gerald Segal, *China and the Arms Trade* (London, Croom Helm, 1985).
99   Yitshak Shichor, 'The Middle East', in Segal and Tow, *Chinese Defence Policy*, pp. 266–7.
100   *Time*, 6 October 1986.
101   *The Economist*, 17 November 1984; *International Herald Tribune*, 4 April 1984; *Aviation Week and Space Technology*, 11 April 1983, pp. 16–18.

102 Shichor, 'The Middle East', pp. 271–2.
103 *International Defense Review*, December 1984, p. 1,795.
104 See, for example, *Washington Post*, 31 October 1983.
105 See, for example, Pierre Sprey, 'The Case for Better and Cheaper Weapons', in Asa A. Clark, Peter W. Chiarelli, Jeffrey S. McKitrick and James W. Reed, eds., *The Defense Reform Debate: Issues and Analysis* (Baltimore, The Johns Hopkins University Press, 1984), pp. 193–208, esp. p. 205.
106 Shichor, 'The Middle East', p. 270.
107 *Die Welt* in Note 40.

Chapter 6: Reforming the PLA: Professionalism First

1 *Hongqi*, no. 15, 1 August 1982; in FBIS, 25 August 1982, pp. K/24–5.
2 *Hongqi*, no. 21, 1 November 1982; in FBIS, 19 November 1982, p. K/22.
3 *Hongqi*, no. 15, 1 August 1984; in FBIS, 21 August 1984, p. K/14.
4 *Jiefangjun Huabao* (Liberation Army Pictorial). no. 1, 1981; in JPRS, 77978, 1 May 1981, no. 188, p. 1.
5 XINHUA, 8 October 1979; in FBIS, 11 October 1979, p. L/18.
6 *Selected Works of Deng Xiaoping* (Beijing: Foreign Languages Press, 1984), p. 32.
7 *Ibid.*, p. 90.
8 See, for example, interview with Chief of Staff Yang Dezhi in *China Daily*, 11 June 1983; in FBIS, 13 June 1983, p. K/30. See also article in *Jiefangjun Bao* by Xiao Ke, vice-minister of national defence and commandant of the PLA Military Academy, XINHUA, 22 February 1983; in FBIS, 23 February 1983, p. K/30.
9 XINHUA, 24 April 1982; in FBIS, 27 April 1982, p. K/8. Also XINHUA, 22 April 1984; in FBIS, 24 April 1984, p. K/18.
10 XINHUA, 24 July 1984; in FBIS, 27 July 1984, p. K/2.
11 XINHUA, 30 June 1980; in FBIS, 2 July 1980, p L/5.
12 *Renmin Ribao*, 3 October 1983; in FBIS, 5 October 1983, p. K/8.
13 Article by Xiao Ke in *Liaowang*, no. 7, 20 July 1983; in JPRS, 84273, 8 September 1983, no. 454, p. 74.
14 *Ibid.*
15 *Ibid.*
16 XINHUA, 3 March 1983; in FBIS, 7 March 1983, p. K/15.
17 *Ibid.*
18 XINHUA, 25 February 1986; in FBIS, 26 February 1986, p. K/20.
19 XINHUA, 24 July 1984; in FBIS, 25 July 1984, p. K/3.
20 *Zhongguo Xinwen She*, 13 June 1985; in FBIS, 18 June 1985, pp. K/6–7.
21 *Ibid.*
22 Beijing Domestic Service, 6 October 1984; in FBIS, 9 October 1984, p. K/8.
23 William R. Heaton, Jr, 'Professional Military Education in China: A Visit to the Military Academy of the People's Liberation Army', *China Quarterly*, March 1980, no. 1, pp. 122–8.
24 XINHUA, 1 September 1983; in FBIS, 8 September 1983, p. K/16; and XINHUA,

31 January 1985; in JPRS-CPS-85-019, 1 March 1985, p. 143.

25   Beijing Hong Kong Service, 18 December 1985; in FBIS, 18 December 1985, p. K/1.

26   *Ibid.*

27   XINHUA, 18 December 1985; in FBIS, 19 December 1985, p. K/3.

28   XINHUA, 19 November 1984; in JPRS-CPS-84-085, 11 December 1984, p. 137.

29   Beijing Domestic Service, 21 November 1984; in FBIS, 23 November 1984, pp. K/8–9.

30   XINHUA, 4 May 1983; in FBIS, 10 May 1983, pp. K/8–9.

31   *Ibid.*, p. K/9.

32   Shenyang Liaoning Provincial Service, 6 May 1983; in FBIS, 16 May 1983, p. S/1.

33   Nanzhang Jiangxi Provincial Service, 1 April 1983; in JPRS, 83563, 27 May 1983, p. 94.

34   XINHUA, 15 March 1983; in FBIS, 17 March 1983, p. K/7.

35   XINHUA, 23 February 1983; in FBIS, 25 February 1983, pp. K/6–7.

36   XINHUA, 31 May 1983; in FBIS, 3 June 1983, p. K/15.

37   *Renmin Ribao*, 9 May 1983; in FBIS, 11 May 1983, p. K/5.

38   *Hongqi*, no. 5, 1 March 1983; in FBIS, 17 March 1983, p. K/6.

39   Radio Beijing Domestic Service, 22 July 1982; in FBIS, 29 July 1982, p. K/6.

40   XINHUA, 24 January 1983; in FBIS, 31 January 1983, p. K/7.

41   XINHUA, 26 May 1983; in FBIS, 27 May 1983, pp. K/7–8.

42   Note 12, p.K/9.

43   Remarks by Yu Qiuli, director of the General Political Department in *Jiefangjun Bao*, 3 March 1983; XINHUA in English, 3 March 1983; in FBIS, 3 March 1983, pp. K/1–2.

44   Zhang Aiping's address to the Party committee of the Commission of Science, Technology and Industry for National Defence, XINHUA, 27 January 1983; in FBIS, 31 January 1983, p. K/7.

45   Yang Shangkun's speech at a conference of PLA academies, XINHUA, 19 February 1983; in FBIS, 23 February 1983, p. K/29.

46   *Ming Pao* (Hong Kong), interview with Xiao Ke, 30 July 1983; in JPRS, 84173, 23 August 1983, p. 117.

47   *Jiefangjun Bao*, 22 February 1983; XINHUA s.d.; in FBIS, 23 February 1983, p. K/30.

48   Military Service Law, XINHUA, 4 June 1984; in FBIS, 6 June 1984, p. K/4.

49   *Ibid.*, p. K/1.

50   Article by He Zhengwen, deputy chief of the General Staff, XINHUA, 7 June 1984; in FBIS, 8 June 1984, p. K/5.

51   Radio Beijing Home Service, 9 October 1978; in BBC/FE/5946/B11/7–8.

52   XINHUA in English, 12 February 1985; in FBIS, 13 February 1985, p. K/1.

53   *Ibid.*

54   Radio Beijing Domestic Service, 3 October 1983; in FBIS, 4 October 1983, p. K/3.

55   Changsha Provincial Service, 29 July 1983; in JPRS, 84173, 23 August 1983, p. 96.

56   XINHUA, 5 January 1982; in FBIS, 5 January 1982, p. K/13.

57   *Renmin Ribao*, 25 February 1980; in JPRS, 75488, 14 April 1980, no. 76, p. 47.
58   *Zhongguo Xinwen She*, 18 September 1985; in FBIS, 19 September 1985, p. K/18.
59   *Ta Kung Pao* (Hong Kong), 16 June 1985; in FBIS, 17 June 1985, p. W/1.
60   *Ming Pao* (Hong Kong), 13 March 1985; in FBIS, 19 March 1985, p. W/2.
61   *Selected Works of Deng Xiaoping*, p. 271.
62   *Hongqi*, no. 15, 1 August 1984; in FBIS, 21 August 1984, p. K/12.
63   XINHUA, 4 September 1982; in FBIS, 7 September 1982, pp. K/20–1.
64   *Selected Works of Deng Xiaoping*, pp. 271–2.
65   Guangxi Regional Service, 18 June 1983; in FBIS, 30 June 1983, pp. P/8–9.
66   Beijing Domestic Service, 8 February 1983; in FBIS, 15 February 1983, p. K/17.
67   XINHUA in English, 5 March 1985; in FBIS, 6 March 1985, p. K/1.
68   Ibid.
69   *China Daily*, 25 January 1986; in FBIS, 27 January 1986, p. K/3.
70   XINHUA, 13 March 1985; in FBIS, 18 March 1985, p. K/24.
71   XINHUA, 23 June 1985; in FBIS, 24 June 1985, pp. K/9–10.
72   *Zhongguo Xinwen She*, 29 June 1985; in FBIS, 1 July 1985, p. K/11.
73   XINHUA, 6 July 1985; in FBIS, 8 July 1985, p. K/1.
74   *Renmin Ribao*, 14 March 1985; in FBIS, 19 March 1985, pp. K/11–12.
75   Edgar Snow, *The Long Revolution* (New York, Random House, 1971); cited in Harvey Nelsen, *The Chinese Military System* (Boulder, Colorado: Westview Press, 1977), p. 43.
76   *Selected Works of Deng Xiaoping*, p. 28.
77   *Ibid.*
78   *Ibid.*, pp. 269–70.
79   XINHUA, Hong Kong Service, 7 July 1985; in FBIS, 8 July 1985, p. K/6.
80   XINHUA, 4 June 1984; in FBIS, 6 June 1984, pp. K/1–10.
81   Harlan W. Jencks, *From Muskets to Missiles: Politics and Professionalism in the Chinese Army 1945–1981* (Boulder, Colorado: Westview Press, 1982), p. 49.
82   XINHUA in English, 19 April 1985; in FBIS, 19 April 1985, p. E/3.
83   XINHUA, 11 June 1985; in FBIS, 12 June 1985, p. K/1.
84   *Ibid.*
85   *Ibid.*, p. K/3.
86   Reprinted in *Renmin Ribao*, 14 June 1985; in FBIS, 18 June 1985, pp. K/15–16.
87   BBC, FE/8008/B11/4–7, 20 July 1985.
88   *Zhongguo Xinwen She*, 26 July 1985; in FBIS, 29 July 1985, p. K/5.
89   *Ibid.*, p. K/4.
90   *China Daily*, 2 August 1985; in FBIS, 5 August 1985, p. K/3.
91   *Selected Works of Deng Xiaoping*, p. 32.
92   *Ibid.*, p. 91.
93   *Ibid.*, p. 270.
94   *Ibid.*, p. 269.
95   *Ibid.*, p. 270.
96   *Ibid.*
97   XINHUA in English, 7 March 1985; in FBIS, 8 March 1985, p. K/12.
98   Beijing Domestic Service, 27 April 1985; in FBIS, 30 April 1985, p. K/22.
99   Beijing Domestic Service, 10 May 1985; in FBIS, 14 May 1985, p. K/15.

100 *Renmin Ribao*, 30 May 1985; in FBIS, 3 June 1985, p. K/18.
101 *Ibid.*
102 Note 85.
103 *Wen Wei Pao* (Hong Kong), 14 June 1985; in FBIS, 14 June 1985, p. W/1, and *Ta Kung Pao* (Hong Kong), in English, 20 June 1985; in FBIS, 20 June 1985, p. W/11.
104 *Liaowang*, 8 July 1985; in BBC/FE/8008/B11/6, 20 July 1985.
105 *Hongqi*, no. 4, 16 February 1986; in FBIS, 6 March 1986, p. K/6.
106 XINHUA, 28 September 1985; in FBIS, 30 September 1985, pp. K/19–22.
107 XINHUA, 31 December 1981; in FBIS, 31 December 1985, pp. K/10–11.
108 XINHUA, 28 November 1982; in FBIS, 29 November 1982, p. K/28.
109 XINHUA, 18 November 1982; in FBIS, 19 November 1982, p. K/2.
110 XINHUA interview with Hong Xuezhi, director of the General Logistics Department, Beijing Domestic Service, 5 December 1982; in FBIS, 9 December 1982, p. K/12.
111 *Ibid.*, pp. K/12–13.
112 Beijing Domestic Service, 27 July 1984; in FBIS, 30 July 1984, p. K/9.
113 *Zhongguo Xinwen She*, 7 February 1986; in FBIS, 10 February 1986, p. K/8.
114 *China Daily*, 26 June 1985; in FBIS, 26 June 1985, p. K/1.
115 XINHUA, 28 January 1981; in FBIS, s.d., p. L/10.
116 XINHUA, 3 March 1985; in FBIS, 4 March 1985, p. K/12.
117 XINHUA, 14 January 1982; in FBIS, 15 January 1982, p. K/7.
118 Lhasa Xizang Regional Service, 13 February 1982; in FBIS, 16 February 1982, pp. Q/1–2; also XINHUA, 20 January 1983; in FBIS, 27 January 1983, p. K/21.
119 XINHUA, 27 August 1983; in FBIS, 29 August 1983, p. K/17.
120 *Ming Pao* (Hong Kong), 12 November 1984; in FBIS, 14 November 1984, pp. W/2–3.
121 See Chapter 1.
122 *Selected Works of Deng Xiaoping*, pp. 27–32. See also Richard J. Latham, 'The Rectification of "Work Style": Command and Management Problems', in Paul H. B. Godwin, ed., *The Chinese Defense Establishment: Continuity and Change in the 1980s* (Boulder, Colorado: Westview Press, 1983), pp. 89–119.
123 *Hongqi*, no. 15, 1 August 1982; in FBIS, 25 August 1982, p. K/26.
124 *Ibid.*
125 XINHUA, 20 January 1983; in FBIS, 27 January 1983, p. K/21.
126 XINHUA, 18 January 1980; in JPRS, 75074, 5 February 1980, no. 57, pp. 53–5.
127 *Renmin Ribao*, 24 March 1982; in JPRS, 83360, 28 April 1983, no. 413, pp. 29–30.
128 XINHUA, 8 May 1985; in FBIS, 13 May 1985, pp. K/5–6.
129 *Hongqi*, no. 15, 1 August 1984; in FBIS, 21 August 1984, p. K/12.
130 *Gansu Ribao* (Lanzhou), 15 August 1983; JPRS-CPS-84-013, 10 February 1984, p. 55.
131 *Jiefangjun Huabao*, no. 1, 1981, interview with Han Huaizhi, assistant to the chief of the General Staff on current year's military training; in JPRS 77978, 1 May 1981, no. 188, p. 1.
132 *Jiefangjun Bao*, 24 January 1978, XINHUA, 25 January 1978; in FBIS, 26 January 1978, p. E/3.

133 Note 130.
134 Note 131, p. 2.
135 XINHUA interview with Zhang Zhen, deputy chief of the General Staff, 18 January 1982; in JPRS, 79954, 27 January 1982, no. 264, p. 32.
136 Lanzhou Provincial Service, 17 April 1978; in FBIS, 19 April 1978, p. M/1.
137 XINHUA, 20 July 1982; in FBIS, 22 July 1982, p. K/1.
138 *Selected Works of Deng Xiaoping*, p. 372.
139 *Ningxia Ribao*, 29 June 1982; in FBIS, 3 August 1982, pp. K/7–9.
140 XINHUA, 1 August 1983; in JPRS, 84173, 23 August 1983, no. 449, p. 113.
141 See, for example, *Hangkong Zhishi* (Aerospace Knowledge Magazine), August 1982; in JPRS, 82011, 18 October 1982, p. 75. Beijing Domestic Service, 20 March 1981; in FBIS, 23 March 1981, pp. L/20–1. *Jiefang Ribao* (Shanghai), 20 July and 16 October 1982; in FBIS, 29 July 1982, p. O/5, and in JPRS, 82449, 13 December 1982, p. 19. See also *Jiefangjun Huabao*; in FBIS, 7 June 1983, p. K/27.
142 See, for example, note 135.
143 Note 140, p. 113.
144 XINHUA, 27 July 1984; in FBIS, 31 July 1984, p. O/3.
145 *Ibid.*, p. O/1.
146 *Liaowang*, no. 16, 22 April 1985; in FBIS, 3 May 1985, p. K/7.
147 XINHUA, 6 September 1984; in FBIS, 10 September 1984, p. S/3.
148 Note 146.
149 XINHUA, 25 October 1985; in JPRS-CPS-85-114, 15 November 1985, p. 36.
150 Beijing Domestic Service, 28 June 1977; in FBIS, 1 July 1977, pp. E/1–6.
151 *Jiefangjun Bao*, 13 April 1980, reported by XINHUA, s.d.; in FBIS, 15 April 1980, p. L/1.
152 *Ibid.*, p. L/2.
153 XINHUA, 10 June 1981; in FBIS, 12 June 1981, p. K/4.
154 XINHUA, 21 January 1983; in FBIS, 25 January 1983, p. K/15.
155 Lhasa Xizang Regional Service, 20 December 1983; in FBIS, 21 December 1983, p. O/2.
156 *Shaansi Ribao*, 2 April 1982, in JPRS, 81033, 11 June 1982, no. 308, pp. 14–15.
157 Beijing Domestic Service, 15 January 1983; in FBIS, 21 January 1983, p. K/22; and Shanghai City Service, 22 December 1982; in JPRS, 82955, 28 February 1983, no. 395, p. 100.
158 Beijing Domestic Service, 16 June 1981; in FBIS, 18 June 1981, p. K/3.
159 Hong Kong AFP, 5 May 1981; in FBIS, 6 May 1981, p. K/2; also Urumqi Xinjiang Regional Service, 15 April 1982; in FBIS, 5 May 1982, p. T/4.
160 XINHUA, 2 March 1981; in FBIS, 3 March 1981, pp. L/3–4.
161 Beijing Xinhua Hong Kong Service, 23 April 1985; in FBIS, 26 April 1985, p. K/19.
162 XINHUA, 6 October 1984; in FBIS, 9 October 1984, pp. K/6–7.
163 *Jingji Ribao*, 23 May 1985; in FBIS, 31 May 1985, p. K/11.
164 *Renmin Ribao*, 8 December 1982; in FBIS, 13 December 1982, p. O/2.
165 *Renmin Ribao*, 25 February 1983; in FBIS, 1 March 1983, p. K/6.
166 XINHUA, 23 July 1983; in FBIS, 27 July 1983, pp. K/18–19.

Chapter 7: Civil–Military Relations: Deng in Command

1   A. Doak Barnett, *Uncertain Future: China's Transition to the Post-Mao Era* (Washington, DC: The Brookings Institution, 1974), p. 85.

2   *Ibid.*

3   *Ibid.*

4   *Liaowang*, 20 January 1983; in FBIS, 23 March 1983, p. K/14.

5   For details see Richard J. Latham, 'The Rectification of "Work Style": Command and Management Problems', in Paul H. B. Godwin, ed., *The Chinese Defense Establishment: Continuity and Change in the 1980s* (Boulder, Colorado: Westview Press, 1983), pp. 89–119.

6   *Bianjiang Wenyi* (Frontier Literature and Art) (Yunnan), no. 13, 5 December 1980; in FBIS, 3 March 1981, p. L/4.

7   Latham, 'The Rectification of "Work Style" ', p. 102.

8   See, for example, *Wen Hui Bao* (Shanghai), 27 February 1981; in FBIS, 3 March 1981, p. L/5; and *Jiefangjun Wenyi* (PLA Literature and Art) (Beijing), no. 11, November 1981; in JPRS, 79938, 26 January 1982, no. 263, pp. 110–21.

9   See, for example, *International Herald Tribune*, 16 October 1979.

10   XINHUA, 29 July 1981; in FBIS, 31 July 1981, p. K/4.

11   XINHUA, 1 February 1983; in FBIS, 2 February 1983, p. K/1.

12   XINHUA, 5 April 1983; in FBIS, 6 April 1983, p. K/5.

13   Alastair I. Johnston, 'Changing Party–Army Relations in China, 1979–1984', *Asian Survey*, vol. XXIV, no. 10, October 1984, p. 1,019.

14   *Liaowang*, no. 33, 19 August 1983; in JPRS-CRS-85-104, 10 October 1985, p. 104.

15   *Ibid.*

16   Note 12, p. K/4.

17   XINHUA, 13 December 1983; in FBIS, s.d., p. K/1.

18   For example, note 10, pp. K/4–5.

19   Beijing Domestic Service, 1 November 1984; in FBIS, 2 November 1984, p. K/11.

20   XINHUA, 22 January 1985; in JPRS-CRS-85-104, 12 February 1985, p. 113.

21   XINHUA, 28 March 1985; in FBIS, 29 March 1985, p. K/18.

22   *Renmin Ribao*, 8 February 1983; in FBIS, 10 February 1983, p. K/8.

23   Note 4.

24   *Ibid.*

25   *Selected Works of Deng Xiaoping* (Beijing: Foreign Languages Press, 1984), p. 358.

26   *Beijing Review*, no. 27, 6 July 1981, p. 22.

27   Beijing Domestic Service, 2 September 1984; in FBIS, 11 September 1984, p. K/3.

28   *Renmin Ribao*, 5 December 1984; in FBIS, 10 December 1984, p. K/1.

29   *Renmin Ribao*, 20 May 1984; in FBIS, 21 May 1984, p. K/22.

30   Reprinted in *Guangming Ribao*, 28 July 1984; in FBIS, 3 August 1984, p. K/6.

31   *Ibid.*, p. K/5.

32   *Ibid.*, p. K/6.

33   For details see Ellis Joffe, 'The PLA After the Cultural Revolution: The Effects of Intervention', *China Quarterly*, no. 55, July–September 1973, pp. 464–8.

34   *Ibid.*

35 *Far Eastern Economic Review*, 7 April 1983, p. 20.
36 Yu Yu-lin, 'Politics in Teng Hsiao-p'ing's Army-Building Strategy, (1977–1984)', *Issues and Studies*, October 1985, p. 53.
37 *Selected Works of Deng Xiaoping*, p. 98.
38 Paul Godwin, 'Towards a New Strategy?', in Gerald Segal and William T. Tow, eds., *Chinese Defence Policy* (London: Macmillan, 1984), p. 46.
39 XINHUA, 11 June 1985; in FBIS, 12 June 1985, p. K/3.
40 *Ibid.*
41 *Wei Wei Pao* (Hong Kong), 17 October 1985; in FBIS, 22 October 1985, p. W/1.
42 Harlan W. Jencks, *From Muskets to Missiles: Politics and Professionalism in the Chinese Army 1945–1981* (Boulder, Colorado: Westview Press, 1982), p. 28.
43 Ye Jianying, Nie Rongzhen, Xu Xiangqian, Wei Guoqing, Li Desheng, Zhang Tingfa and Wang Zhen.
44 Ulf Sundhausen, 'Military Withdrawal from Government Responsibility', *Armed Forces and Society*, vol. 10, no. 4, Summer 1984, p. 544.
45 At the local level, the most outstanding was Chen Zaidao, who openly disregarded central directives and supported a conservative Red Guard organization in Wuhan against the radical one favoured by the Beijing leadership. At the central level, Lin Biao and his associates did not respond to pressure from Mao and other Party leaders to remove the PLA from positions of power.
46 The term 'political quiescence' is taken from Timothy J. Colton, *Commissars, Commanders, and Civilian Authority: The Structure of Soviet Military Politics* (Harvard University Press, 1979).
47 Ellis Joffe, *Party and Army: Professionalism and Political Control in the Chinese Officer Corps, 1949–1964* (Harvard University: East Asian Research Center, 1965), pp. 137–8.
48 Johnston, 'Changing Party–Army Relations', pp. 1,016–17.
49 See, for example, XINHUA (Beijing) Hong Kong Service, 27 October 1985; in JPRS-CPS-85-115, 19 November 1985, pp. 96–7.
50 *Hongqi*, no. 14, 16 July 1984; in FBIS, 17 August 1984, p. K/6.
51 *Renmin Ribao*, 12 April 1985; in FBIS, 17 April 1985, p. K/14.
52 Beijing Domestic Service, 9 November 1984; in FBIS, 15 November 1984, p. K/12.
53 *Ibid.*, p. K/13.
54 XINHUA, 9 February 1983; in FBIS, 10 February 1983, p. K/5.
55 Beijing Domestic Service, 31 May 1985; in FBIS, 7 June 1985, p. K/14.
56 XINHUA, 30 October 1983; in FBIS, 1 November 1983, p. K/4.
57 Kunming Yunnan Provincial Service, 5 February 1981; in FBIS, 6 February 1981, p. Q/3.
58 See, for example, *Beijing Review*, no.10, 4 March 1977, p. 9.
59 Richard Nethercut, 'Deng and the Gun: Party–Military Relations in the People's Republic of China', *Asian Survey*, August 1982, p. 696.
60 The full text of Ye's speech is carried in FBIS, 1 October 1979, pp. L/8–34.
61 XINHUA, 30 June 1981; in FBIS, 1 July 1981, p. K/18.
62 Beijing Domestic Service, 2 January 1981; in FBIS, 6 January 1981, p. L/25.

63   *Ibid.*
64   *Lilun Yu Shijian* (Liaoning), no. 4, 1983, reprinted in *Renmin Ribao*, 13 April 1983; in FBIS, 14 April 1983, p. K/4.
65   Guangzhou Guangdong Provincial Service, 26 March 1981; in FBIS, 30 March 1981, p. P/1.
66   Shijiazhuang Hebei Provincial Service, 14 April 1982; in FBIS, 28 April 1982, p. R/1.
67   Shanghai City Service, 20 April 1981; in FBIS, 22 April 1981, p. K/1.
68   *Jiefang Ribao* (Shanghai), 28 August 1982; in FBIS, 29 September 1982, pp. K/4–6.
69   *Ibid.*, p.K/4.
70   *Ibid.*
71   *Ibid.*, p. K/6.
72   The *Jiefangjun Bao* critique of Zhao's article was reprinted in *Jiefang Ribao*, 28 September 1982; in FBIS, 4 October 1982, p. K/1.
73   *Ibid.*
74   *Ibid.*, p. K/8.
75   Beijing Domestic Service, 8 May 1980; in FBIS, 9 May 1980, p. L/3.
76   *Ibid.*, p. L/4.
77   XINHUA, 13 January 1982; in FBIS, 15 January 1982, p. K/3.
78   Hainan Island Regional Service, 13 February 1981; in FBIS, 18 February 1981, p. P/1.
79   Shijiazhuang Hebei Provincial Service, 14 April 1982; in FBIS, 28 April 1982, p. R/1.
80   XINHUA, 5 April 1981; in FBIS, 9 April 1981, p. P/1.
81   Beijing Domestic Service, 27 March 1981; in FBIS, 1 April 1981, p. K/6.
82   According to some accounts, Wei and Xu were strong supporters of Deng and fought to have him reinstated after his second ouster from power. See Parris H. Chang, 'Chinese Politics: Deng's Turbulent Quest', *Problems of Communism*, January–February 1981, p. 3. If so, they obviously parted ways with Deng – Wei for reasons already noted, and Xu either because, like Ye, he favoured closer adherence to Maoist values or because of personal reasons, such as his reported but unfulfilled desire to be defence minister.
83   The assumption with regard to Ye Fei is speculative and is based on the somewhat flimsy evidence of his speech to a naval congress in which he seemed to take the line of the dissidents. *Guangming Ribao*, 15 August 1981; in FBIS, 25 August 1981, pp. K/17–18.
84   The assumption with regard to Xiao Hua is based on his emphasis on the importance of political work during military modernization. See *Hongqi*, no. 6, 1 June 1979; in JPRS, no. 73956, 3 August 1979, pp. 54–66.
85   XINHUA, 24 April 1981; in FBIS, 28 April 1981, p. K/19.
86   XINHUA, 20 January 1982; in FBIS, 21 January 1982, p. K/13.
87   See, for example, Guangzhou Guangdong Provincial Service, 26 March 1981; in FBIS, 27 March 1981, p. P/1; and Xian Shaanxi Provincial Service, 26 March 1981; in FBIS, 27 March 1981, p. T/2.
88   See, for example, note 85. See also Lanzhou Gansu Provincial Service, 4 April 1981; in FBIS, 8 April 1981, pp. T/1–2; XINHUA, 5 April 1981; in FBIS, 9 April

1981, pp. P/1–2; and *Renmin Ribao*, 8 February 1982; in FBIS, 11 February 1982, pp. K/9–10.

89 XINHUA, 12 March 1981; in FBIS, 13 March 1981, pp. L/13–14.

90 XINHUA, 20 January 1983; in FBIS, 27 January 1983, p. K/21.

91 *Renmin Ribao*, 25 July 1983; in FBIS, 25 July 1983, p. K/12.

92 *Ibid.*, p. K/15.

93 *Ibid.*, p. K/14.

94 *Ibid.*

95 The article in the army paper was reprinted in *Guangming Ribao*, 28 July 1984; in FBIS, 3 August 1984, p. K/10.

96 *Ibid.*

Index